THE TOTAL SHRED GUITARIST

A Fun and Comprehensive Overview of Shred Guitar Playing

GERMAN SCHAUSS

Alfred, the leader in educational music publishing, and the National Guitar Workshop, one of America's finest guitar schools, have joined forces to bring you the best, most progressive educational tools possible. We hope you will enjoy this book and encourage you to look for other fine products from Alfred and the National Guitar Workshop.

National Guitar Workshop Method
Approved Curriculum

Alfred Music Publishing Co., Inc.
P.O. Box 10003
Van Nuys, CA 91410-0003
alfred.com

ISBN-10: 0-7390-7478-4 (Book & CD)
ISBN-13: 978-0-7390-7478-7 (Book & CD)

This book was acquired, edited, and produced by Workshop Arts, Inc., the publishing arm of the National Guitar Workshop.
Nathaniel Gunod, acquisitions, managing editor
Burgess Speed, acquisitions, senior editor
Timothy Phelps, interior design
Ante Gelo, music typesetter
CD recorded by German Schauss and mastered by Collin Tilton at Bar None Studio, Northford, CT

Cover photograph by Kaley Nelson
Guitar on cover courtesy Schecter Guitar Research

Alfred Cares. Contents printed on 100% recycled paper.

Contents

A compact disc is available with this book. Using the disc will help make learning more enjoyable and the information more meaningful. Listening to the CD will help you correctly interpret the rhythms and feel of each example. The symbol to the left appears next to each song or example that is performed on the CD. Example numbers are above the symbol. The track number below each symbol corresponds directly to the song or example you want to hear. In some cases, there is more than one example per track; this is reflected in the track numbers (for example: track 2.1, track 2.2, track 2.3, etc.). Only the examples that are on the CD are numbered, and the example numbers start at 1 with each new chapter. Track 1 will help you tune to this CD.

About the Author

German Schauss is a guitarist, composer, author, and educator who teaches at Berklee College of Music and the Los Angeles Music Academy. He performs and tours as the leader of his own band and with other internationally known artists. Schauss writes music for commercials, TV, and video games, and has been named one of the 50 fastest guitarists of all time by *Guitar World* magazine. He is the author of *Shredding Bach* (Alfred/NGW #34922) and writes the popular monthly column "Instant Shredding" for Germany's biggest guitar magazine, *Gitarre & Bass*.

PHOTO BY JI YEON SONG

German uses and proudly endorses: Ernie Ball/Music Man, Bogner, Rocktron, PreSonus, Native Instruments, Maxon, Guyatone, Morley, Dunlop, Voodoo Labs, Pigtronix Pedals, DiMarzio, Zoom, Tremol-No, DR Strings, MakeMusic, and Pedaltrain products.

For more about German Schauss and his music, please visit: www.germanschauss.com

Acknowledgements

I would like to thank my wife Ji Yeon for her never-ending patience, guidance, and love. Furthermore, I would like to thank my family for their love and belief in me and my music. I would also like to express my sincere gratitude and thanks to Helmut Gattung, my first guitar teacher, who guided me through all the ups and downs of learning an instrument. Thanks to all of my friends and fans around the world for their support, positive thoughts, and love—you are all an inspiration to me! Additionally, thanks to Burgess Speed and the teams at Workshop Arts and Alfred Music Publishing.

Introduction

Welcome to *The Total Shred Guitarist.* This book is intended for intermediate to advanced guitarists who are ready to expand their technique by learning to shred. To get the most out of this book, you should have a firm grasp on basic playing technique and theory. You should also be able to read standard music notation or tablature (TAB). For a refresher on some of these topics, refer to the next page.

Shredding, which can be defined as a technically virtuosic approach to playing an instrument, has been around for centuries. Composer/musician J. S. Bach (1685–1750) was a shredder, as was violinist Niccolò Paganini (1782–1840). However, shredding as we know it became popular in the 1970s with the playing of guitarists like Ritchie Blackmore (Deep Purple) and then in the 1980s with the dazzling neo-classical sounds of Yngwie Malmsteen and Jason Becker. In recent years, shredding has experienced a huge comeback with the playing of John Petrucci (Dream Theater), Buckethead, Steve Vai, Joe Satriani, Jeff Loomis (Nevermore), and many others.

The Total Shred Guitarist starts with the basics of developing greater technical fluency and builds on this foundation toward many advanced concepts and techniques. This book will help you develop your own sound and style, and will help you incorporate the awesome power of shred into your own playing.

Chapter 1: Notation and Basic Technique Review

On this page, you will find important information on basic notation and guitar technique. You may read it now or refer to it later if you have questions.

Reading Tablature (TAB)

Tablature, or TAB, is a system of notation used for guitar and other fretted instruments. There are six lines that represent the strings. Numbers are placed on the lines; these numbers tell you what frets to play. Numbers under the TAB staff tell you which left-hand fingers to use. The top line represents the 1st string and the bottom line represents the 6th string. In this book, TAB is written below the corresponding standard music notation.

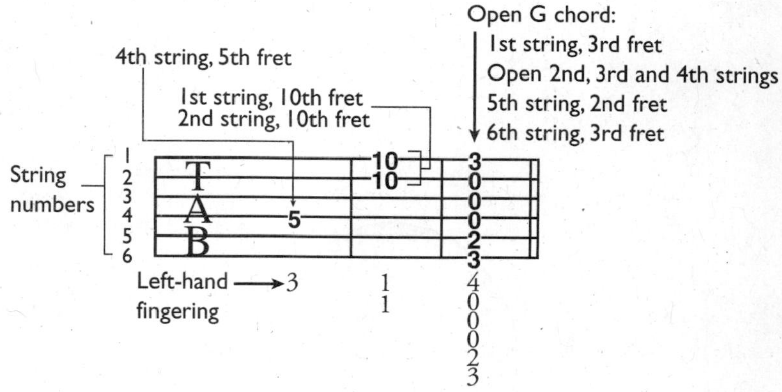

Scale Diagrams

Scale diagrams are horizontal representations of the guitar fretboard that are used to display scale fingerings.

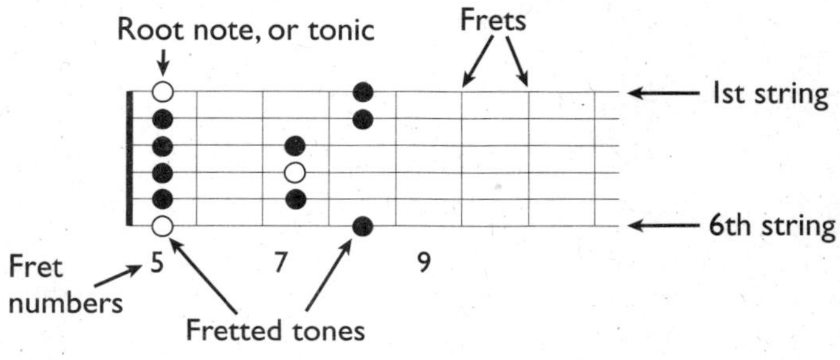

Notation Legend

H 0 2 — *Hammer-on:* Pick the first note normally, then "hammer" your left-hand finger onto the fret to sound the second note. Do not pick the second note with your right hand.

P 2 0 — *Pull-off:* Pick the first note normally, then pull your left-hand finger off the fret to sound the second note. Do not pick the second note with your right hand.

SL 14 16 — *Slide:* While maintaining pressure on the string with your left-hand finger, slide your left hand up or down to the next note, resulting in a continuous sound.

1 — *Bend:* While maintaining pressure on the string with your left-hand finger, press or pull the string perpendicular to the neck so that the note goes up in pitch. The number above the arrow indicates how many steps the note should rise in pitch (quarter step, half step, whole step, etc.).

1 — *Bend-and-release:* Perform a bend, then release the bend so that the note returns to its original pitch while continuing to sustain.

T 12 — *Tap:* Hammer-on to the indicated fret with your right-hand finger. T2 and T3 are used in multi-finger tapping to indicate second and third fingers of the right hand.

Vibrato: A series of small, quick bends that create a "singing" sound that fluctuates in pitch.

8va - - - - — *All'ottava:* Play the bracketed notes one octave higher than written.

p, i, m, a, c — The right-hand fingers starting with the thumb (*p* = thumb, *i* = index, *m* = middle, *a* = ring, and *c* = pinky).

Chapter 2: Warming Up and Body Awareness

Shredding is very similar to any type of athletic sport. It requires rigorous practice, patience, discipline, and routine. Also, like a sport, it requires warming up.

Getting your entire body ready (especially your arms and hands) for the physical demands of shred can be tricky. In general, you should set aside at least 10–15 minutes before you begin a practice session and 5–10 minutes after a practice session for cooling down and stretching out your muscles. This might sound like a tedious thing to do, but it is really important to begin and end your practice with warmed-up and stretched muscles, as well as properly aligned bones to guarantee the best flow of nerve impulses.

There are many ways to warm up and you will have to explore this for yourself further, as everyone will develop a preference and special need for particular exercises. For now, here are a few tips and tricks to get you started.

One way of developing a great warm-up routine is to start by warming up your entire body, paying special attention to your back, shoulders, and arms. After that, you should work on your hands. Please refer to a professional for the right exercises and correct postures that will help you. Of course, if you should have more questions or develop any pain, please consult a physician immediately.

If you are interested in alternative ways of warming up and creating body awareness, I recommend the following practices:

- Qigong (pronounced: Chi Kung)
- Tai Chi
- Alexander Technique
- Rolfing

Though there is not enough space on this page to discuss each of the above practices, a quick internet search on each term will yield a lot of useful information. Personally, I perform Qigong every morning before my practice session. After the session, I cool down with some stretches of the arms and hands.

Practice Routines and Habits

As an active musician, composer, clinician, and teacher, I am often asked by students about the best ways to practice. First of all, I would like to say there is no single "best" way to practice. Good practice with great results can be different for everyone. However, I employ the following methods in my own practice so I suggest these same methods to all my students.

Consistency—This is the first and most fundamental aspect of practicing. Practice every day. Once you have identified the best time of day to practice, it is important to practice every day at that time. Daily practice at a regular time will become a non-negotiable routine that will help you achieve consistent quality in performance. You won't have any more excuses about why you couldn't practice that D♭ altered XYZ scale!

Organization—Organize your practice material into different categories. Create as many categories as you like. For example: picking, sweeping, legato, tapping, chords, sight-reading, improvisation, etc. Place all your exercises from their various sources (like guitar-lesson handouts, books, magazines, websites, etc.) into a folder or box. Take a sheet (or two) from each category every day and practice it. After you are done, place this sheet in the back of the category. This method of organizing your practice material will allow you to be thorough in your daily practice, and it will prevent you from repeating the same material over and over again.

Keep a musical journal—The third and most important aspect of practice is to keep a record of your practice in the form of a musical journal. This will help you objectively review your progress. Sometimes, it is hard to see the progress you have made because you do not have a point of reference for comparison. With a record of your daily practice, you will be able to compare your actual progress and also plan your next step or goal.

It is good to remember that maintaining one goal can sometimes be a tricky thing. Very often, your goals will change as your knowledge increases and your skills advance.

I always compare this to the story of the boy with the carrot and the donkey. The boy dangles the carrot in front of the donkey so that it will continue to move forward towards the carrot. However, the donkey never gets the carrot because the boy will always dangle the carrot a little ahead of the donkey. And so, the goal is not the actual carrot dangling in front of you (mastering a particular technique, etc.); it is the process of trying to attain the ever-changing carrot that enables you to learn and improve every day.

Chapter 3: Basic Warm-Up Exercises

In order to perform the most complex finger movements at rapid speeds, you will need to condition your fingers and synchronize your hands. This chapter gives you a complete workout for your hands and mind that will help you develop proper playing technique and a great way to warm up.

The following example is a simple *chromatic scale* utilizing open strings and, mostly, four fingers on each string. The chromatic scale consists of 12 notes connected by a series of *half steps*. A half step on the guitar is the distance of one fret. Try playing this example slowly using a *metronome* (an adjustable time-keeping device that keeps a steady tempo), and pay close attention to your left- and right-hand synchronization. You will use strict *alternate picking* for this one: down-up-down-up, etc.

⊓ = Downstroke
∨ = Upstroke

Chromatic Scale—Ascending and Descending

1 Track 2.1

It's important to develop a great picking hand. This next example is for your right hand only and is designed to build up your picking technique in a simple, but relaxed, way. This exercise utilizes the "rhythm pyramid" idea, which consists of a note played in a simple descending order of basic rhythmic *values,* or durations: whole, half, quarter, eighth, eighth-note *triplets* (see page 11), and sixteenth notes. This example is demonstrated on the high-E string but should be practiced on the other strings as well. Don't forget to use your metronome!

Picking Exercise with Rhythm Pyramid

2
Track 2.2

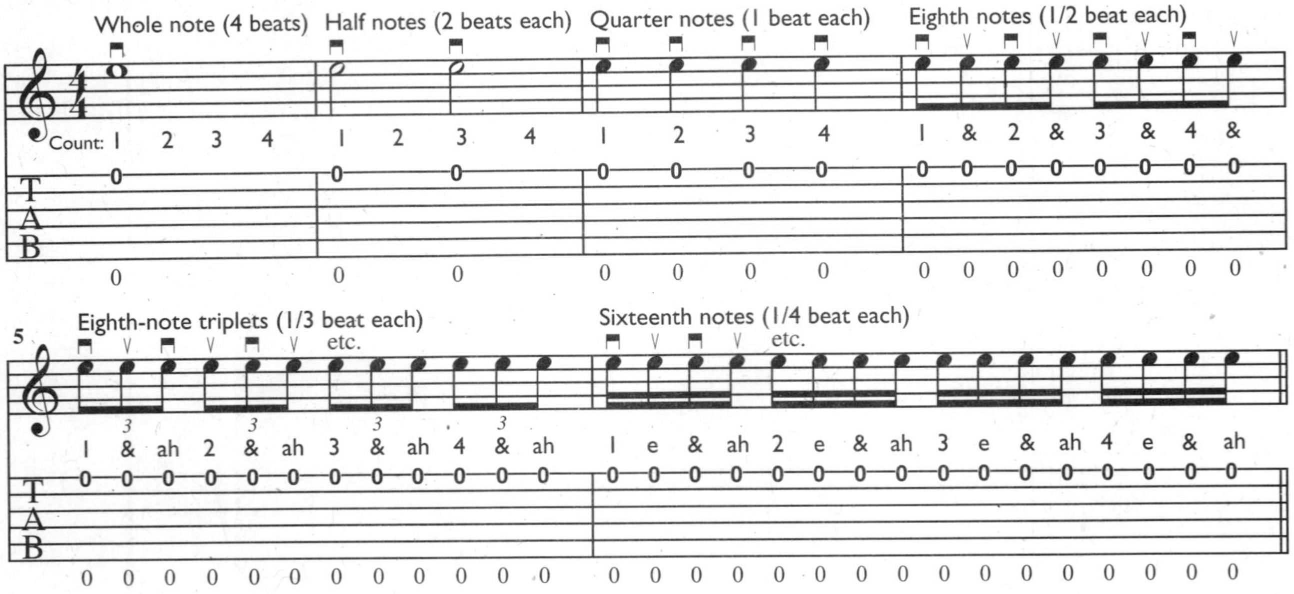

To play fast and accurately, you need to develop great right-hand coordination. For this, we have a few examples featuring *string skipping.* The string skipping technique consists of skipping, or "jumping over," strings as you go from note to note (or groups of notes to groups of notes). Start out slowly, using a metronome and staying aware of the correct picking directions. These ideas can be adjusted to fit any type of rhythmic variation as well. Try playing them as triplets, or uneven groups of notes on each string.

Basic String Skipping

3
Track 2.3

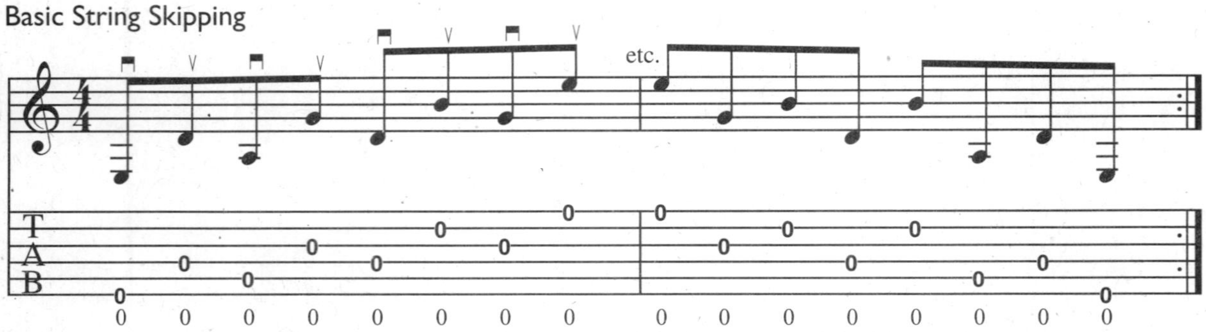

Rhythmic Variation

4
Track 2.4

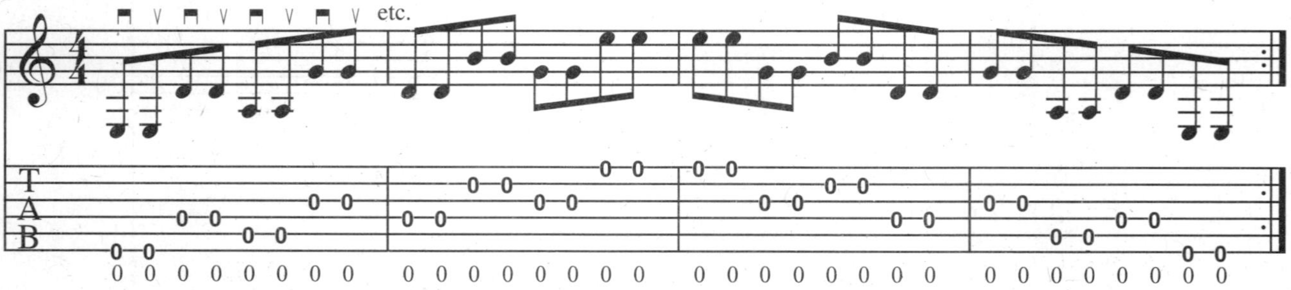

Outside-Inside String Skipping

5
Track 3.1

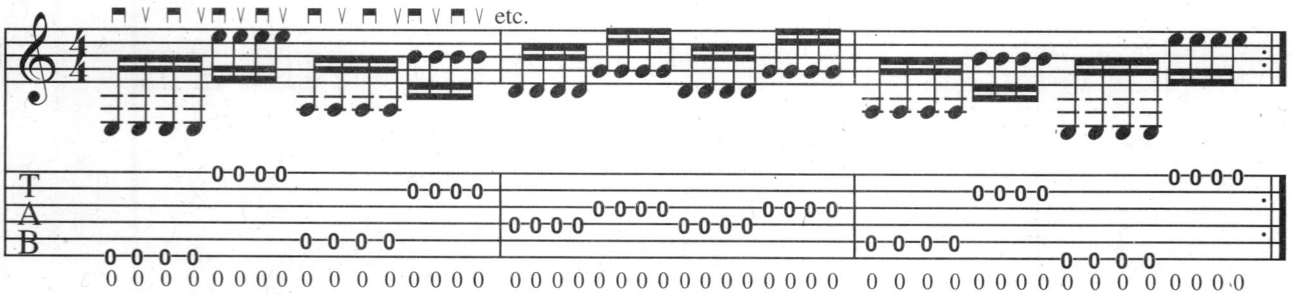

Now, let's shift our focus to speed development. When working on your speed, it's important to start slowly and accurately—practicing within your comfort level—then slowly increase your tempo.

This next exercise is based on the chromatic scale and is played with four fingers per string. Work your way up the fretboard with the ascending pattern, then immediately launch into the descending pattern.

Basic Left- and Right-Hand Synchronization—Ascending

6
Track 3.2

Basic Left- and Right-Hand Synchronization—Descending

The next exercise is designed to help you develop better *cross-picking* technique. Cross-picking consists of alternate picking, across the strings, with only one note per string.

Synchronization Across the Strings

7
Track 3.3

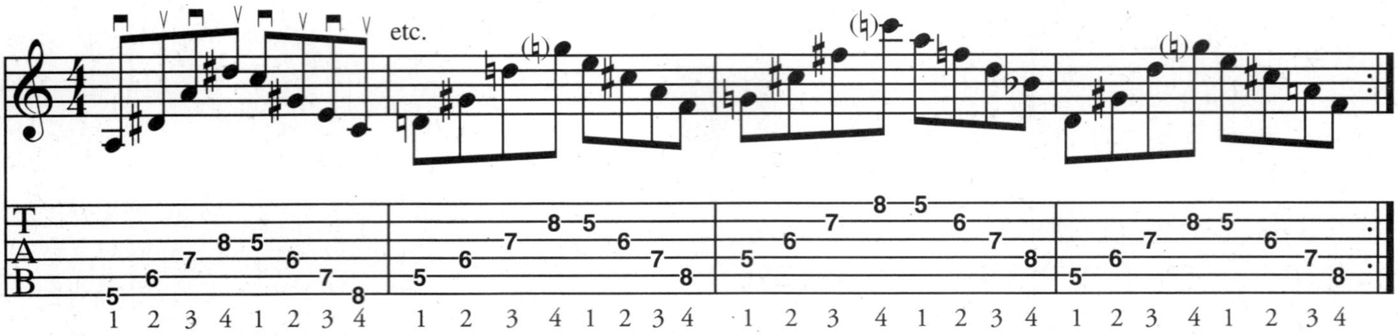

The following example is a variation of the one above. Here, you start off with your 1st finger on the 3rd string and descend down to the lowest string.

Synchronization Across the Strings—Variation

8
Track 3.4

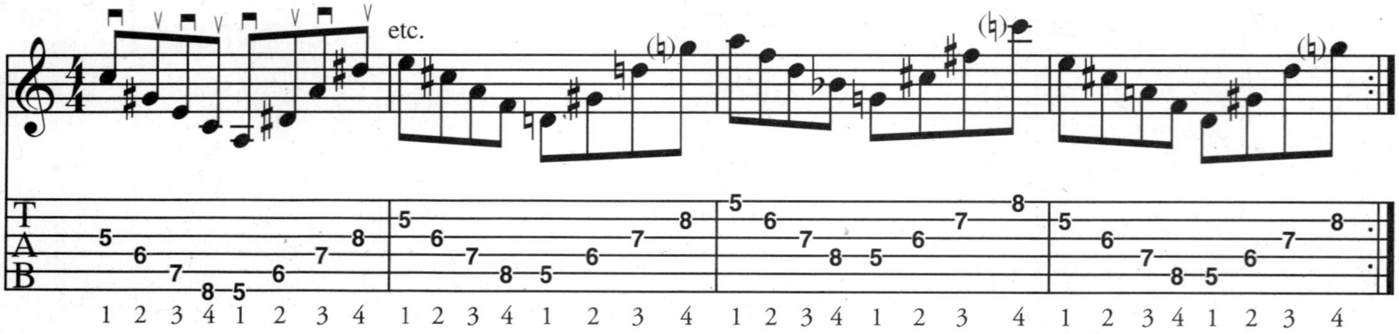

Finger Independence and Conditioning

It is extremely important to develop finger independence and the ability to use any combination of left-hand fingers. The first example is based on the idea of using all possible finger combinations. We can refer to this as a "finger twister." Though this exercise is demonstrated below as starting on the 5th fret, you can play it anywhere on the fretboard. To the right are four columns of numbers. The first column represents all possible finger combinations starting with the 1st finger. The second column represents all possible combinations starting with the 2nd finger, etc. Play the combination "1-2-3-4" across the fretboard, starting on the 6th string and ascending to the 1st, and then descending back to the 6th. See Examples A and B below for the correct ascending and descending sequence. Play through all the possible finger combinations, cleanly and evenly, in all four columns.

1 2 3 4	2 1 3 4	3 1 2 4	4 1 2 3
1 2 4 3	2 1 4 3	3 1 4 2	4 1 3 2
1 3 2 4	2 4 1 3	3 2 1 4	4 2 1 3
1 3 4 2	2 4 3 1	3 2 4 1	4 2 3 1
1 4 2 3	2 3 1 4	3 4 1 2	4 3 1 2
1 4 3 2	2 3 4 1	3 4 2 1	4 3 2 1

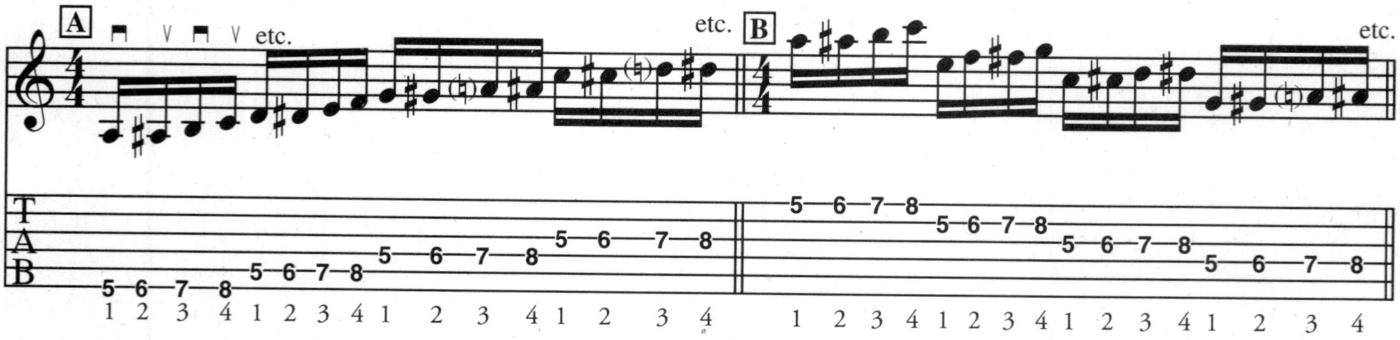

The following examples are variations on the previous exercise. In examples C and D, the 3rd and 4th fingers are moved to the adjacent string. This can very tricky, but it is a great way to develop the independence of your 3rd and 4th fingers.

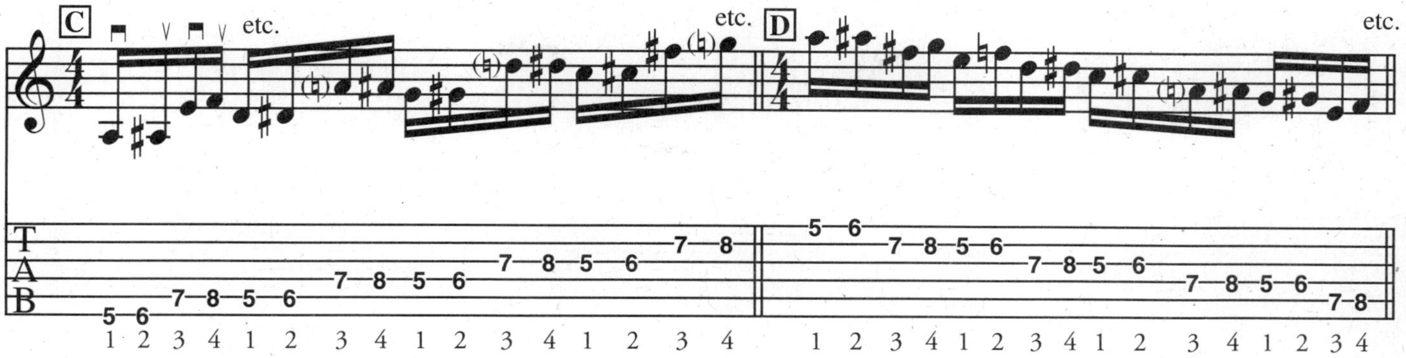

In Examples E and F, we go one step further by skipping the adjacent string. This requires great coordination and concentration. Strive for accuracy and a good, clean sound. Do not be impatient—the speed will come!

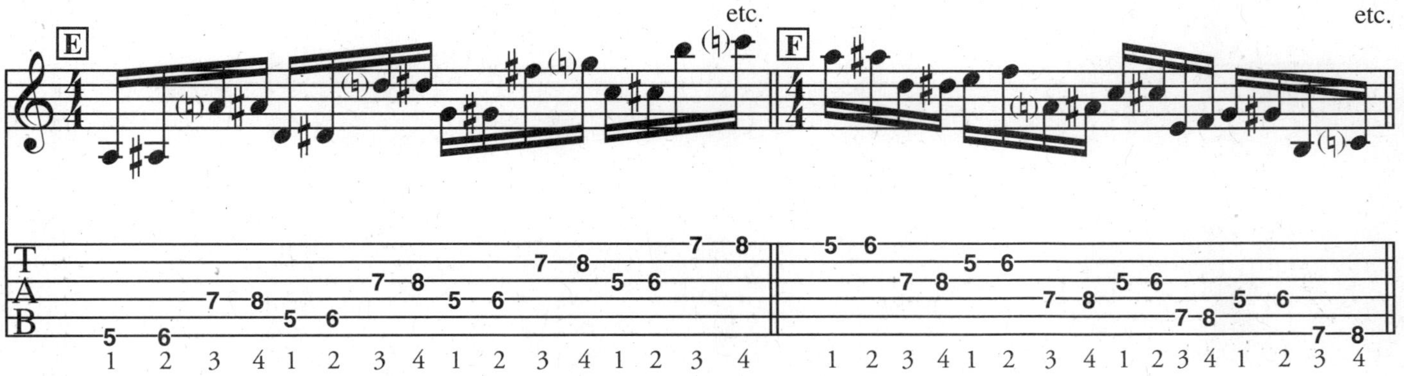

Below, we have three-note ascending and descending patterns played in *triplets.* A triplet consists of three notes played in the time of two notes of equal value. For instance, an eighth-note triplet consists of three eighth notes in the time of two normal eighth notes (one beat). Each note in an eighth-note triplet lasts for one third of a beat. Play all the patterns using strict alternate picking, and use a metronome to monitor your speed while always striving for accuracy.

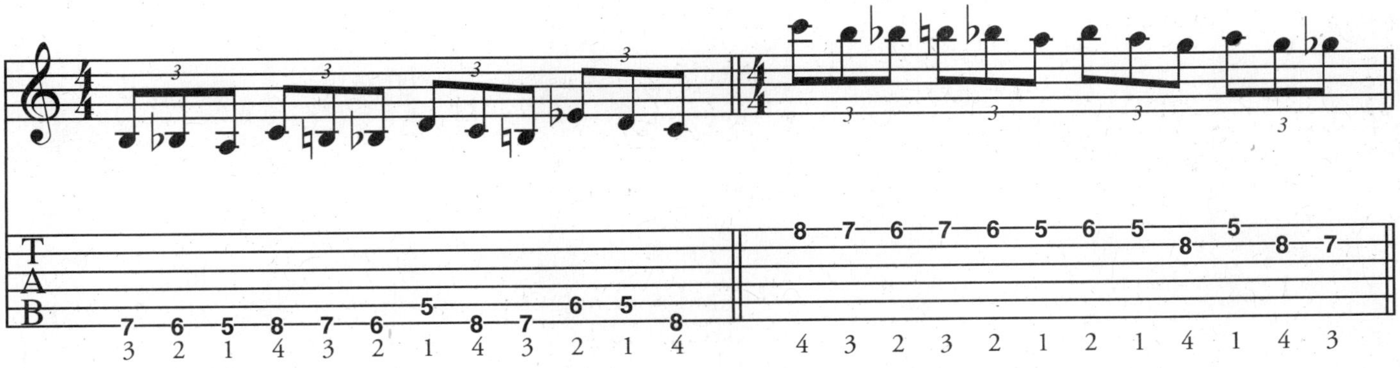

The following examples are combinations of the previous exercises. For example, three notes ascending and three notes descending, and so on.

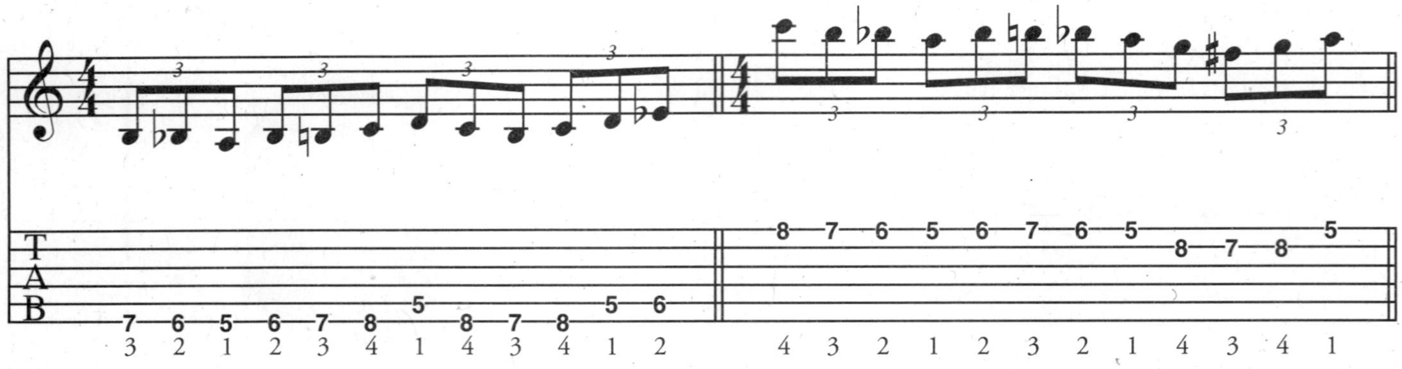

Here, we have more ascending and descending three-note patterns. These are based on an interval known as the 2nd (for more on intervals, see pages 16 and 21).

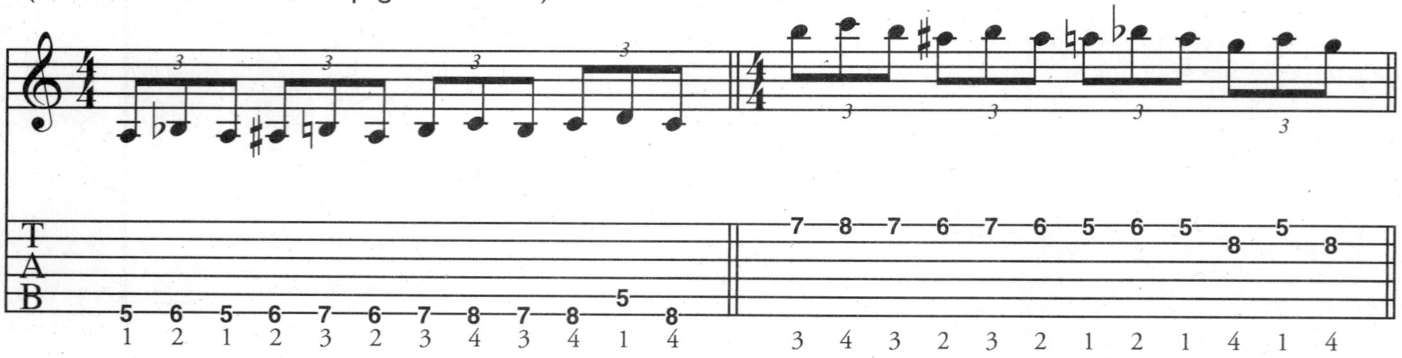

Following is a series of ascending and descending four-note patterns.

The next example is based on 2nds.

The examples below are based on 3rds.

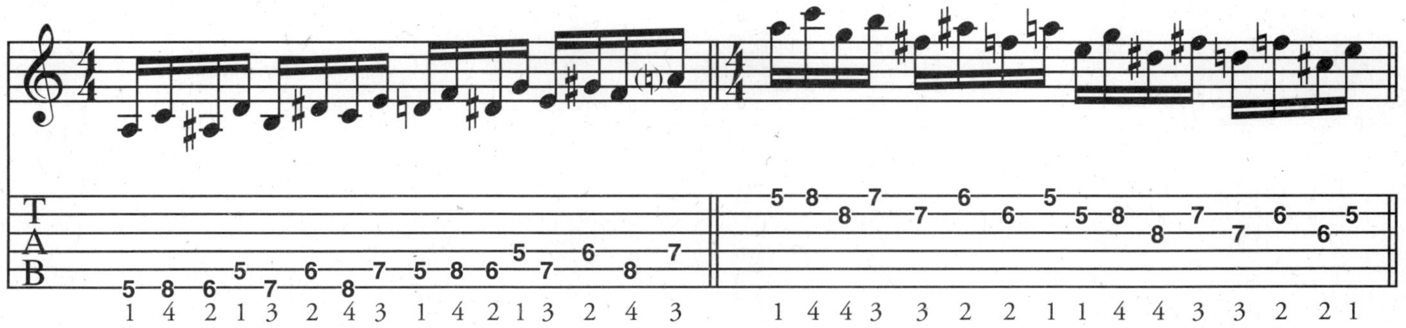

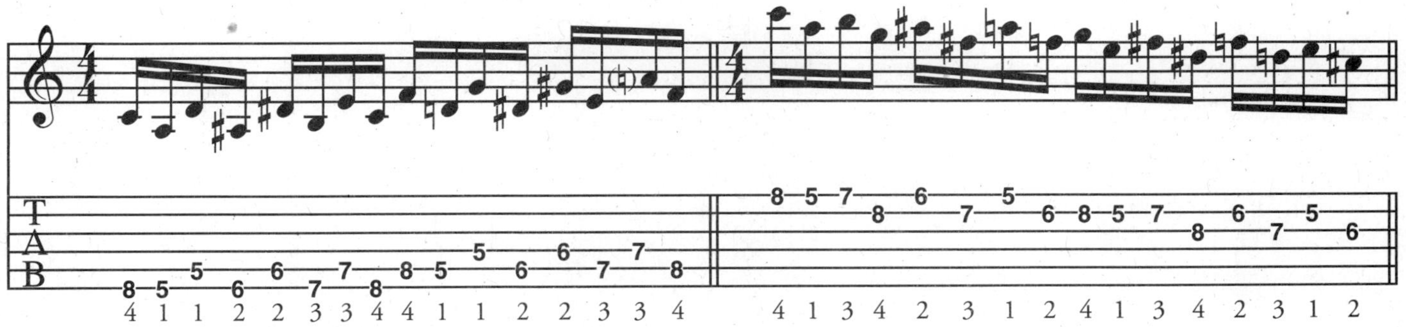

The next examples are ascending and descending patterns in groups of five. Pay close attention to your picking hand, as it is very easy to make a mistake.

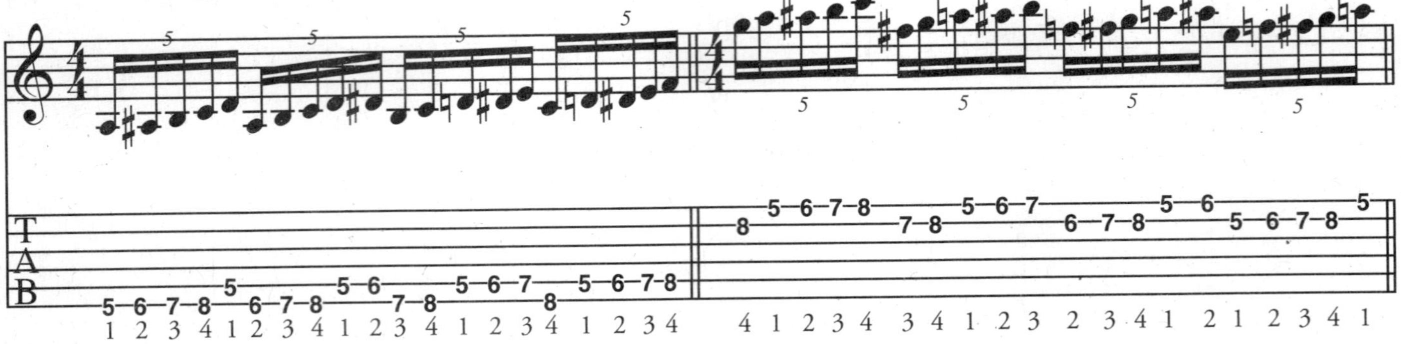

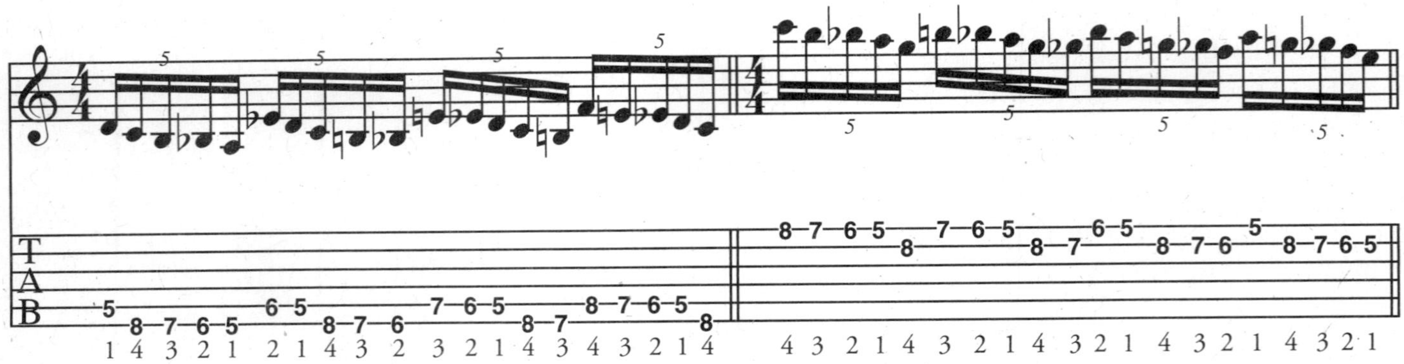

Below are more ascending and descending five-note patterns similar to the exercises on the previous pages.

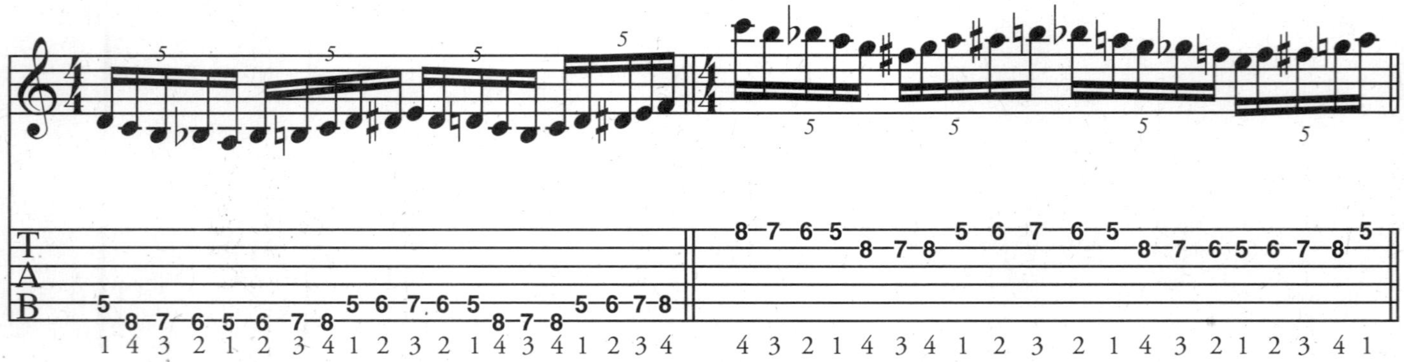

The examples and patterns in this chapter will help you develop excellent picking technique. They can also serve as a great warm-up routine, as they train the muscles and movements of your hand. As always, warm up slowly and with care. Speed is a result of accuracy, so be patient and diligent.

Chapter 4: Diatonic Theory

To be a great shredder and musician, you should know scale theory, chord theory, and diatonic harmony. All of this falls under the blanket of *diatonic* theory. The word "diatonic" means of a scale or key. Let's start by looking at the major scale.

The Major Scale

To understand the major scale, we need to first look at another scale. Western music consists of 12 notes that are organized in half steps. These 12 half steps make up what is known as the chromatic scale. The example below illustrates the chromatic scale starting on C. As you can see, the notes move in half steps from one fret to the next. The word "chromatic" is derived from the Greek word for color.

Note: When a slide is written in the music, but without a slur (⁀), it is indicating a *shift slide.* A shift slide facilitates a position change, and both the first and second notes are sounded with the pick.

The Chromatic Scale

1
Track 4.1

One of the most commonly used scales in music is the *major scale.* A major scale consists of seven notes organized in the following order of whole steps (W) and half steps (H): W–W–H–W–W–W–H.

Half steps occur between the 3rd and 4th notes and the 7th and 8th notes of the scale. (The 8th note is really the 1st note, just an *octave,* or 12 half steps, higher.)

Take a look at the keyboard illustration below, and you will see white keys separated by black keys (whole steps) and adjacent white keys with no black keys separating them (half steps).

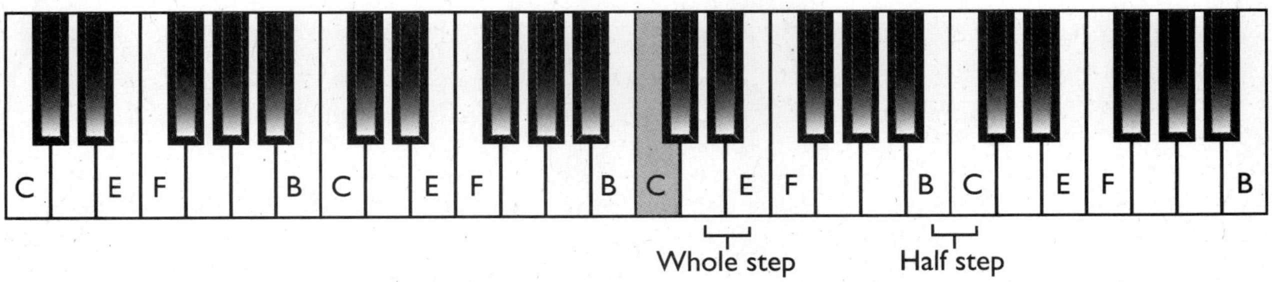

The adjacent white keys are the pitches E and F, and B and C. The diagram starts on the pitch C. If you count the number of pitches until you get to the half steps, you will find that the half steps are located between the 3rd and 4th notes, and the 7th and 8th notes. This is the case for all major scales.

Let's look first at a C Major scale. Like all major scales, its formula in terms of whole steps and half steps is: W–W–H–W–W–W–H. The seven notes of the major scale are assigned numbers, or *scale degrees:* 1–2–3–4–5–6–7. The 1 is the *root,* or *tonic,* of the scale. This is the note upon which the scale is built and from which it gets its name. The 8th scale degree can also be referred to as a 1 or root. (Notice in the scale below that the 1 is a C note, as is the 8.)

C Major Scale

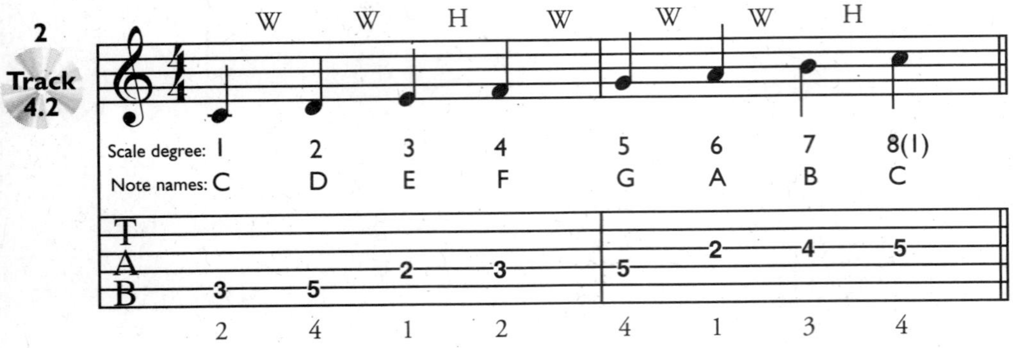

W = Whole step
H = Half step

You can create a major scale starting from any of the 12 pitches of the chromatic scale. All you need to do is follow the major scale formula of: W–W–H–W–W–W–H. You will need to raise or lower notes to create this formula. This is done by using either a *sharp* ♯, which raises a note by a half step, or a *flat* ♭, which lowers a note by a half step.

The example below shows a G Major scale. If you compare the order of whole steps and half steps, you will notice that it is exactly the same as the C Major scale above. To maintain the correct order of whole steps and half steps, we had to adjust a note. The interval between the 6 and 7, if we left the F as it was, would have been a half step. But because we needed a whole step in that place, we had to raise the 7 with a sharp, thereby creating the whole step interval between 6 and 7 (E and F♯), which at the same time created the half step we needed between 7 and 8 (F♯ and G).

G Major Scale

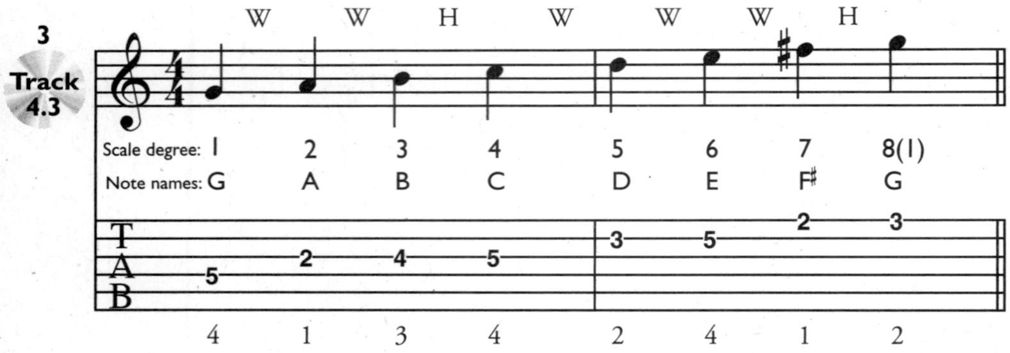

Intervals

An *interval* is the distance between two notes. Whole steps and half steps are two examples of intervals. In relation to the tonic, any note in the major scale can be considered an interval. Scale degree 2 can be referred to as a 2nd, scale degree 3 as a 3rd, etc.

Note: Any scale degree or interval can be altered with a sharp or flat (♯4, ♭3, etc.). So, referring to the G Major scale above, the 3 (or 3rd) is B, while a ♭3 (or ♭3rd) would be a B♭.

Triads

Scales can be used to build *chords.* (A chord is three or more notes played simultaneously.) A *triad* is the most basic kind of chord, consisting of three notes that are "stacked" from the root in intervals of 3rds (every other note in the scale).

There are four types, or *qualities,* of triads:

1. Major
2. Minor
3. Augmented
4. Diminished

The quality is determined by the order of major and minor 3rds within the chords. A *minor 3rd* (m3) consists of three half steps, or one and a half steps, and a *major 3rd* (M3) consists of four half steps, or two whole steps. Below, you will see chord tones, or scale degrees, that make up each type of triad, plus the structure of 3rds within the chords, from one note to the next (root to 3rd and 3rd to 5th).

M3 = Major 3rd
m3 = Minor 3rd

C Major Triad

C E G = 1 3 5
M3 m3

C Minor Triad

C E♭ G = 1 ♭3 5
m3 M3

C Augmented Triad

C E G♯ = 1 3 ♯5
M3 M3

C Diminished Triad

C E♭ G♭ = 1 ♭3 ♭5
m3 m3

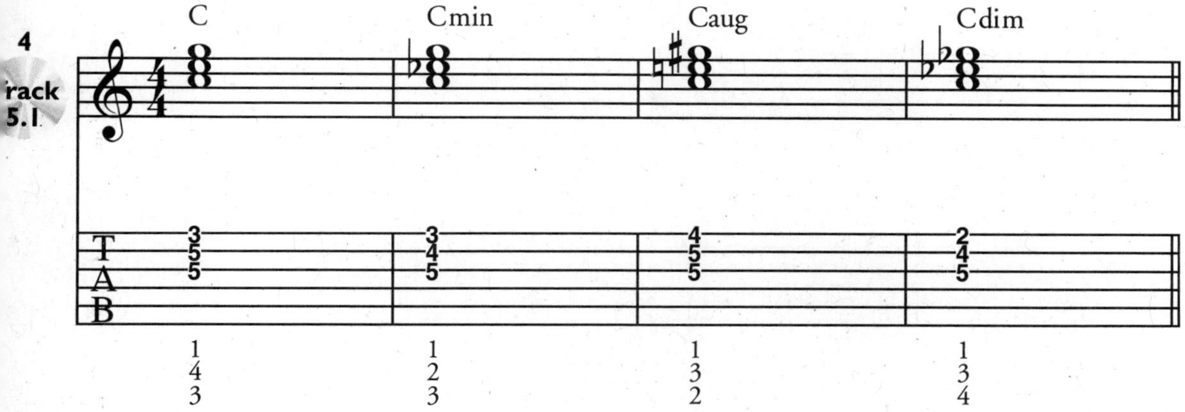

7th Chords

7th chords are four-note chords consisting of a basic triad with an added 7th on top. Another way to look at 7th chords is that they are basic triads with an additional 3rd interval on top. Below, you will see the five most common types of 7th chords.

C Major 7 (CMaj7)

C E G B = 1 3 5 7

M3 m3 M3

Maj. Triad

C Dominant 7 (C7)

C E G B♭ = 1 3 5 ♭7

M3 m3 m3

Maj. Triad

C Minor7 (Cmin7)

C E♭ G B♭ = 1 ♭3 5 ♭7

m3 M3 m3

Min. Triad

C Minor7♭5 (Cmin7♭5)

C E♭ G♭ B♭ = 1 ♭3 ♭5 ♭7

m3 m3 M3

Dim. Triad

C Diminished 7 (Cdim7)

C E♭ G♭ B♭♭ = 1 ♭3 ♭5 ♭♭7

m3 m3 m3

Dim. Triad

5
Track 5.2

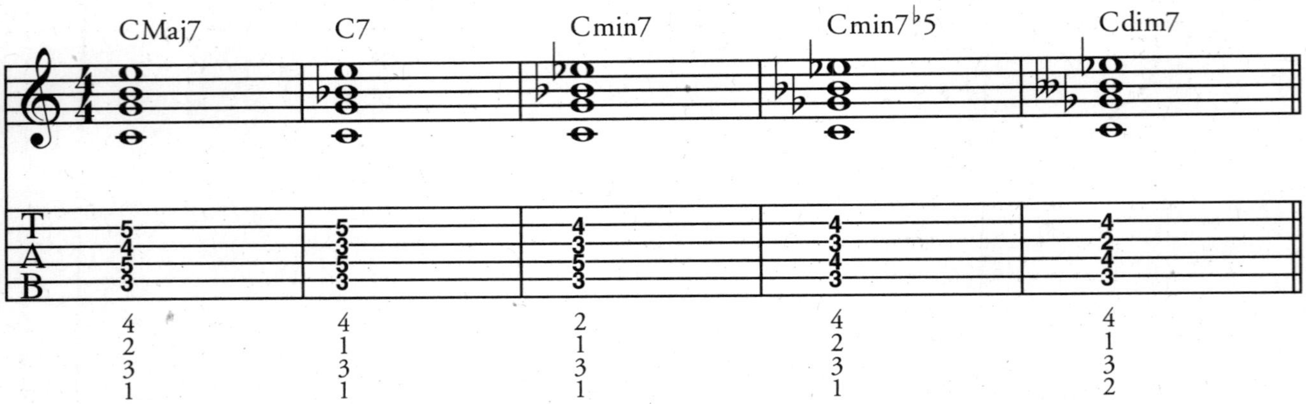

Diatonic Harmony

Diatonic harmony refers to all the chords that belong to a particular key, or that can be made using the notes of a particular scale. The example below shows the diatonic triads of the C Major scale.

6
Track 6.1

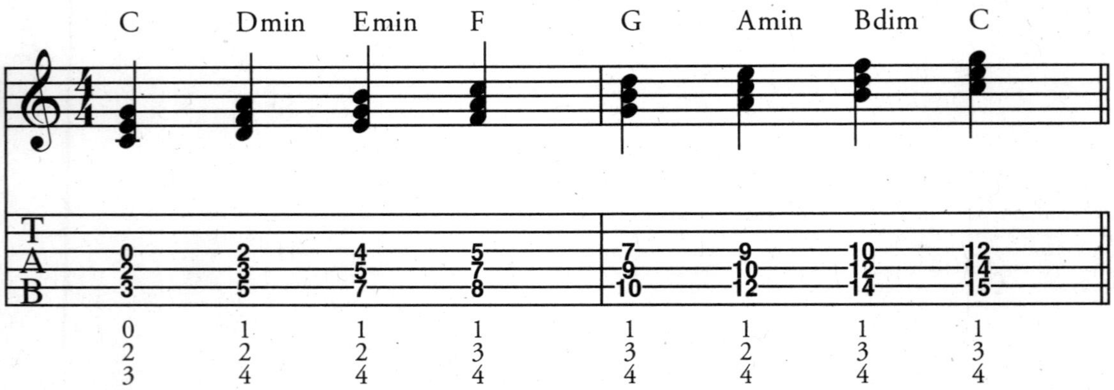

The example below shows the diatonic 7th chords built from the C Major scale.

7 Track 6.2

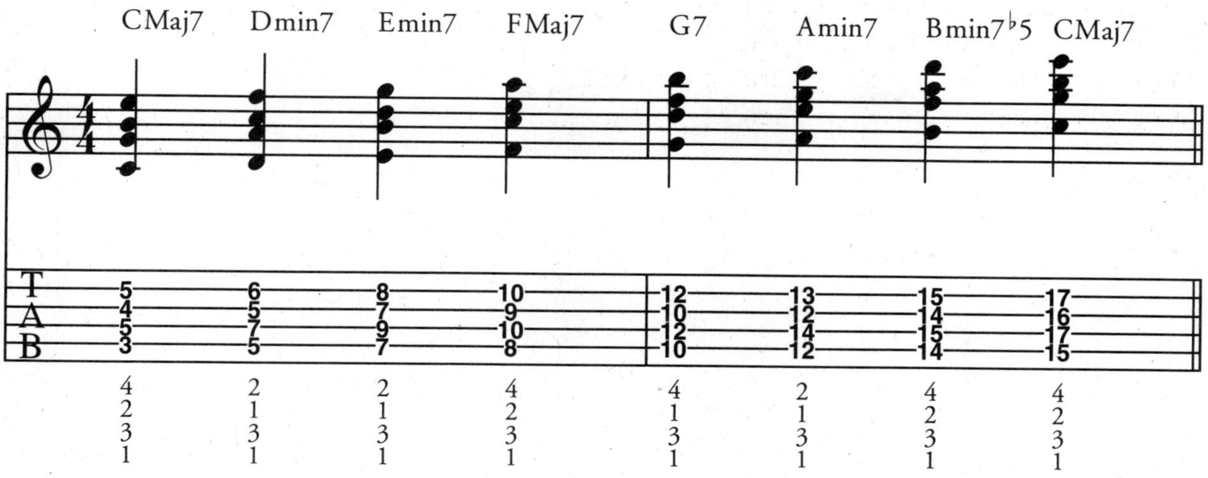

Roman Numerals and Chord Progressions

In diatonic harmony, chords can be referred to using Roman numerals. The chord built on the 1st scale degree is a I chord, the chord built on the 2nd scale degree is a ii chord, etc. Uppercase Romans indicate major chords, while lowercase Romans indicate minor or diminished (◦) chords.

Triads in C Major

I	ii	iii	IV	V	vi	vii°
C	Dmin	Emin	F	G	Amin	Bdim

7th Chords in C Major

I7	ii7	iii7	IV7	V7	vi7	vii min7♭5
CMaj7	Dmin7	Emin7	FMaj7	G7	Amin7	Bmin7♭5

Roman Numeral Review

I or i............... 1	V or v............ 5
II or ii............ 2	VI or vi.......... 6
III or iii.......... 3	VII or vii........ 7
IV or iv.......... 4	

This system makes it easier to analyze a *chord progression* (series of chords) and to *transpose* it, or move it to different keys.

The chord progression below is a simple I–vi–ii–V7 progression in the key of C.

Try moving this progression to a different key by using the relative positions indicated by the Roman numerals. For instance, if we started with a G chord, and used the chords of a harmonized G Major scale, we would get the progression: G(I)–Emin(vi)–Amin(ii)–D7(V7).

Practice analyzing chord progressions this way. It will help deepen your understanding of scales, chords, and music in general.

Natural Minor Scale

The *natural minor scale* is also known as the *relative minor scale*. It is derived from the 6th scale degree of a major scale. For example, the 6th scale degree of a C Major scale is the note A. If you build a seven-note scale starting from this note and follow the remaining pitches of the C Major scale, you will get an A Natural Minor scale. It's referred to as "relative" because it uses the same notes and chords as the major scale from which it is derived.

The scale degrees of the natural minor scale are as follows:

1	2	♭3	4	5	♭6	♭7	1
A	B	C	D	E	F	G	A

The formula in terms of whole steps and half steps is: W–H–W–W–H–W–W. The example below illustrates the A Natural Minor scale.

A Natural Minor Scale

8
Track 7.1

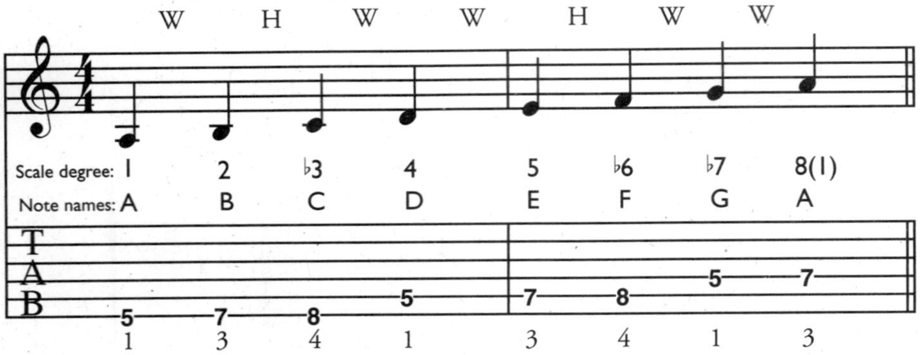

Major Key	Relative Minor
C Major	A Minor
G Major	E Minor
D Major	B Minor
A Major	F♯ Minor
E Major	C♯ Minor
B Major	G♯ Minor
F♯ Major	D♯ Minor
F Major	D Minor
B♭ Major	G Minor
E♭ Major	C Minor
A♭ Major	F Minor
D♭ Major	B♭ Minor
G♭ Major	E♭ Minor

Every major scale has a relative minor scale with which it shares the same notes, chords, and sharps or flats. An easy way to figure out a major scale's relative minor is to go down one and a half steps from the root note. (One and a half steps down from C is A, one and a half steps down from G is E, etc.). To the right is a chart listing all of the major scales and their corresponding relative minors.

The natural minor scale can also be harmonized as triads and 7th chords, as seen below using the A Natural Minor scale.

9
Track 7.2

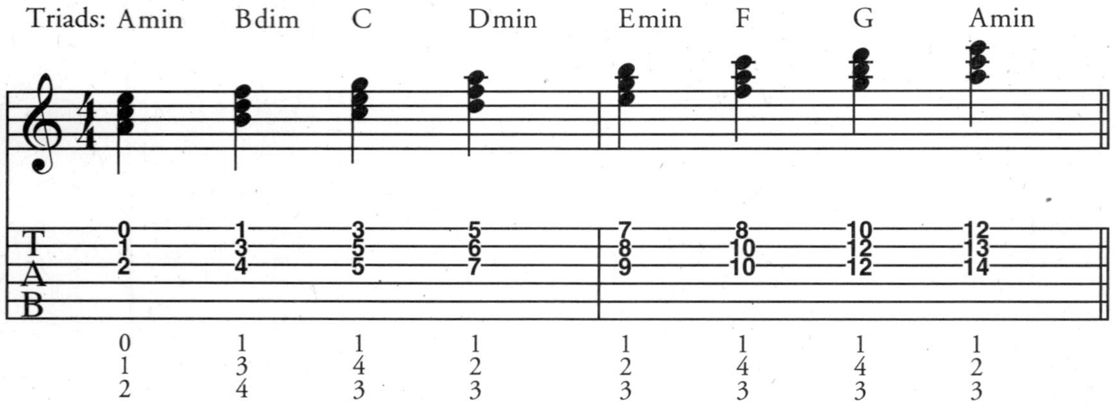

10
Track 7.3

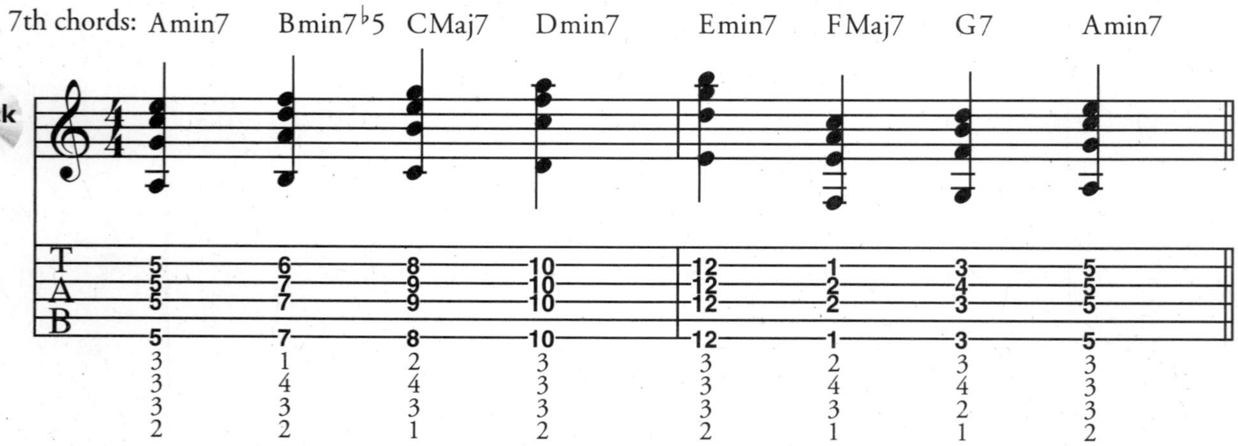

More on Intervals

Intervals can be measured by counting the half steps between two notes. The half step, as you'll see below, is also known as the *minor 2nd*, and it is the smallest interval between two notes.

11
Track 8

Minor 2nd (1 half step)

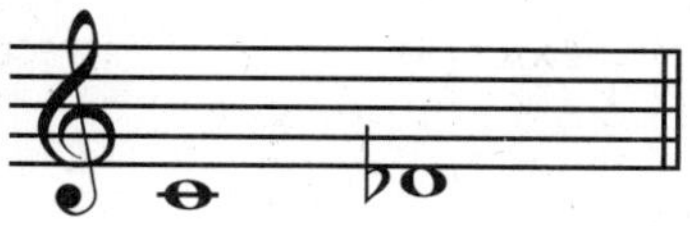

C D♭

Major 2nd (2 half steps)

C D

Minor 3rd (3 half steps)

C E♭

Major 3rd (4 half steps)

C E

Perfect 4th (5 half steps)

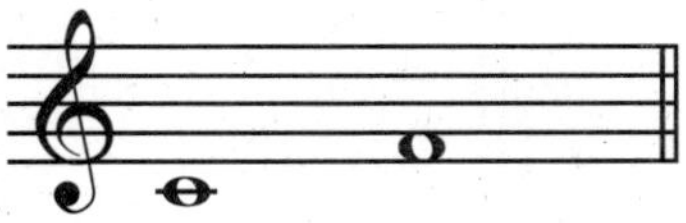

C F

Augmented 4th (6 half steps)

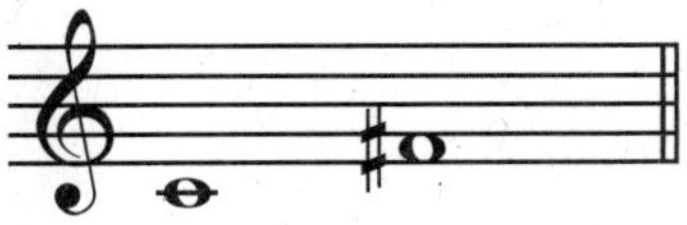

C F♯

Perfect 5th (7 half steps)

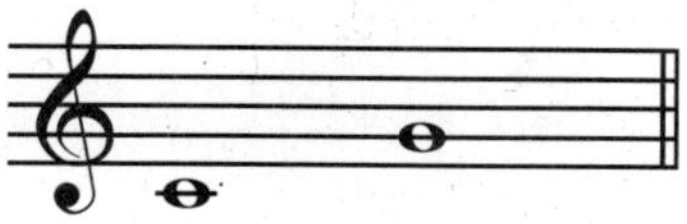

C G

Minor 6th (8 half steps)

C D♭

Major 6th (9 half steps)

C A

Minor 7th (10 half steps)

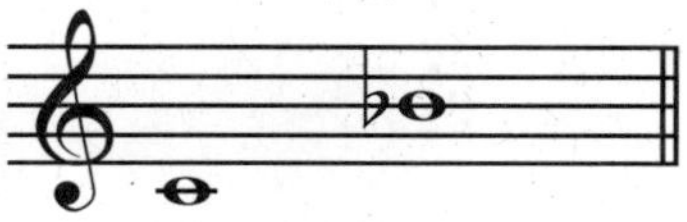

C B♭

Major 7th (11 half steps)

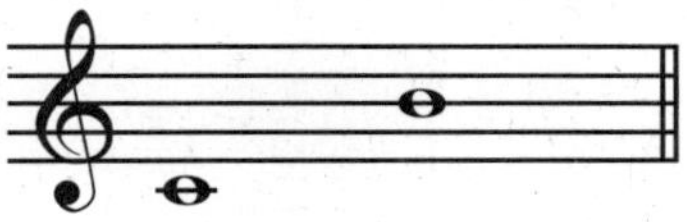

C B

Perfect Octave (12 half steps)

C C

Try to memorize all of the intervals above, as well as their distance in half steps. This will help you better understand how scales and chords are built and named.

Interval Inversions

Another way to organize intervals is according to their *inversions.* To invert an interval, you simply place the bottom note on top. This changes the name and quality of the interval. The sum of the interval and its inversion is always 9. (If you look at the first example below, you will see a 7th and a 2nd: 7+2=9. In the example after that, you have a 3rd and a 6th: 3+6=9, etc.) When you invert an interval, you are also changing its quality. A major interval becomes minor, minor becomes major, augmented becomes diminished, and diminished becomes augmented. Perfect intervals are the only ones in which the quality remains the same. You will notice that each interval and its inversion spans one octave.

Below are examples of intervals and their inversions.

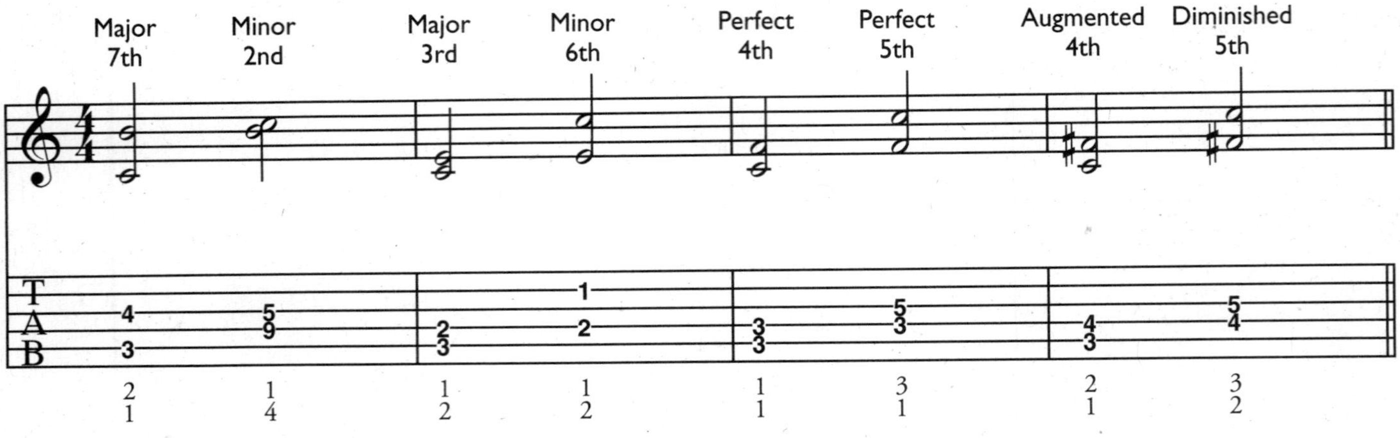

Extended Intervals and Chords

The term *extended chords* refers to chords that include *extensions,* or notes that lie beyond a one-octave major scale. (The most common tones we add to chords are the 9th, 11th, and 13th.)

C Major Scale (Two Octaves) Extended Intervals

A Note about Simple and Compound Intervals

Intervals that stay within one octave are known as *simple intervals,* whereas those that go beyond an octave are referred to as *compound* intervals. The extensions 9, 11, and 13 are actually not new intervals; they are the compound versions of the simple 2nd, 4th, and 6th intervals. In other words, these intervals are the same, except the notes are in a higher octave.

Below is an extended C Major 7th chord. Although, technically, this would be called CMaj13, for now, we will call it CMaj7 and show all the extensions.

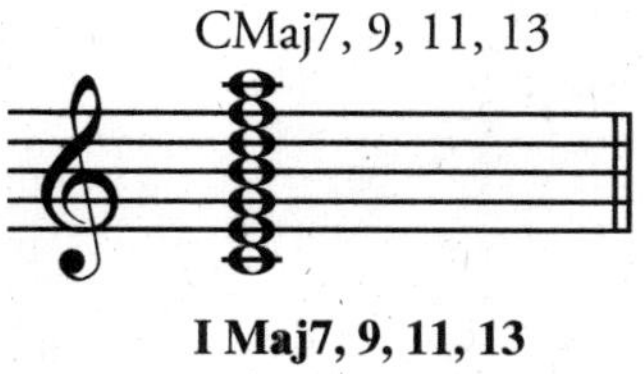

And following are the remaining extended chords in the key of C Major. Note that all chord tones and extensions are relative to the root of each chord, but they are all diatonic to the key of C.

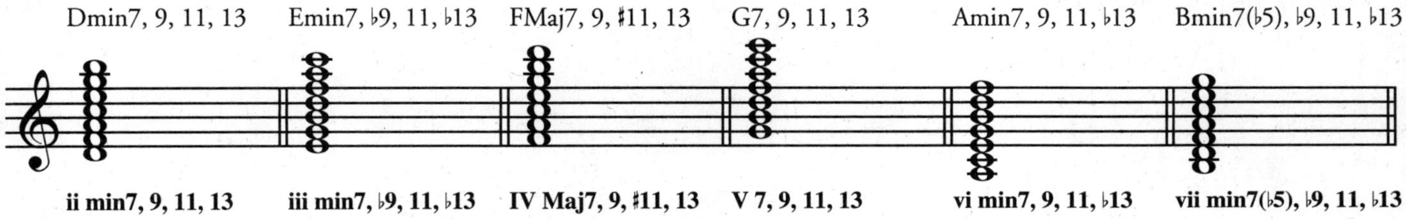

Extensions, which can be applied to any chord derived from any scale, can add interesting colors to chords and help you with note choices when soloing.

Circle of 5ths

The *circle of 5ths* refers to the organization of the 12 keys—in intervals of 5ths—around a circle.

Starting from the key of C Major (which has no sharps or flats), we go clockwise around the circle and up a 5th to G Major (which has one sharp). Then we go up another 5th to D Major (which has two sharps), etc. We continue to go clockwise around the circle, going up a 5th each time—as well as adding a sharp with each new key—until we get to F♯ Major, which is the last key with sharps.

We can also go counterclockwise around the circle, going up a 4th (the inversion of a 5th) with each new key. So, starting from C Major, we go up a 4th to F (which has one flat), then up a 4th to B♭ (which has two flats), etc.

Because this is a circle, if you continue moving clockwise in 5ths or counterclockwise in 4ths, you will end up on the same pitch where you started after cycling through all 12 keys.

Highlighted in the circle below, you will see *enharmonic keys*. *Enharmonic equivalents* are notes that sound the same but are spelled differently (for example, C♯ and D♭). So, enharmonic keys are keys that sound exactly the same, but are spelled differently.

In addition to the major keys, you will also see their corresponding relative minor keys, which share the same key signature.

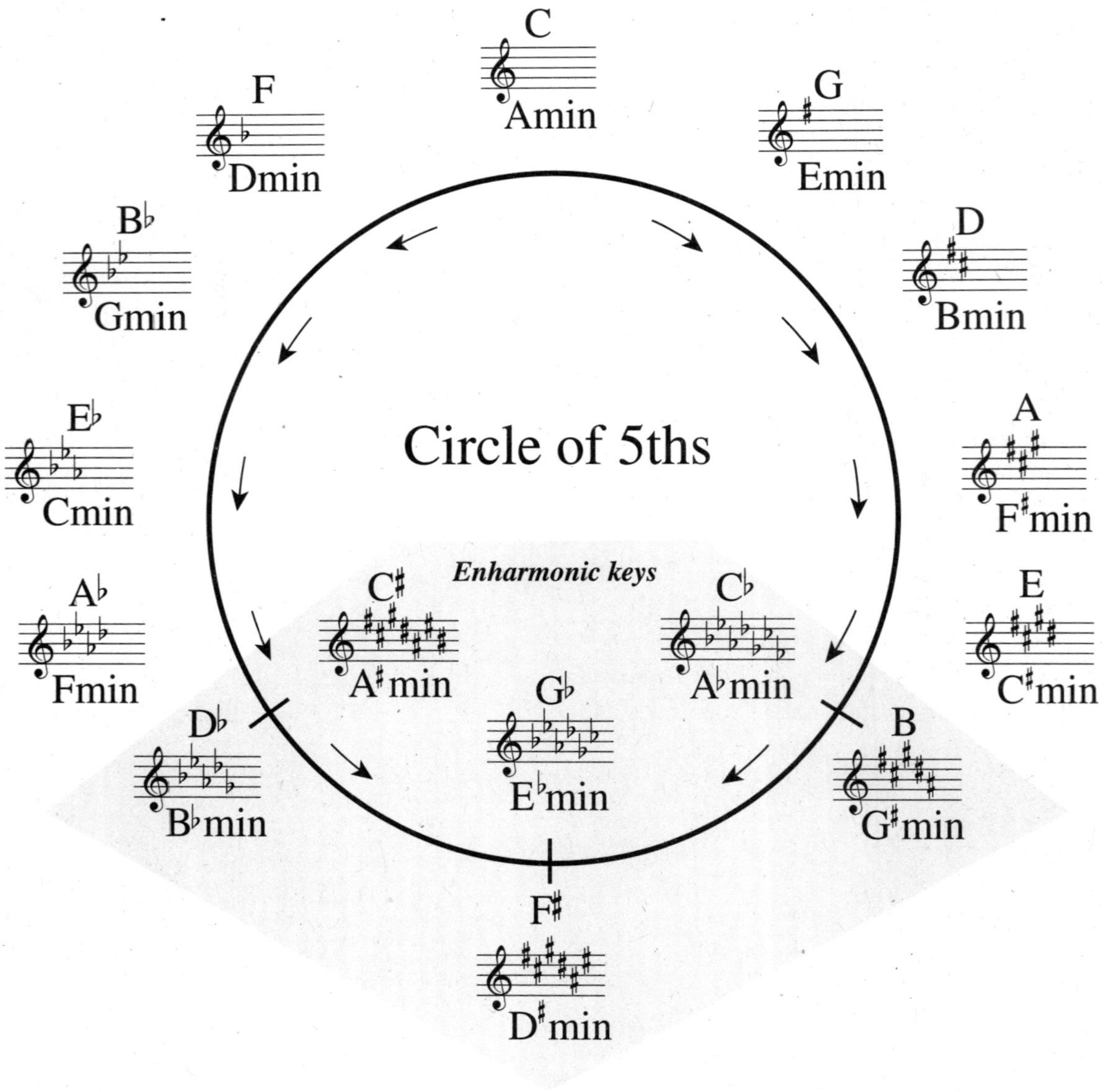

Chapter 5: Minor Pentatonic Scale

One of the first and most common scales used by guitarists and aspiring shredders is the *minor pentatonic scale,* which consists of five notes and has the formula: $1–\flat 3–4–5–\flat 7$.

The example below is the A Minor Pentatonic scale with the notes: A–C–D–E–G.

A Minor Pentatonic Scale

1
Track 9.1

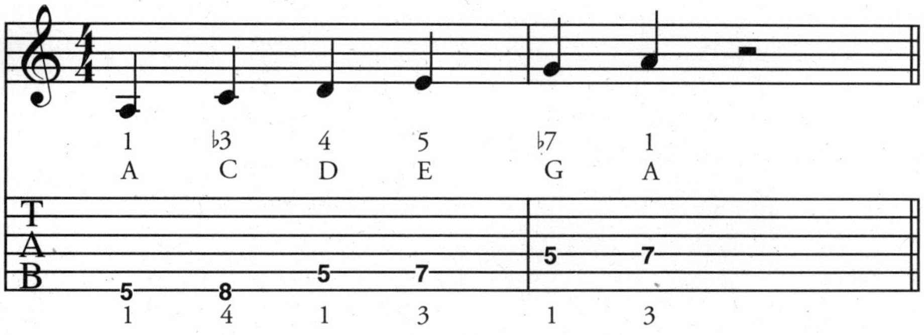

This scale is particularly useful because it can be played in many different stylistic and harmonic contexts. When compared to the A Natural Minor scale, the A Minor Pentatonic scale has two missing notes: 2 and $\flat 6$. The basic fingering pattern for the scale is illustrated to the right. You probably already know this shape, as it the first one most guitarists learn when beginning to study the guitar.

2
Track 9.2

Starting from the Root

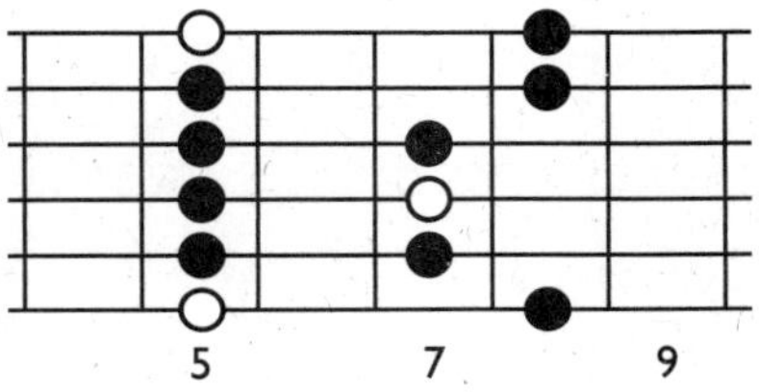

If you play this scale starting on the different scale degrees ($\flat 3$, then 4, then 5, then $\flat 7$), you will produce four more fingering patterns that cover the entire fretboard.

Starting from the $\flat 3$

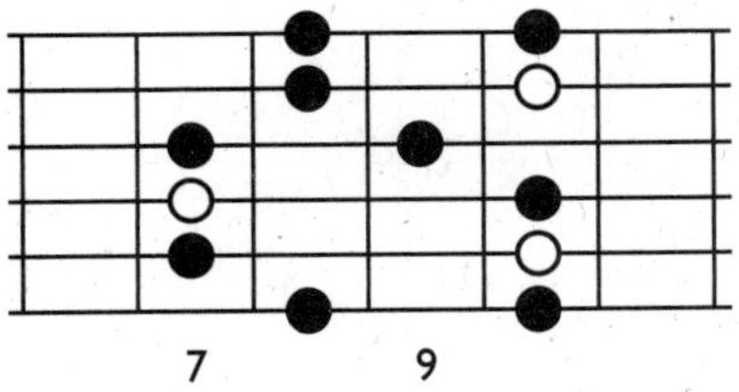

Starting from the 4

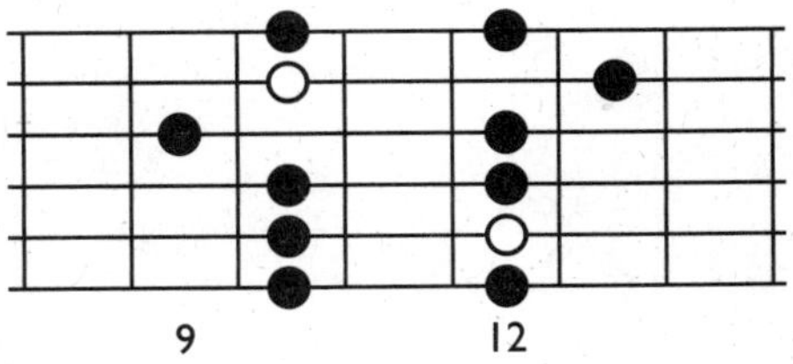

Starting from the 5

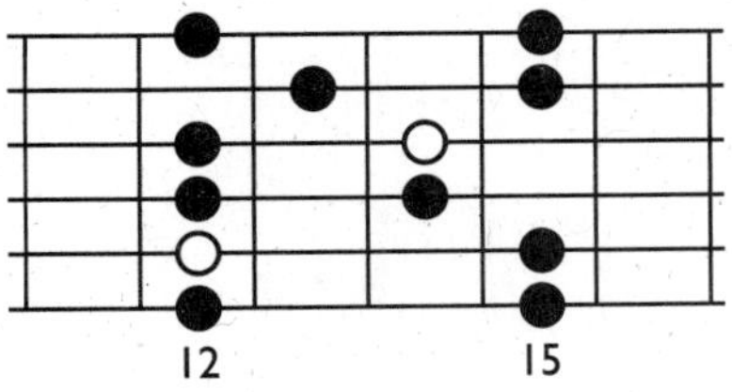

Starting from the $\flat 7$

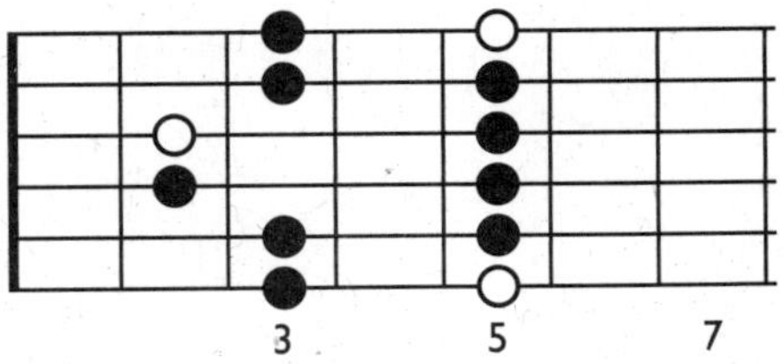

It is very important to learn the notes and formula for the minor pentatonic scale, as well as all five fingering patterns on this page. This will provide a solid base for soloing with this scale across the fretboard.

Exercising with Sequences

When learning scales, it is important to use them in technical exercises to develop dexterity and musical vocabulary. Following is a series of exercises applying the minor pentatonic scale to various patterns and *sequences*. We have already used sequences in the warm-up section of this book; now we will give it the formal definition of a musical phrase that is repeated at different pitch levels. For example: 1–♭3–4, ♭3–4–5, 4–5–♭7, etc. (See first example below.)

All of the examples in this section show the beginning of each sequence; you will have to continue the sequence for the entire scale position. This should be relatively easy, and, at the same time, a great ear-training exercise as you really have to understand the fingering patterns from the previous page before you can practice these exercises. So, keep your brain and hands connected and "switched on" at all times.

Following are three-note sequences in ascending or descending form. Play all of these examples with strict alternate picking.

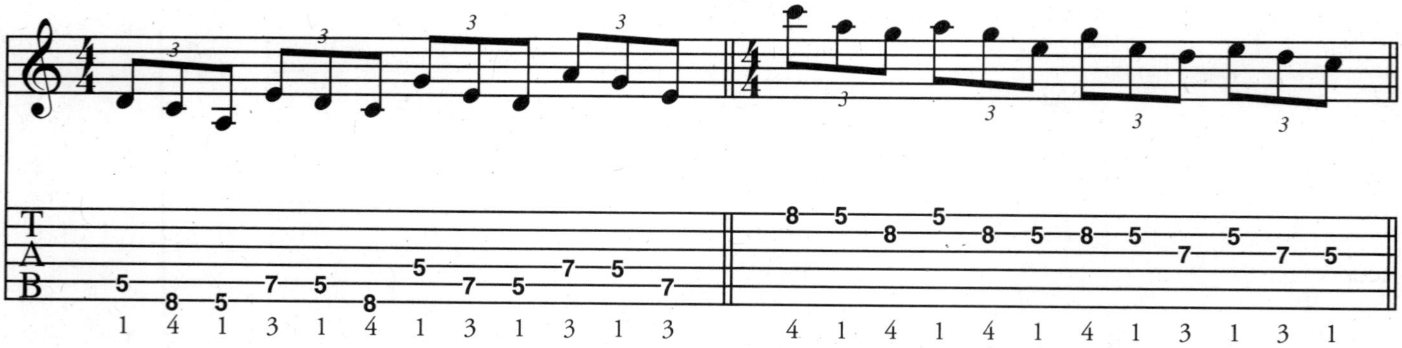

The following sequences combine ascending and descending motions.

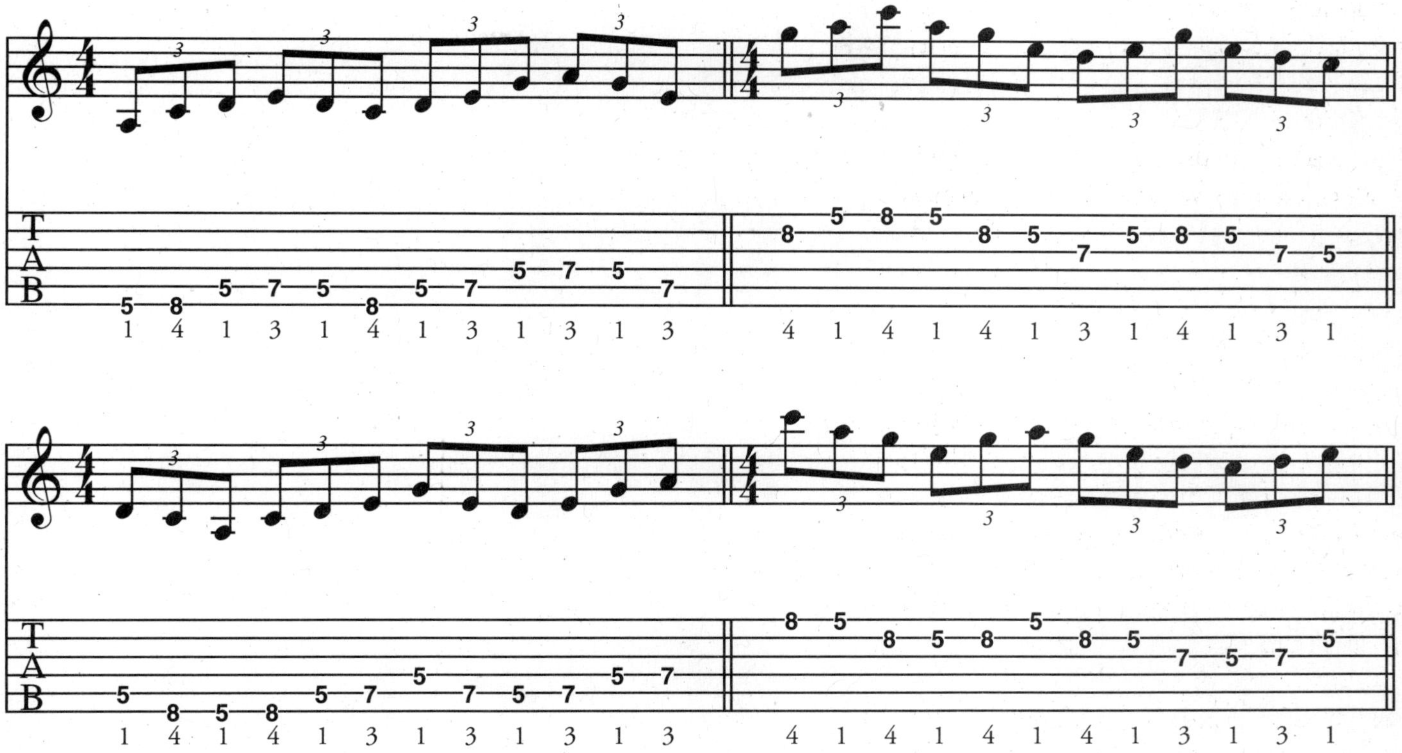

The next examples are four-note sequences in ascending and descending forms.

The following four-note sequences combine ascending and descending motions.

Now that you have covered some basic patterns, let's take a look at some more challenging ones. The following sequences are in five- and six-note groupings. Though these may be less common than those on the previous pages, they will add interest and variation to your playing.

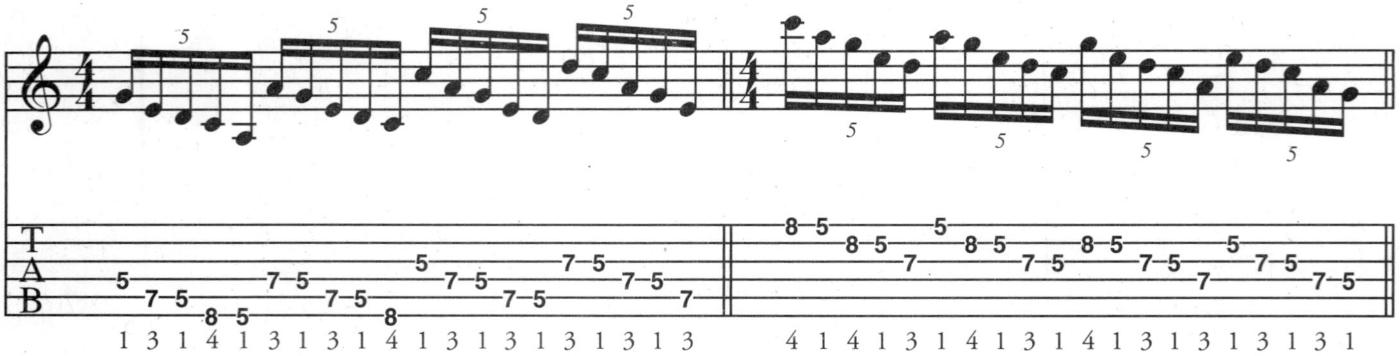

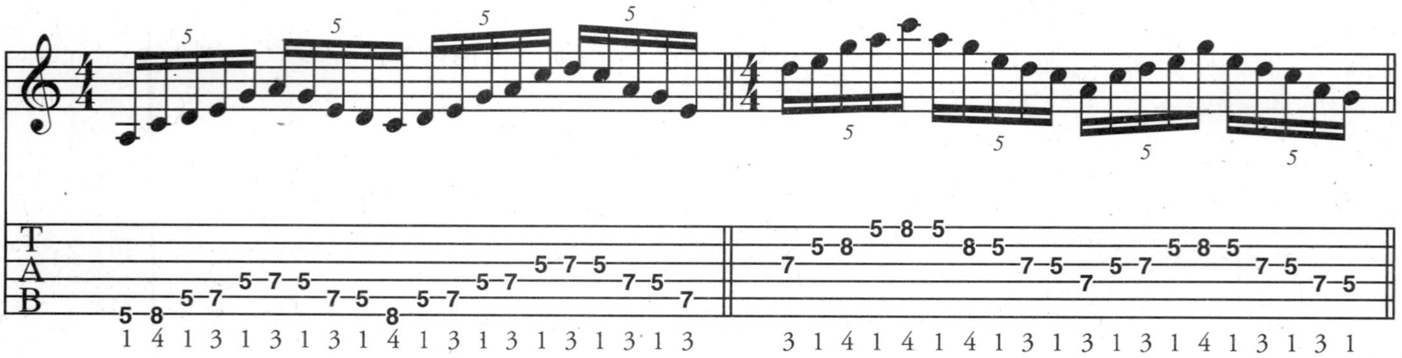

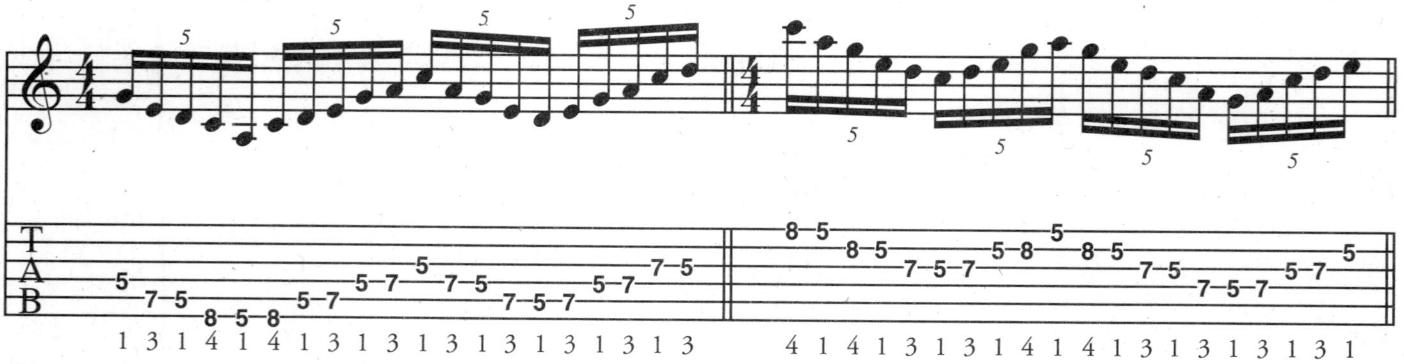

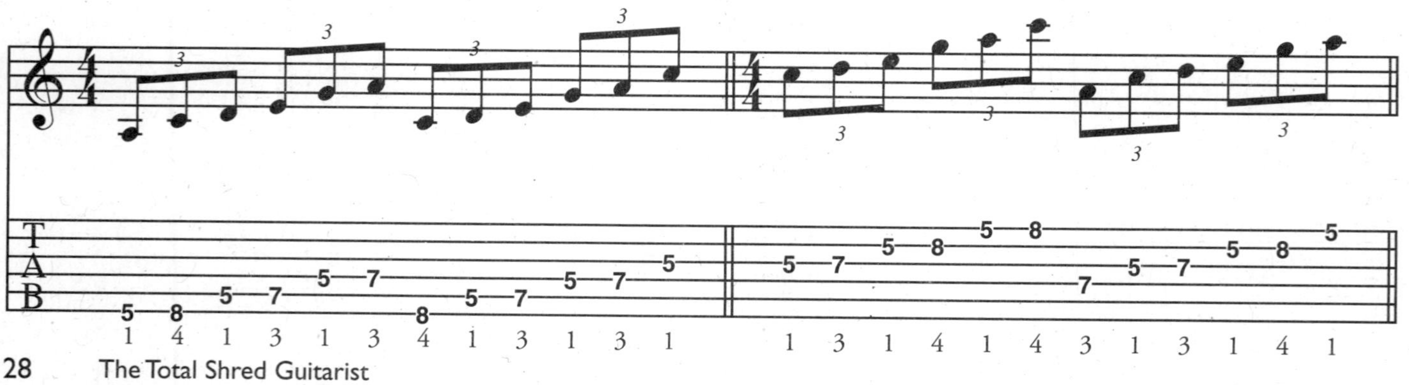

Up Close

Let's take a closer look at the pentatonic scale. By isolating the first four notes of each of the five fingering patterns from page 25, we get five useful shapes. (Forms 3 and 5 look the same but consist of different scale degrees.)

3
Track
9.3

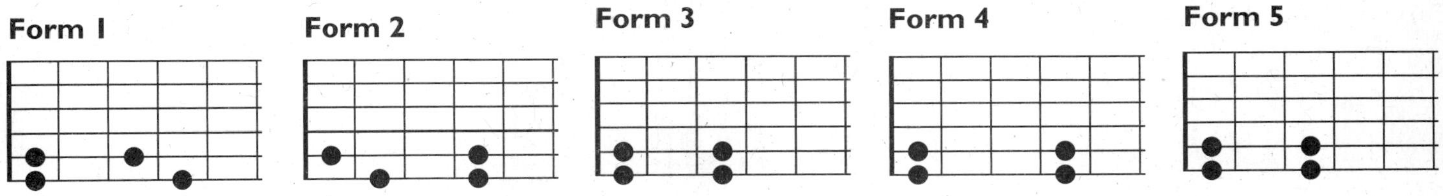

These five shapes represent the basic building blocks of the minor pentatonic scale. (A one-fret adjustment is necessary when dealing with the 2nd and 3rd strings because these strings are tuned a major 3rd apart rather than a perfect 4th; see Study Tip on next page.) If you take a closer look at the five positions of the scale, you can clearly see these different shapes. For example, if you "dissect" the root position fingering pattern, you will find the following basic forms: 1, 3, 5, 2, and 4. This row of numbers represents the order of the cycling patterns. In other words, no matter what pattern you start on, the order will always be the same.

The example below shows the minor pentatonic scale played on two adjacent strings. It is in the key of A Minor, but practice it in all 12 keys.

4
Track
10.1

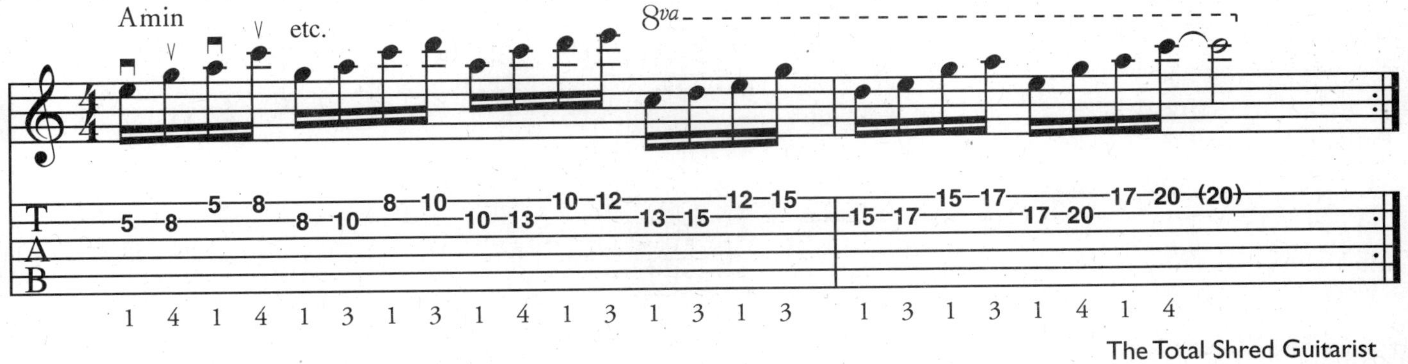

Study Tip: The guitar is tuned mainly in perfect 4ths but the 3rd(G) and 2nd(B) strings are tuned to a major 3rd. This difference in tuning will affect your shapes when applied to those two strings. In these cases, you must adjust each pattern by moving the notes on the 2nd string one fret to the right. This will give the otherwise simple and commonly known shapes a different appearance. Please make sure you can see and understand this adjustment.

To help you, the following example shows the pentatonic scale played across the G and B strings. Try finding the basic five forms as they have been offset by one fret. The ascending sequence starts with Form 1.

5

Track 10.2

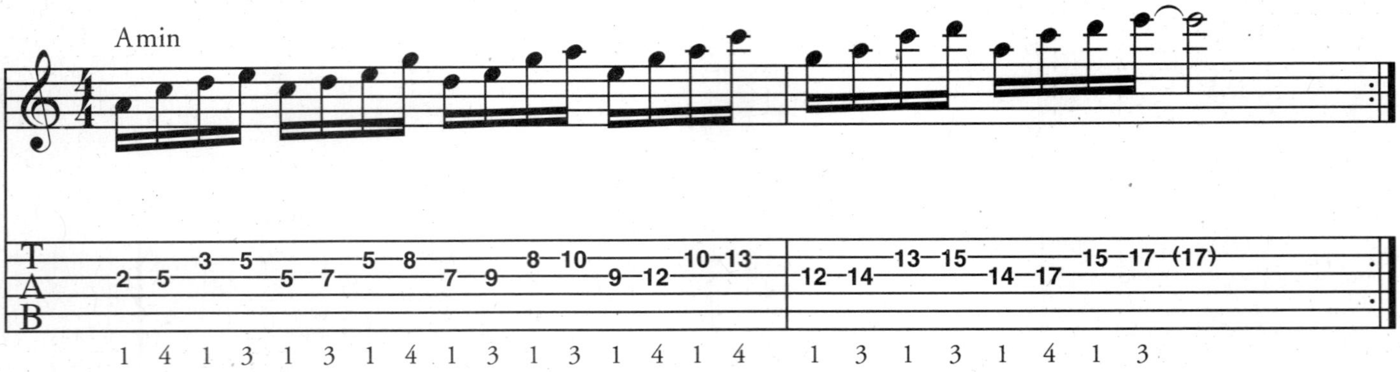

The example below demonstrates Form 5 of the minor pentatonic scale played in three octaves across all the strings.

6

Track 10.3

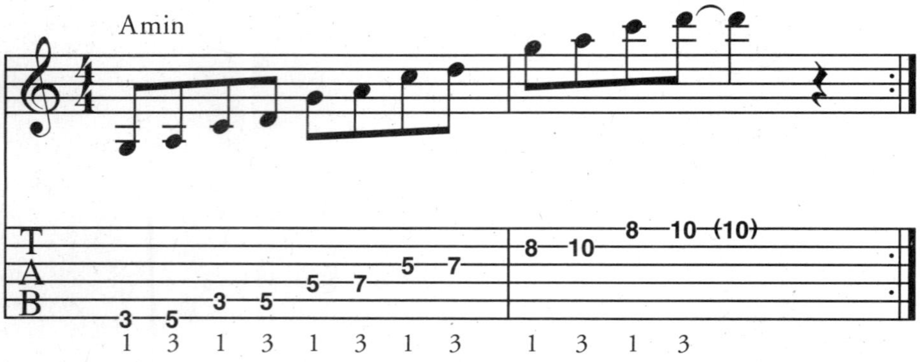

Practice all five forms and connect them horizontally and vertically on the fretboard. It's a great way to deepen your understanding of the minor pentatonic scale.

Licks and Backing Tracks

Now that you have learned the pentatonic scale and worked on patterns and sequences, it is time to put them into a musical context. Use the accompanying backing tracks to practice soloing with pentatonic scales, applying all the patterns and sequences you have learned in this chapter.

In addition, on the next page, you will find examples of common pentatonic licks to try over the backing tracks. (Later, we will introduce many more licks utilizing the pentatonic scale when we discuss different techniques such as tapping, legato, sweep picking, and so on.) If you need a review of bending technique, refer to page 5.

Track 11 — Backing Track 1 ||: Amin | Amin :||

Track 12 — Backing Track 2 ||: Cmin | Fmin :||

Track 13 — Backing Track 3 ||: G C | Emin D :||

Track 14 — Backing Track 4 ||: Bmin A/C# | D A :||

Lick 1 (A Minor Pentatonic String Skipping Lick)

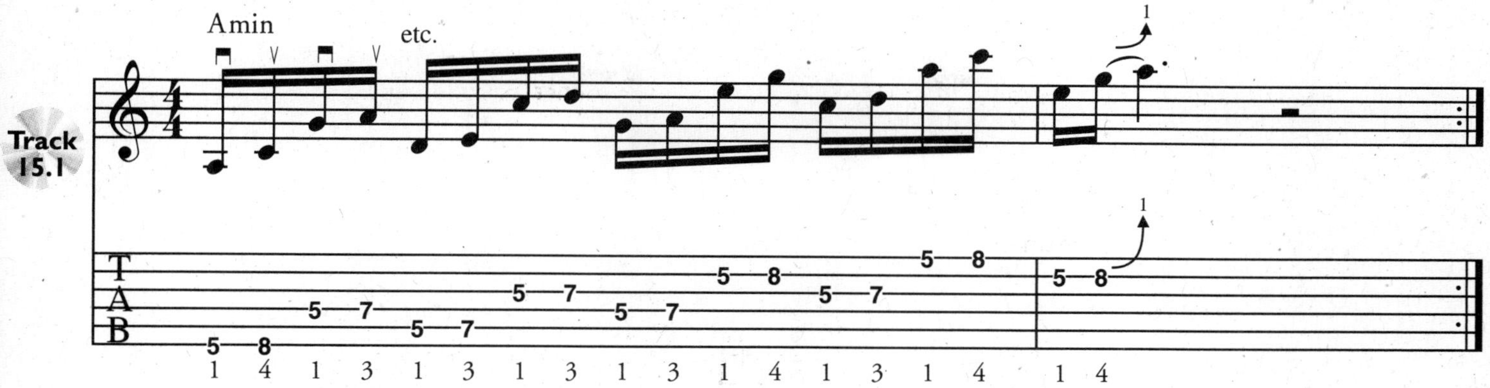

Lick 2 (Rock 'n' Roll Cliché Lick in C Minor Pentatonic)

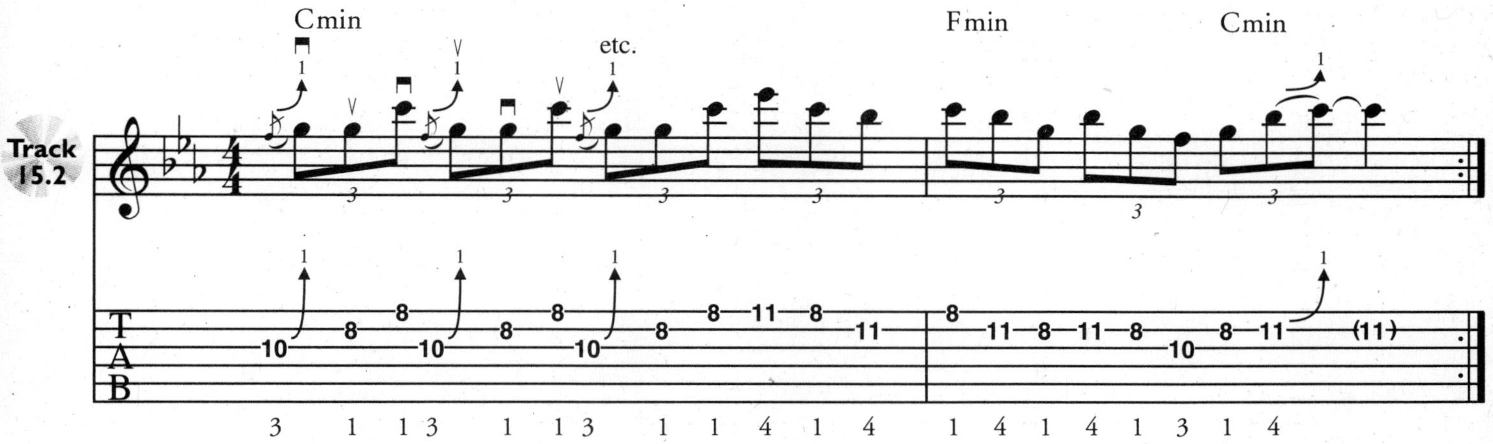

Lick 3 (Fast E Minor Pentatonic Bends in the Style of Eddie Van Halen and Jimi Hendrix)

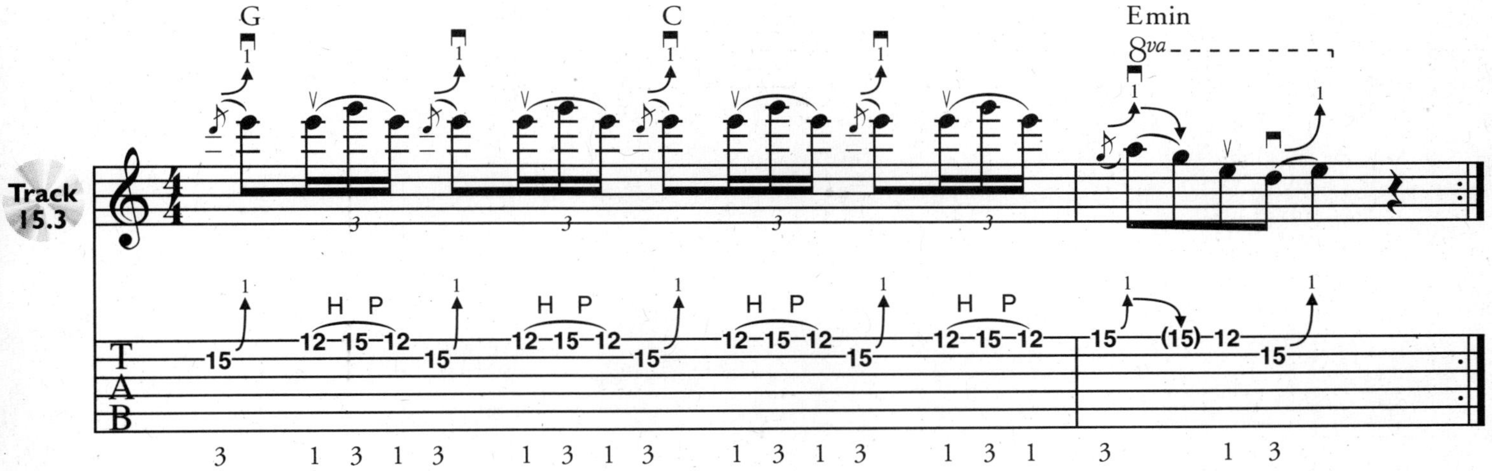

Lick 4 (Three-Note-Per-String/ String-Skipping Pentatonic Lick in the Style of Paul Gilbert)

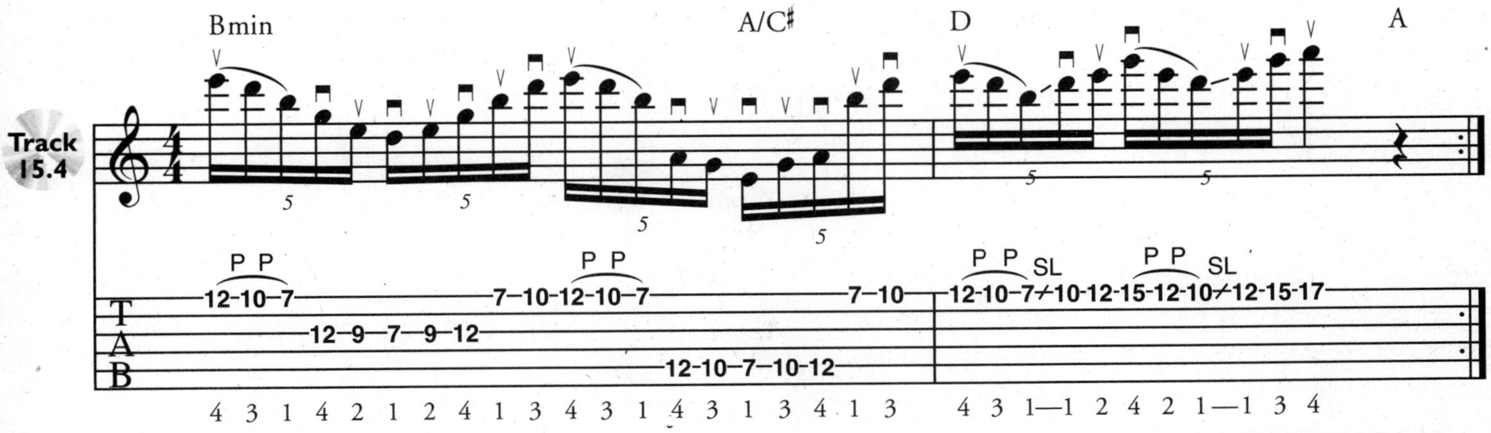

Chapter 6: Patterns for Alternate Picking

Alternate picking, one of the most important and common techniques for guitar is also one of the hardest and most labor intensive techniques to master and maintain. To develop good picking skills and maintain a certain "chops" level, one must practice patiently and daily to achieve perfect speed and synchronicity between picking and fretting hands. A good way to develop this skill is to practice short musical phrases before using them to construct more complex and longer ideas. Practice the following examples slowly at first, and keep track of your tempos as you are able to increase your speed.

Pattern 1 is a simple three-note ascending group. Play it slowly on the 3rd string. Play it as written, then all the way up the fretboard and down again until you reach your original position. Try to keep your picking relaxed and even.

The next example is the descending version of pattern 1. Again, take it slow, and make sure your left- and right-hand coordination is working properly.

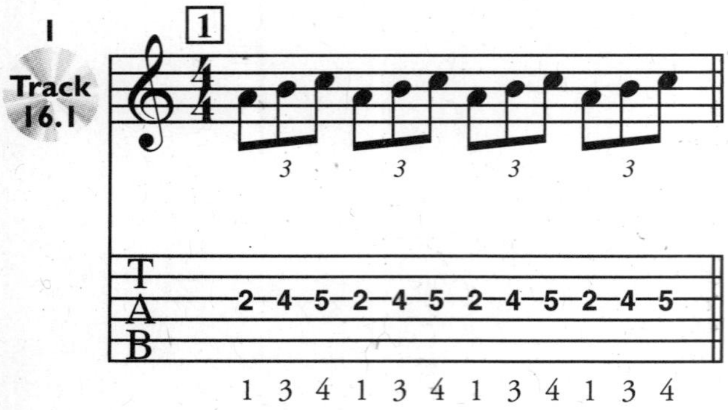

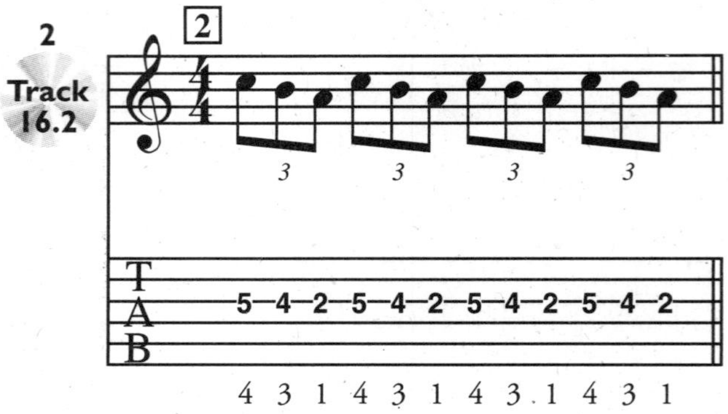

The next examples are also simple one-string patterns. Play them slowly, being attentive to proper picking technique, as it is important to learn the ideas and motions correctly right from the very beginning. When practicing the patterns, move them also to the other five strings and up and down the fretboard.

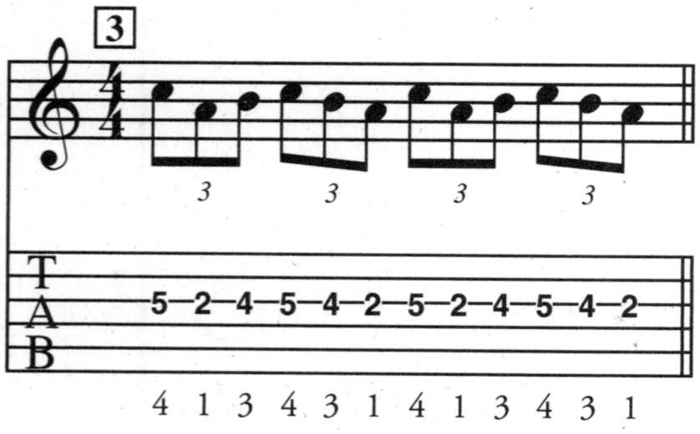

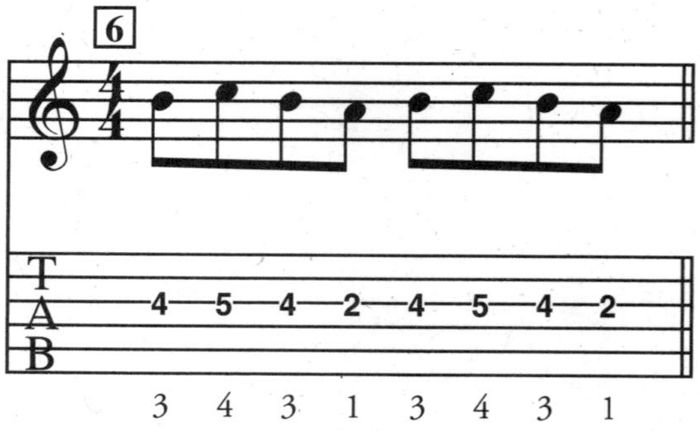

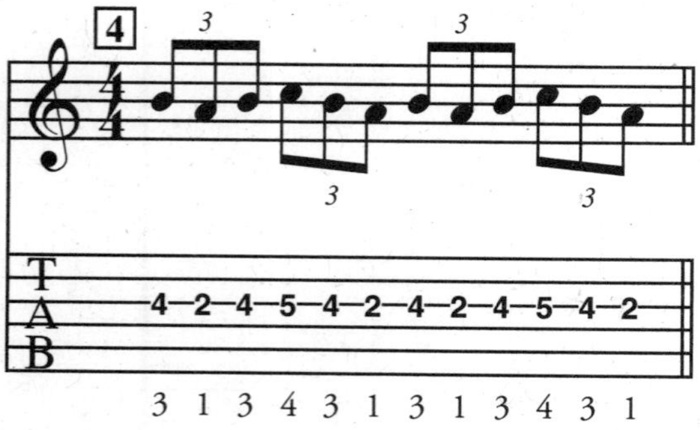

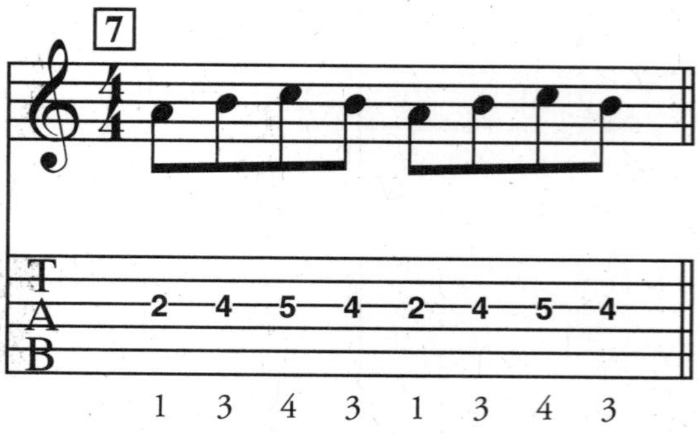

Examples 8, 9, and 10 are also single-string patterns, but they are rhythmically more challenging as they are made up of quintuplets or *septuplets* (seven notes in the time of six notes with the same value). Accent the downbeats (1, 2, 3, and 4) to maintain the proper rhythm and to clearly subdivide the beats. Use a metronome with these patterns.

8

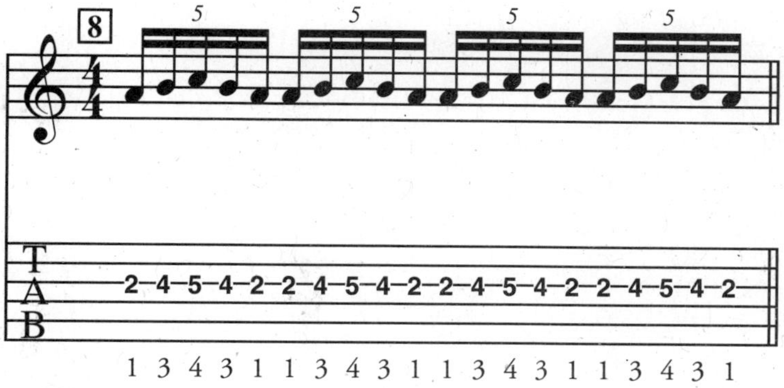

9

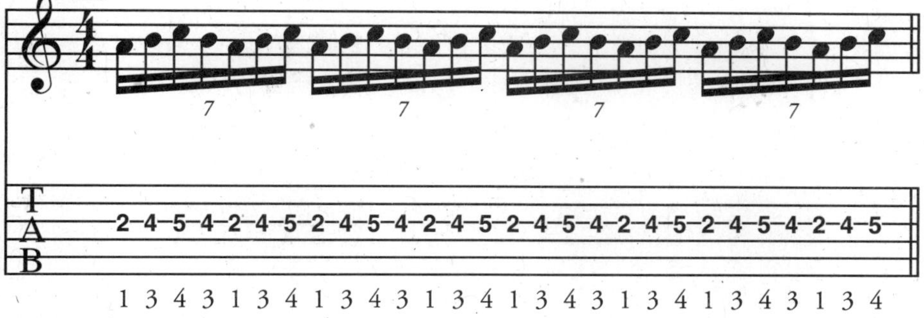

10

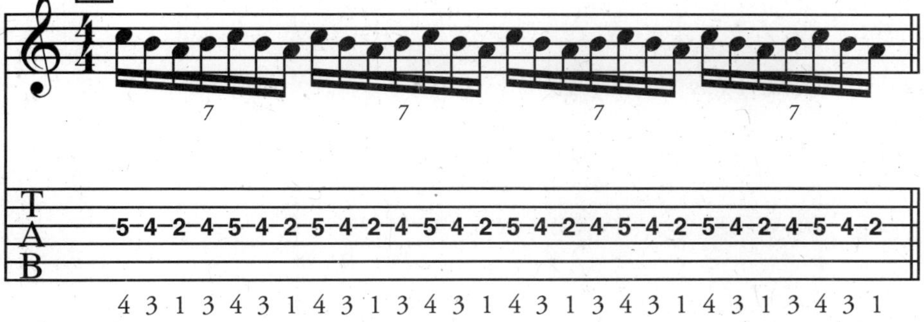

Next up are two-string sequences. These will be more challenging as they use more notes and more complex motions. Again, begin slowly and monitor your right- and left-hand coordination. Example 11 is a basic six-note ascending group and Example 12 is the opposite, a six-note descending group. In Example 13, you are crossing over to an adjacent string for a single upstroke. Because we are using strict alternate picking, you need to play the A note on the G string with an upstroke before returning to the D string. Play this example very carefully and overemphasize the upstroke on the G string to ensure you are playing it correctly. We encounter the same picking situation with Example 14, which is a descending version of Example 13. Examples 15 and 16 are combinations of the previous patterns; Example 15 is a combination of 13 and 11, and Example 16 consists of patterns 14 and 12.

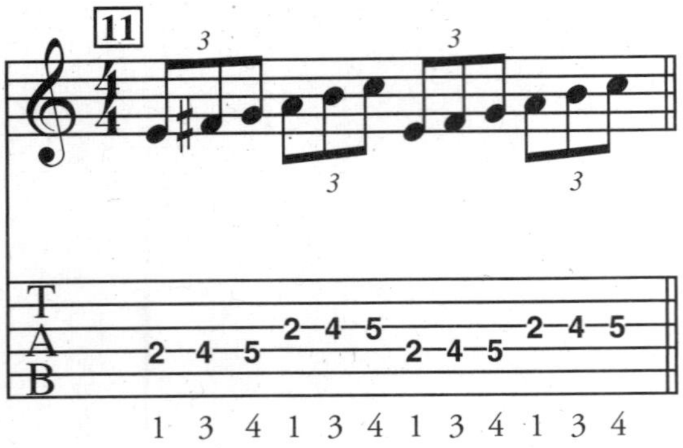

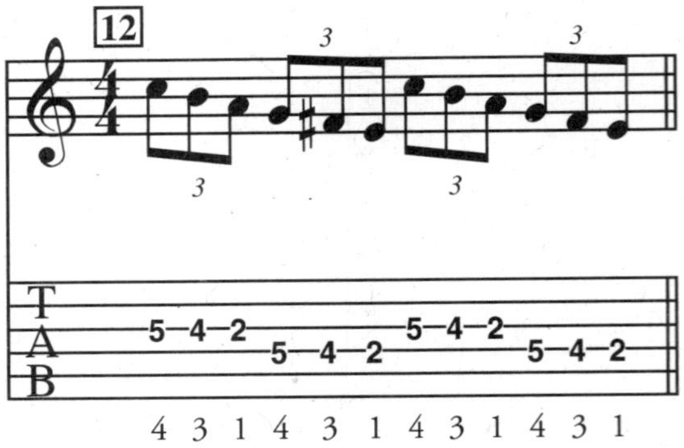

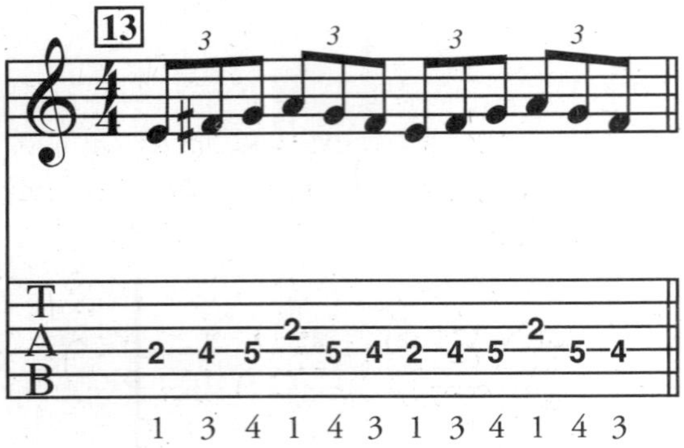

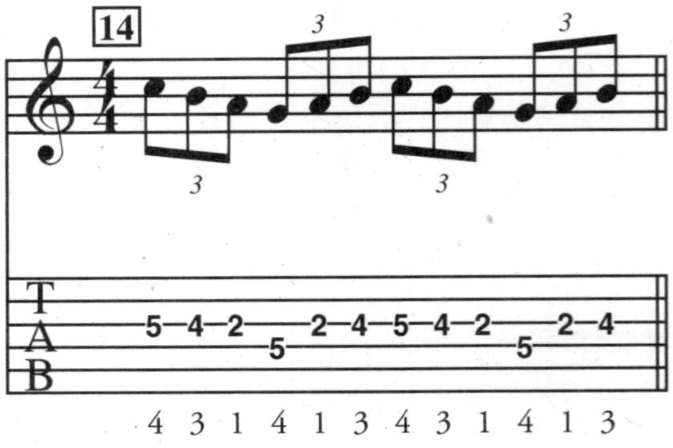

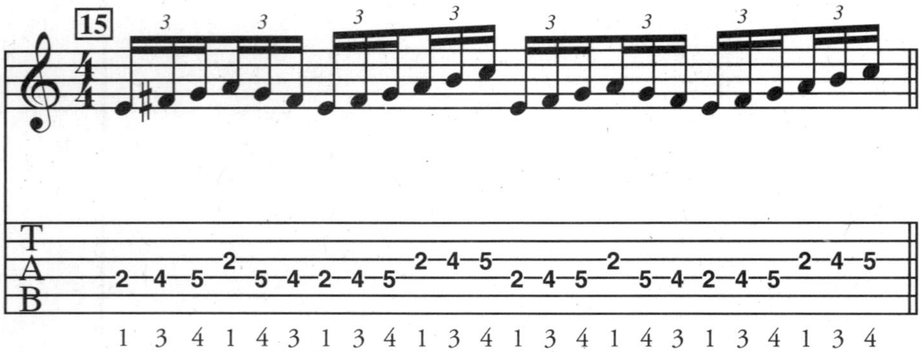

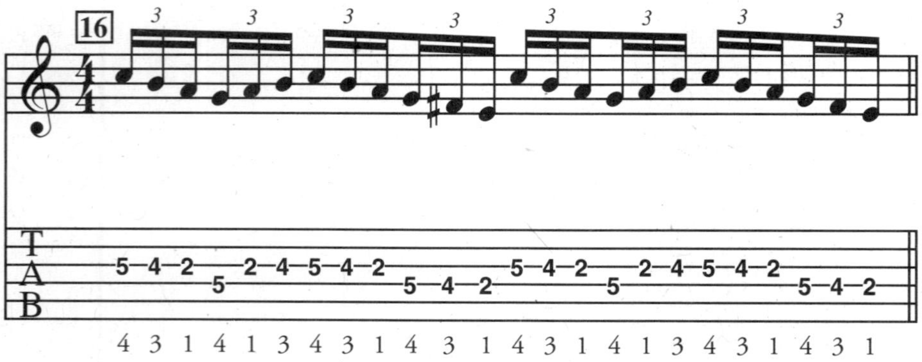

Here are two more variations.

17

18

Example 19 is a simple four-note ascending pattern and Example 20 is the descending version. Play these up and down the fretboard—first on the string pair indicated, then on different pairs across the neck (6th and 5th, 5th and 4th, etc.). Note the $\frac{3}{4}$ time signature, which indicates three beats per measure.

19

20

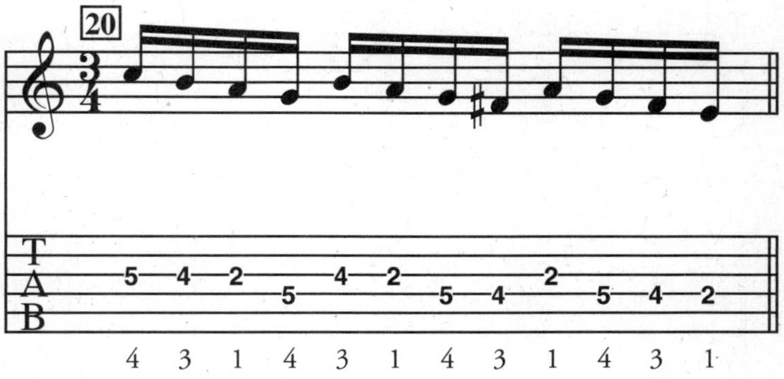

Examples 21 and 22 (next page) are variations of Examples 19 and 20. The pattern begins with an interval skip of a 3rd and is followed by *stepwise* movement upwards or downwards. The term "stepwise" refers to movement of a whole step or half step.

21

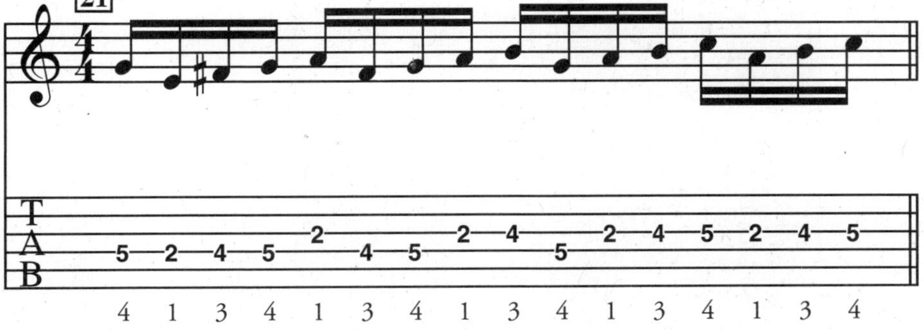

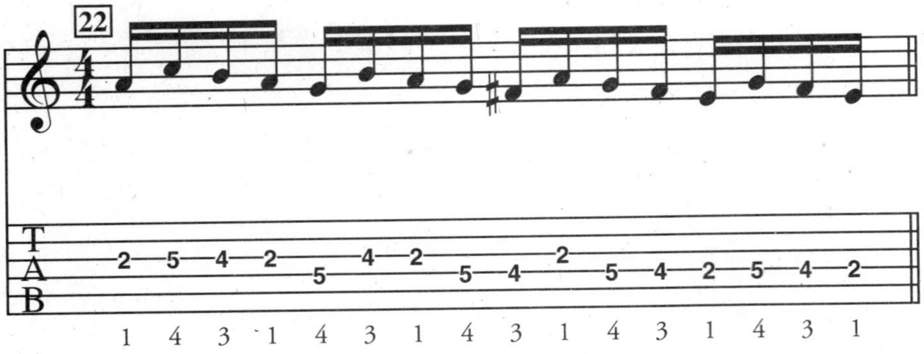

Example 23 is a cool-sounding quintuplet pattern. Example 24 features a wide intervallic leap and is a combination of previous patterns.

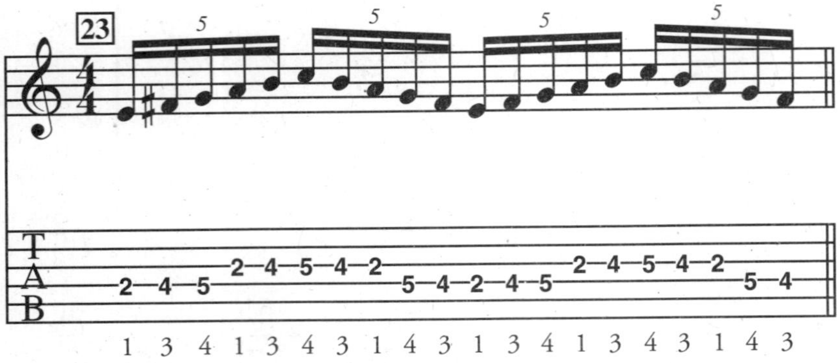

The last example of this section is based on the idea of a *pedal point* lick and will require a lot of finger independence and coordination. A pedal point is a note, or group of notes, that is either sustained or repeated while the melody or harmony above it changes. In the example below, the pedal point is the ascending and descending figure containing the notes E, F♯, and G, while the changing melody above it (highlighted in the music) consists of the notes A, B, C, and B.

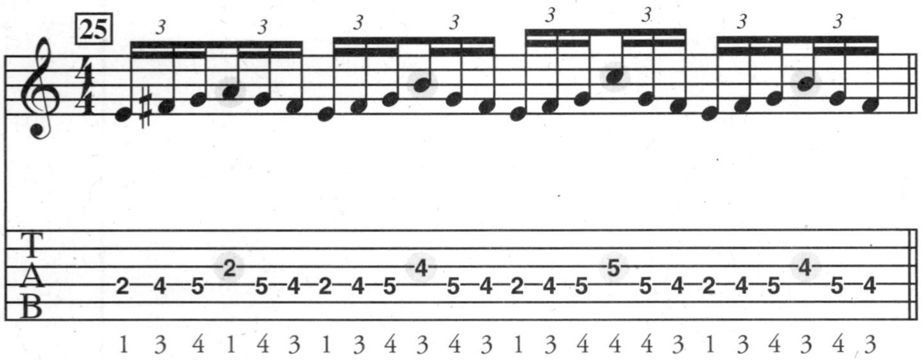

Fretboard Efficiency and Knowledge

The next step, after learning all the short musical phrases and being able to play them in a relaxed manner, is to move them across the strings and eventually cover the entire fretboard. This can be done in two ways: chromatically or diatonically.

When you play the patterns chromatically, you simply take the pattern and move it up or down one fret at a time, maintaining the same shape. In order to practice all possible shapes chromatically, you should consider practicing the different variations of interval structure using the same pattern. This means if you have an ascending three-note phrase, the intervals could be:

1. Whole step–whole step
2. Whole step–half step
3. Half step–whole step

The example below illustrates the chromatic three-note ascending pattern played on the G string. Make sure to move it to the other strings and apply the other interval patterns mentioned above.

Chromatic Ascending Pattern

3

Track 16.3

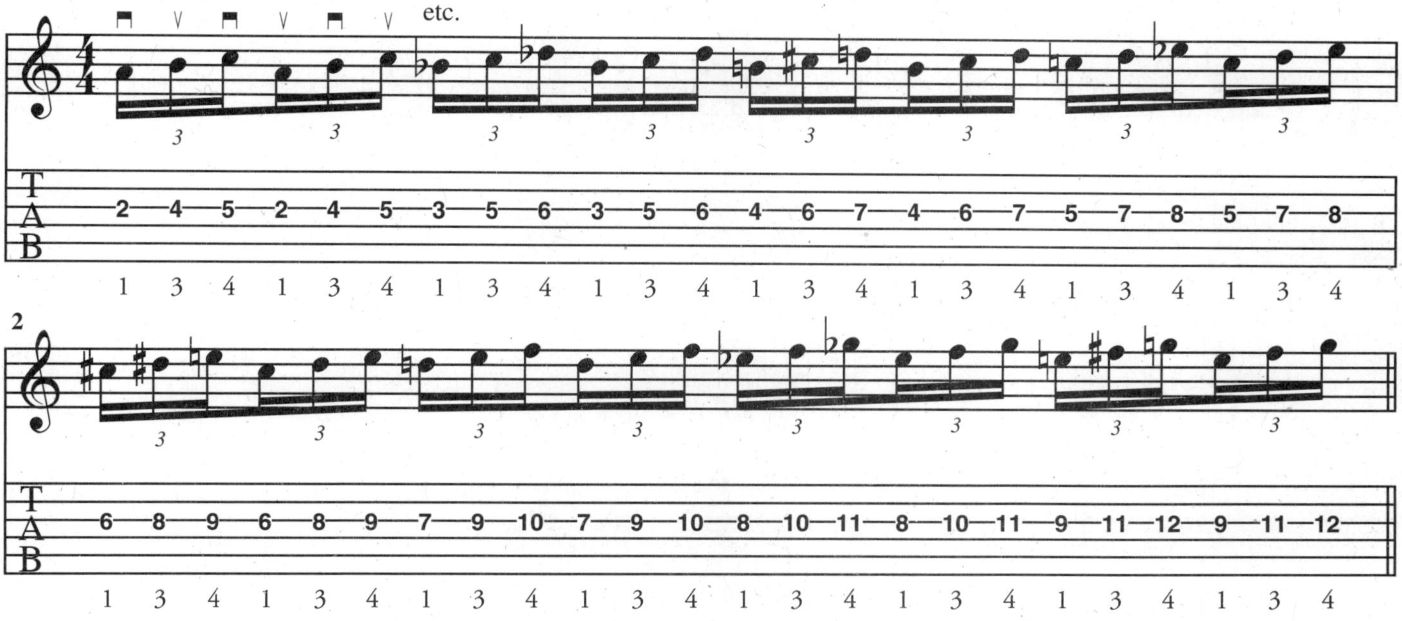

Following is the three-note ascending pattern from above. Here, however, only notes diatonic to the key of C Major are used. Again, play this idea on all strings and make sure you are playing it in the correct key.

Try this with all the remaining patterns. Additionally, use a metronome to control the speed and synchronization between your fretting and picking hands.

Diatonic Ascending Pattern

4

Track 16.4

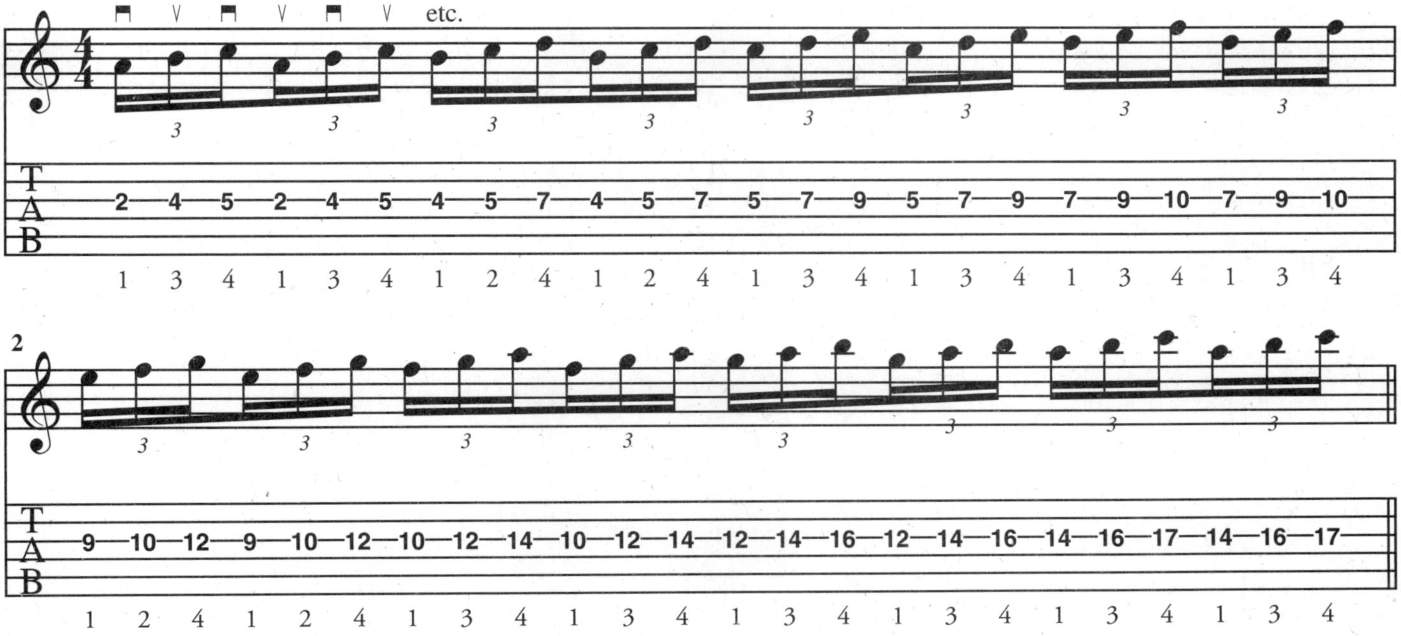

Etudes and Backing Tracks

Following are four *etudes,* or studies, that incorporate all the fragments and patterns we have been looking at. This should give you a great starting point to develop your own examples, practice routines, and technique.

Etude 1

Etude 1 features a classical-sounding note sequence. You can hear this *motif,* or repeated musical idea, in the music of J.S. Bach and other composers. The implied chord progression in this etude is very simple: Amin–F–Dmin–E. This is a typical i–♭VI–iv–V chord progression. Practice the etude slowly, making sure your picking and fretting hands are in perfect synchronization. You can also move this etude, which is a single-string example, to the other strings, or try developing your own chord progression and adapting the pattern.

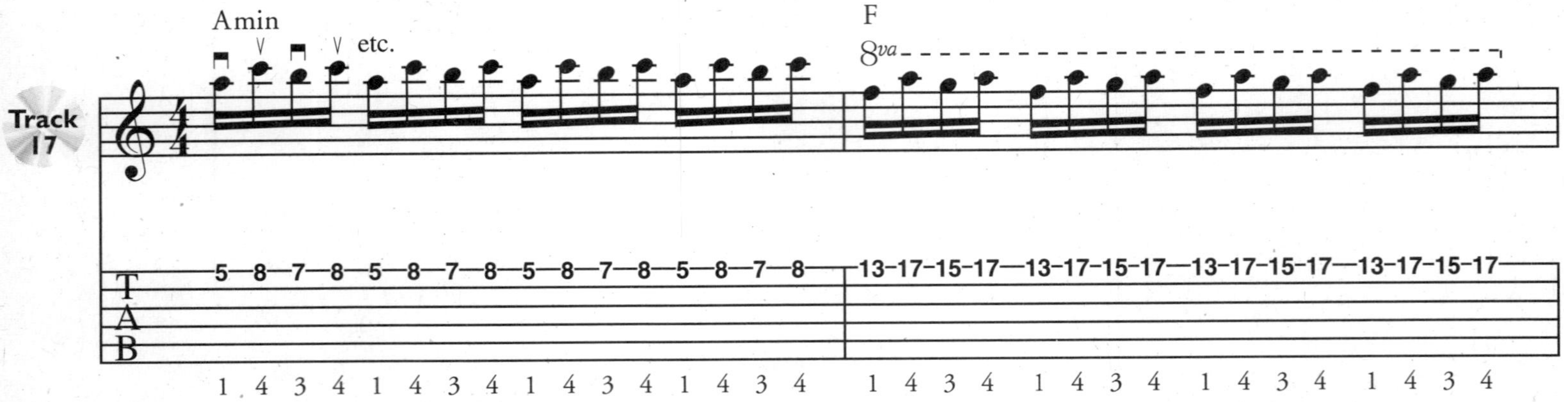

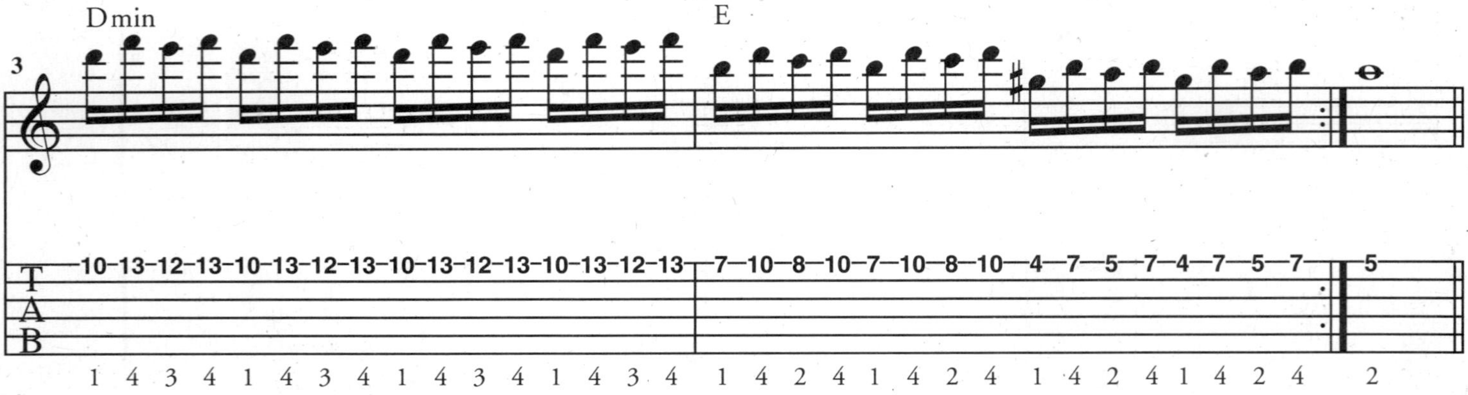

Etude 2

Etude 2 is also in the key of A Minor. It is more complicated and much longer than the previous etude. It features several different one- and two-string patterns across the entire fretboard.

Try to break this exercise down into its components, isolating the short musical phrases and fragments (like we did starting on page 32) and practicing these first. Make sure you use the correct fingering and picking. After practicing the fragments, put them back together and continue to slowly memorize the piece. As always, use a metronome to ensure accuracy and develop speed.

Remember: Start slowly to build stamina and control before trying to take it further. Be patient!

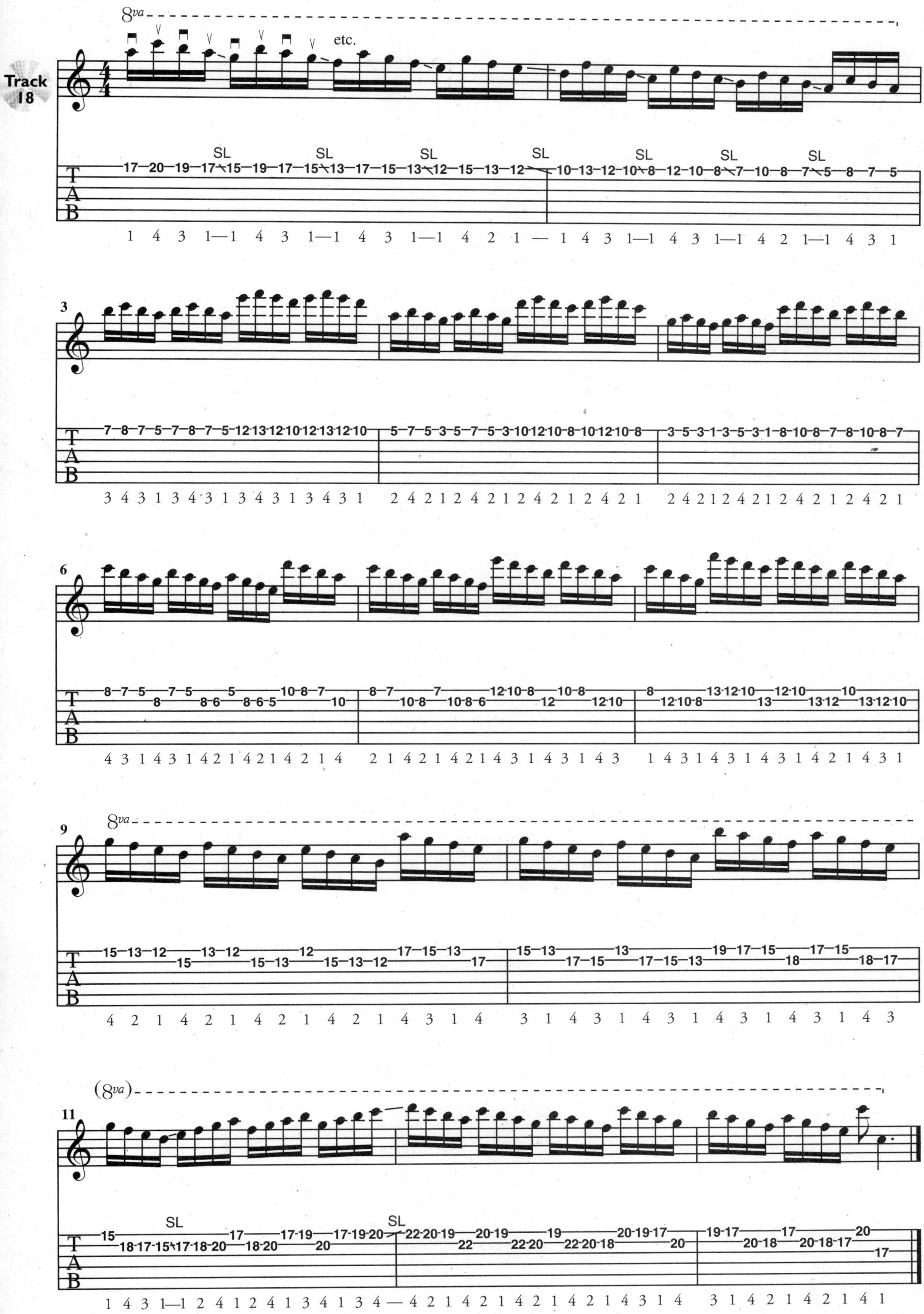
Track 18
8va
etc.
SL
(8va)

Etude 3

Etude 3 is in the key of C Minor. It utilizes five-note groupings, as well as string skipping, and will be harder to master. Again, practice each part separately before attempting to play everything. This exercise is also relatively easy to move around the fretboard. Try extending the idea or transposing it. This is a great way to explore and learn more about the fretboard.

Track 19

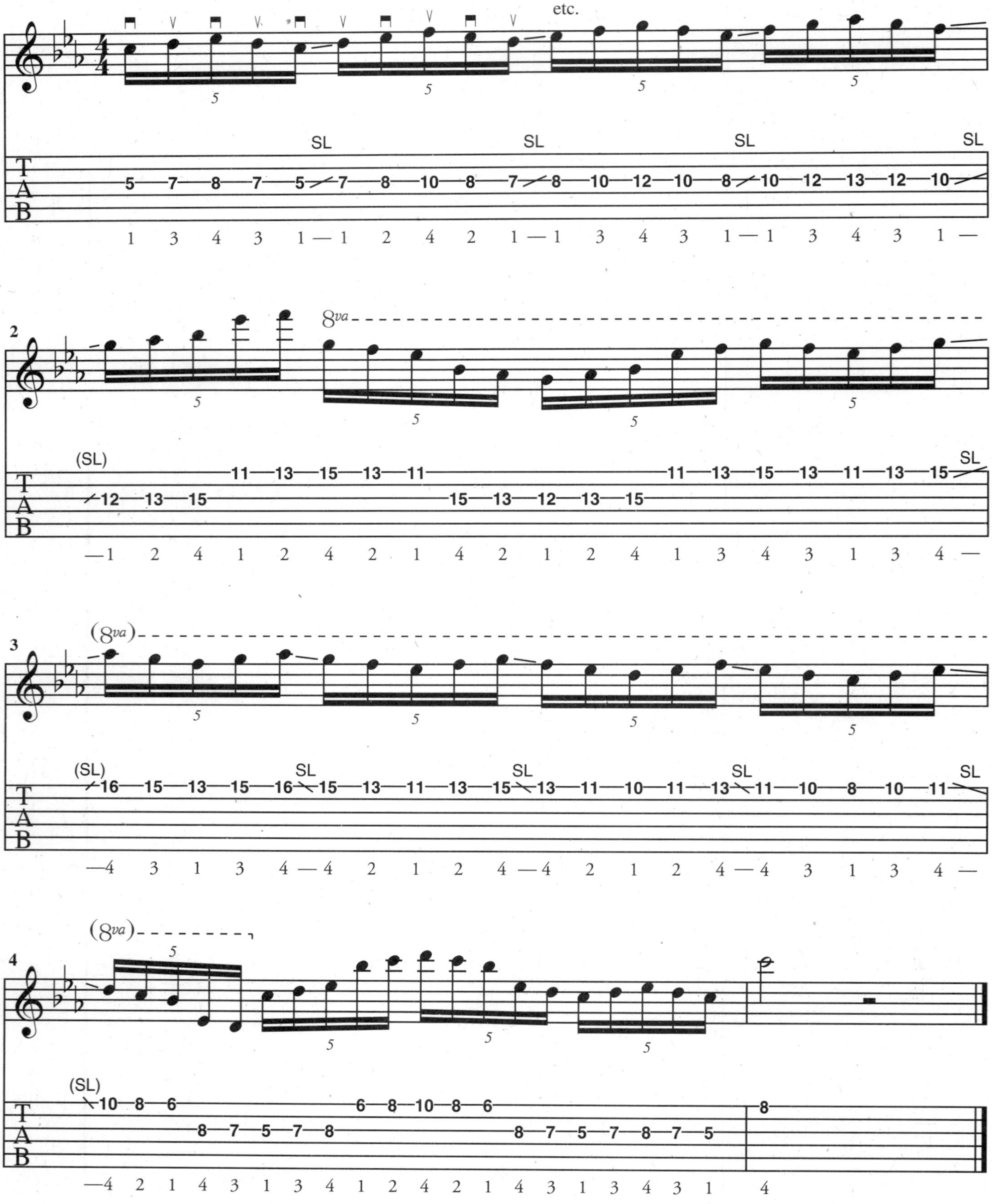

Etude 4

Etude 4 is in the key of D Major. This exercise is also based on string skipping and includes two basic patterns. The chord progression is a simple I–vi–IV–V (D–Bmin–G–A).

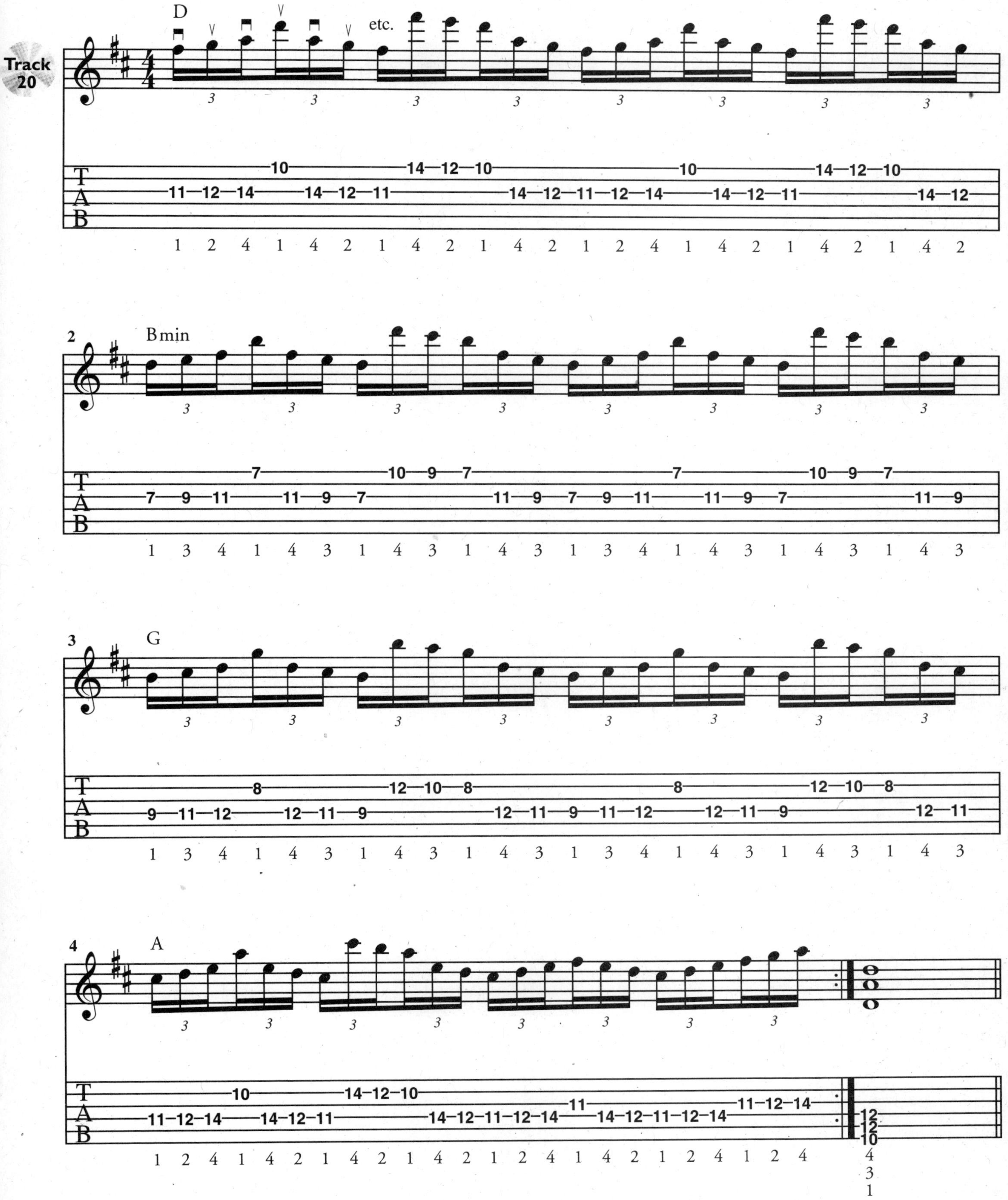

Backing Tracks

The next four examples demonstrate the backing tracks you can use to practice all the patterns and fragments you've been working on. Even though there are only three keys represented here, be sure to practice all of your patterns in all 12 keys. (Also, have fun trying the following rhythm guitar parts.)

Backing Track 1 (Rock, A Minor)

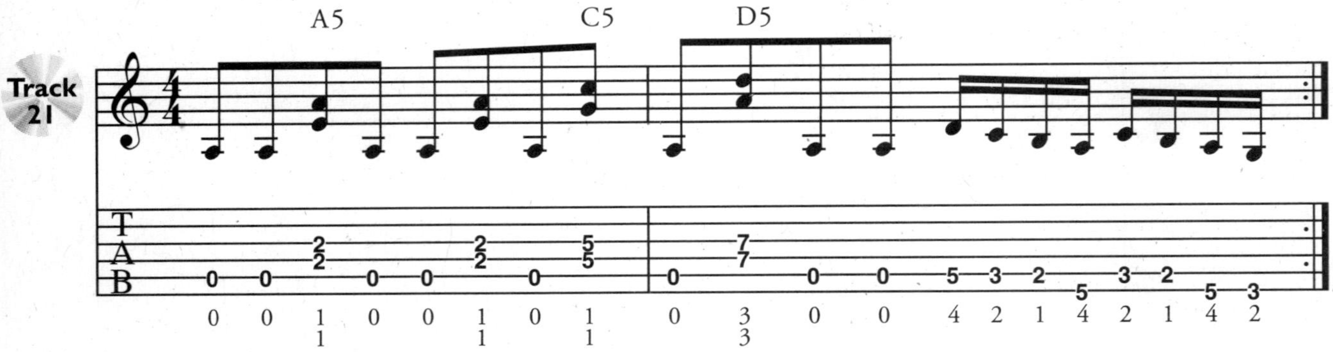

Backing Track 2 (Metal, A Minor)

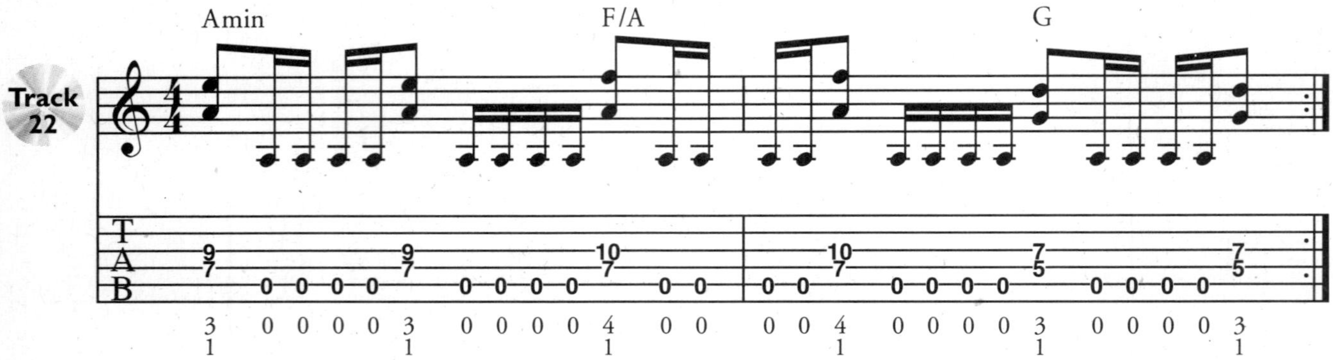

Backing Track 3 (Modern Rock, C Minor)

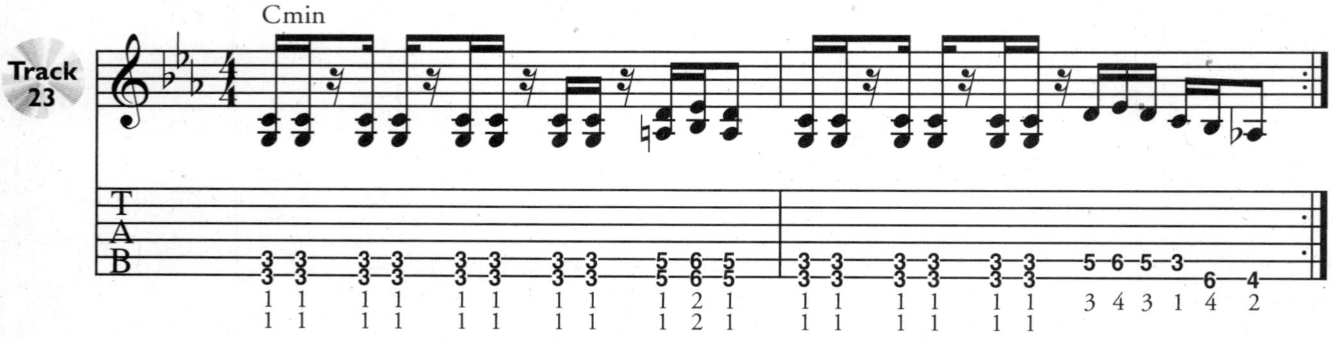

Backing Track 4 (Classic Rock, D Major)

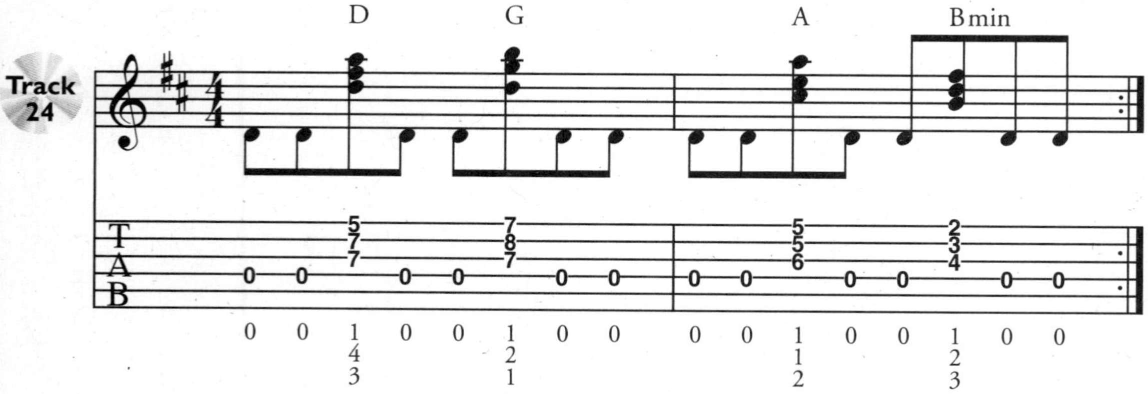

Chapter 7: Three-Note-Per-String Scales

The most common scale form in shred is the three-note-per-string scale. The structure of this form is quite simple: It contains three notes on each of the six strings. The three-note-per-string structure allows your picking and fretting hands greater coordination and lends itself to playing scale patterns and sequences, as the picking (and other techniques) remains predictable and continuous.

Modes of the Major Scale

The three-note-per-string scales below show the C Major scale across the entire neck. Because each of these fingerings starts on a different degree of the C Major scale, they are referred to as *modes*. There are seven modes of the major scale, one for each of the seven scale degrees of the major scale.

The modes of the C Major scale are as follows:

1. Ionian: C–D–E–F–G–A–B–C
2. Dorian: D–E–F–G–A–B–C–D
3. Phrygian: E–F–G–A–B–C–D–E
4. Lydian: F–G–A–B–C–D–E–F
5. Mixolydian: G–A–B–C–D–E–F–G
6. Aeolian: A–B–C–D–E–F–G–A
7. Locrian: B–C–D–E–F–G–A–B

Below, we have all seven modes, or positions, of the major scale. We'll start with the Lydian mode because it is the lowest on the fretboard.

Lydian

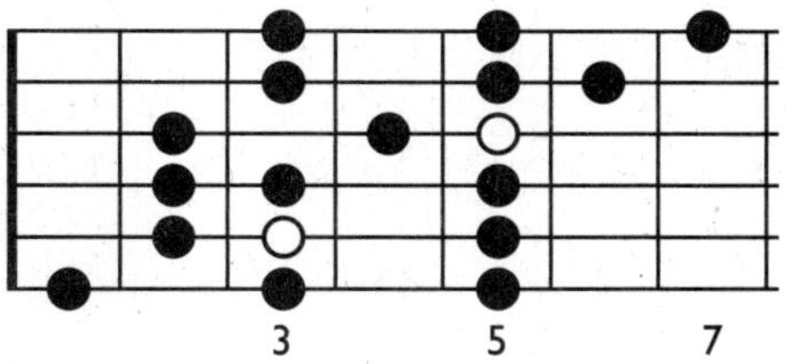

Mixolydian

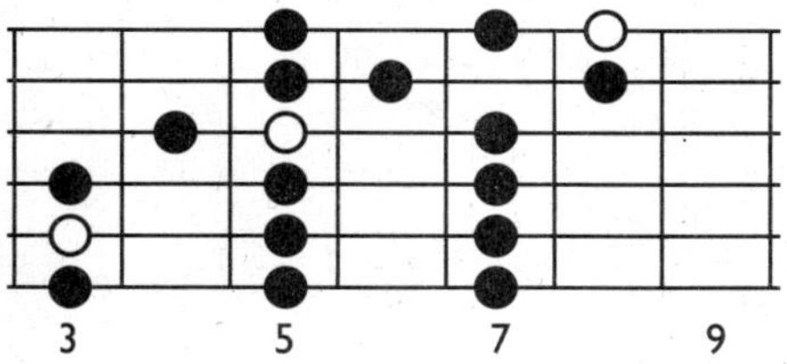

Aeolian (Natural Minor)

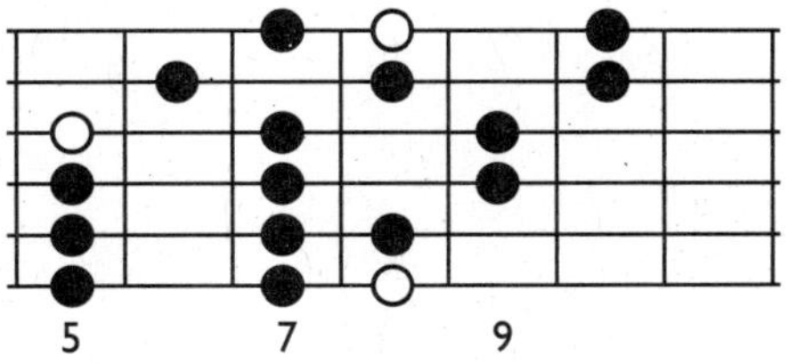

Locrian

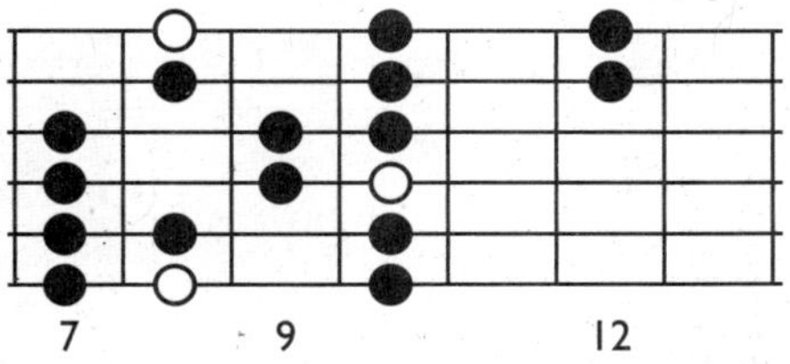

Ionian (Major)

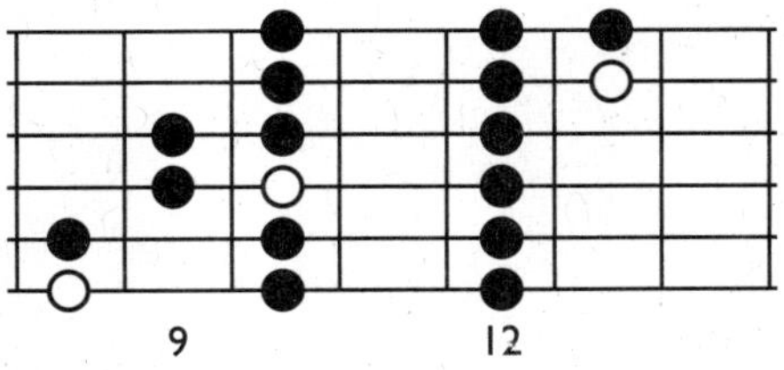

Dorian

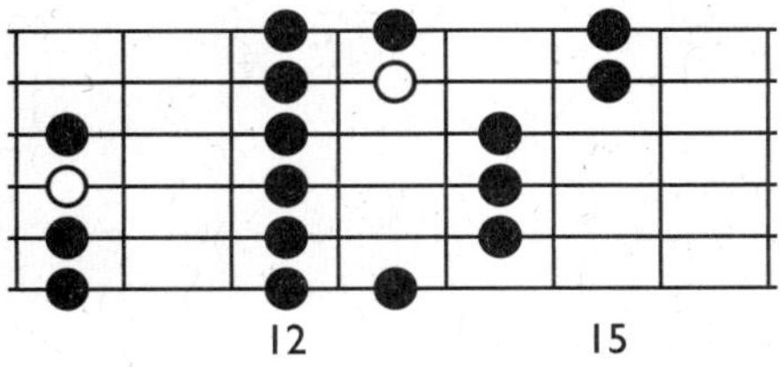

Phrygian

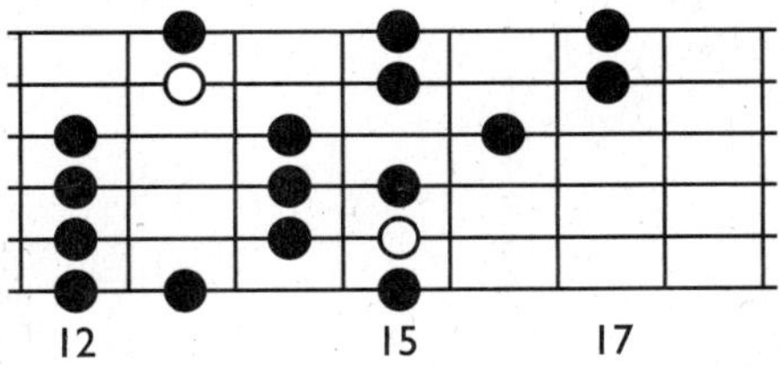

Relative vs. Parallel Approach

Looking at the modes in the way described on the previous page—in relation to the root of the major scale—is referred to as the *relative approach*. With this approach, you are not really thinking "modally," you are simply playing the major scale starting from one of its seven scale degrees. For example, playing the C Major scale from the note F makes it an "F Lydian" mode. But if you are playing over a C Major chord progression, you are using the relative approach and playing the 4th position of the C Major scale.

There is another approach to the modes called the *parallel approach,* which treats the first note of each mode as its own root or tonic. We will discuss this later in the book (see page 114).

Memorize all seven positions of the C Major scale and then practice them in the remaining 11 keys. If you are not sure about your 12 keys, please revisit page 24.

The following exercises will serve not only as a technical challenge, but will also help you develop melodic phrases. All examples are played with strict alternate picking. As usual, start out slowly and increase speed over time as you get more comfortable with the patterns.

To save space, only the first bar of each pattern is demonstrated. It is up to you to follow through with the rest of the pattern in the particular position you are in.

The following example shows a basic ascending four-note pattern using the C Ionian mode.

1

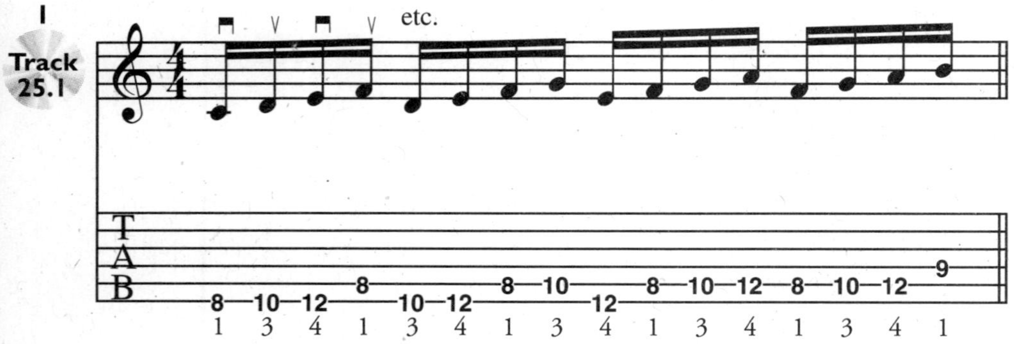

In order to develop variations of musical ideas, you can *reverse, inverse,* or *reverse-inverse* the original idea. This will give you a total of four musical motifs to use.

Take a look at the following examples.

Example 2 shows the reverse (meaning backwards) of the four-note pattern in Example 2. It is descending through the strings rather than ascending.

Reverse

2
Track
25.2

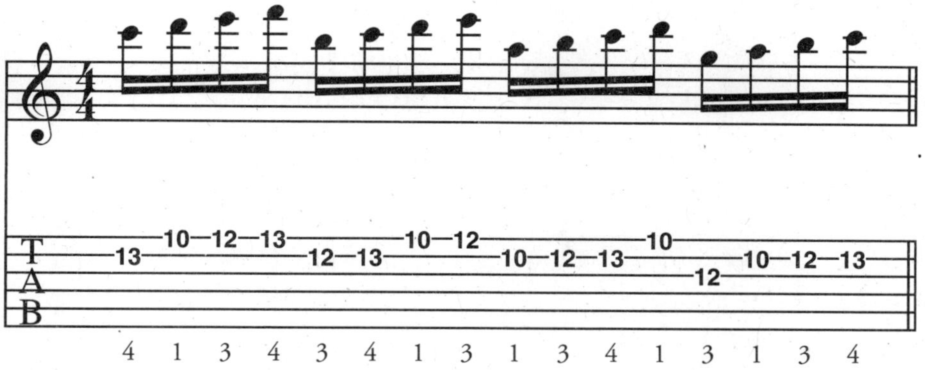

The examples below show the inversion and reverse-inversion of the four-note-pattern in Example 1. The inversion cycles backward through the pattern while ascending the strings. The reverse-inversion uses the inverted pattern but descends through the strings rather than ascending.

Inversion

Reverse-Inversion

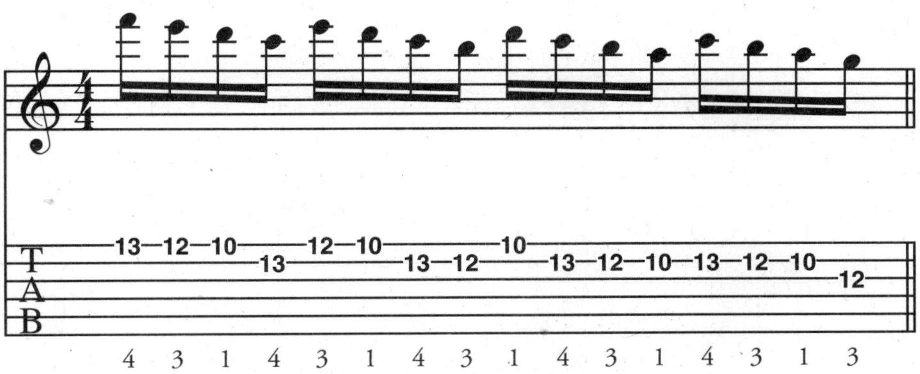

The following examples are combinations of the ascending and descending four-note patterns.

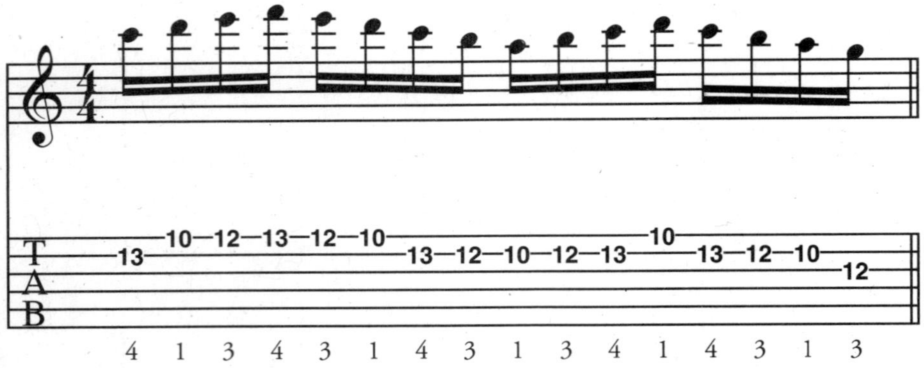

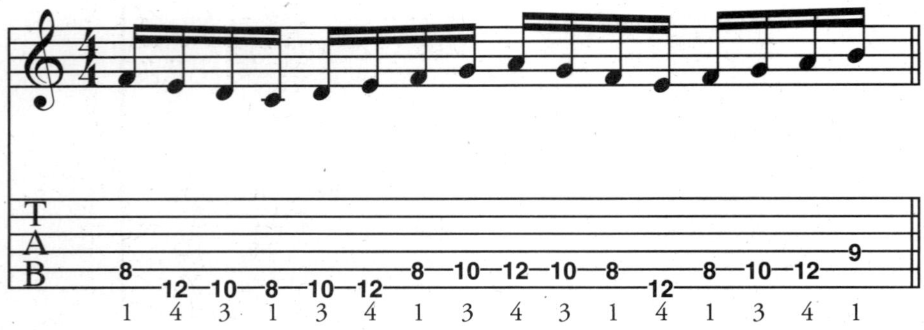

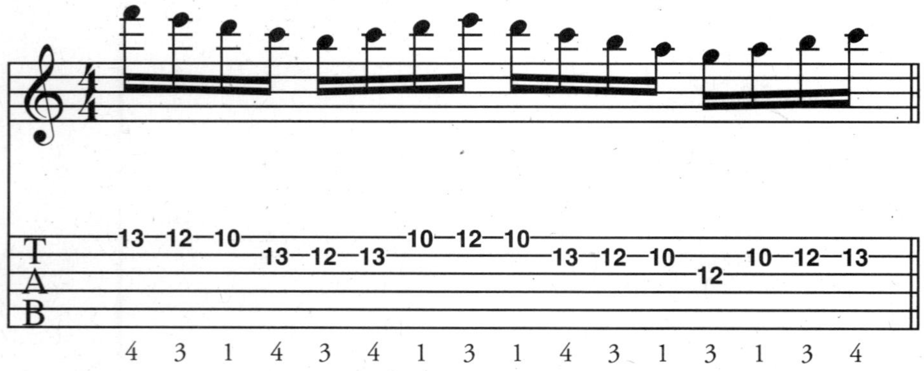

The next examples are based on a three-note sequence, resulting in a triplet rhythm.

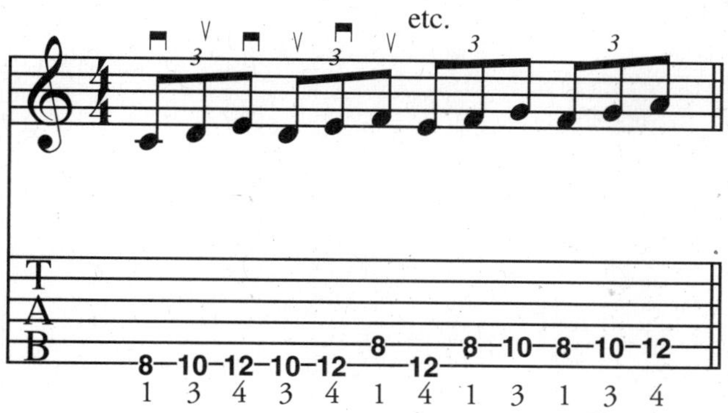

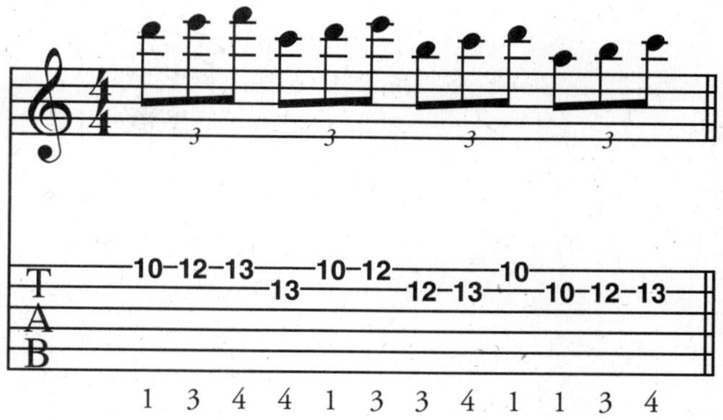

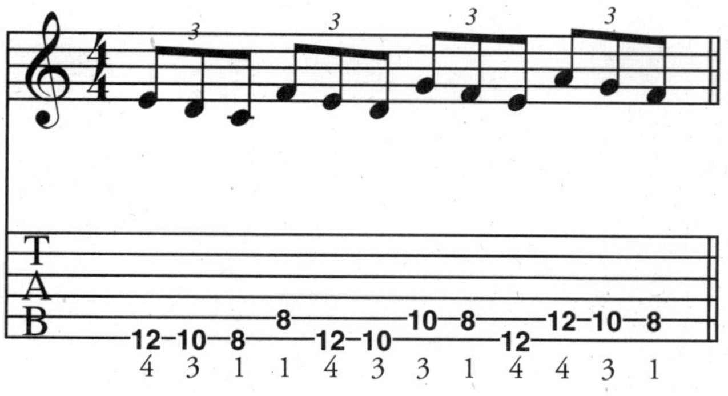

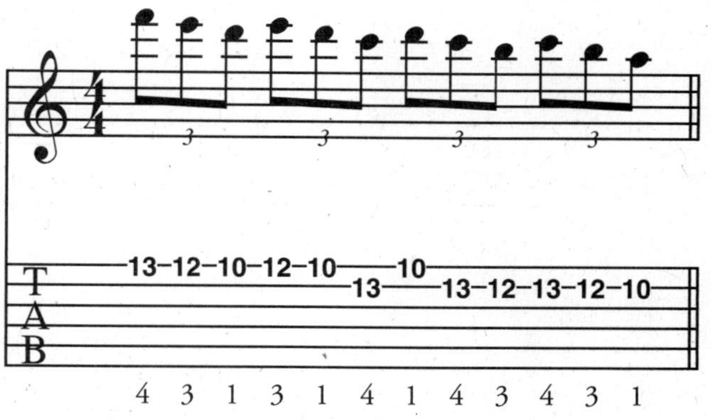

Following are combinations of ascending and descending three-note sequences.

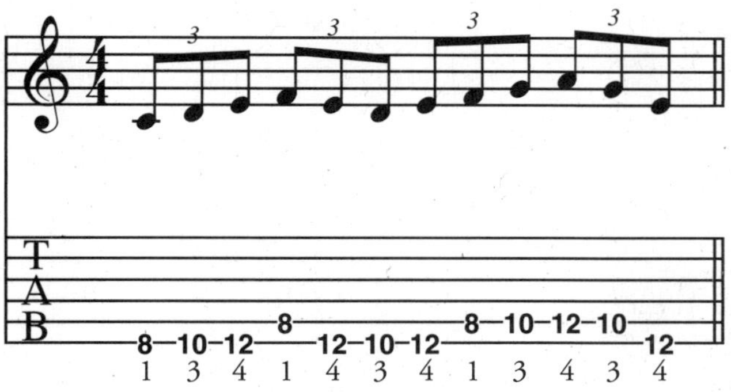

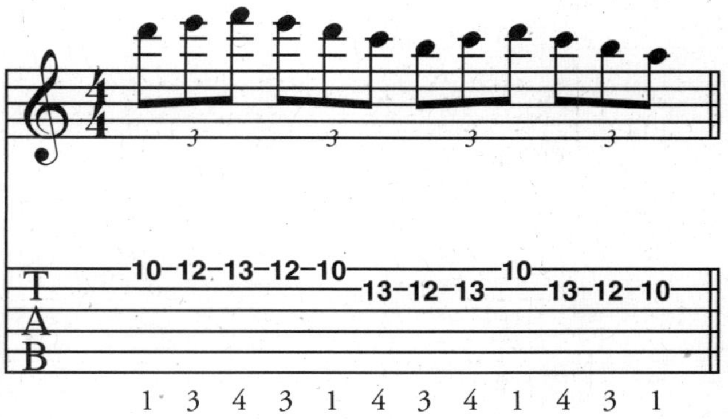

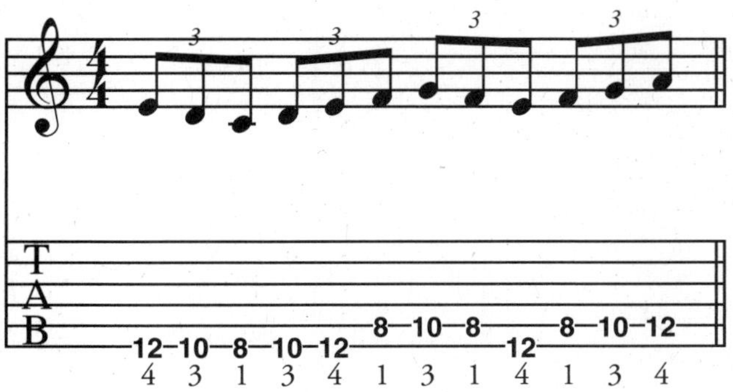

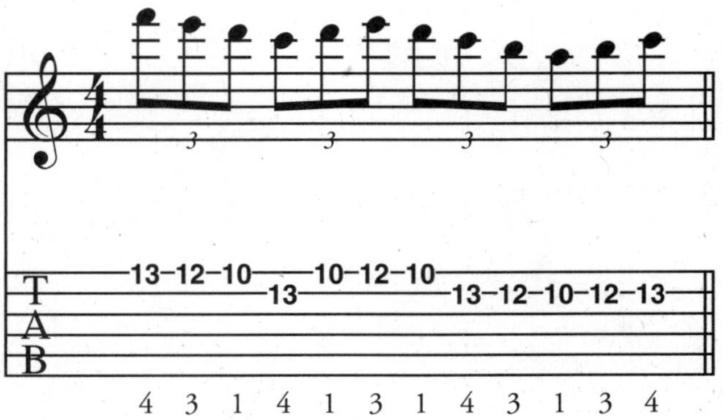

Apply all the patterns in this section to your seven scale positions, paying close attention to the synchronization between your fretting and picking hands. Use a metronome to control your speed and accuracy.

Intervals

So far, we have discussed only linear, step-wise patterns and sequences, but scales can also be played in a more intervallic way, making wider leaps between notes. The following examples are based on patterns of 2nds and 3rds and are very common in the rock/shred guitar language.

The next two examples are ascending and descending sequences in 2nds.

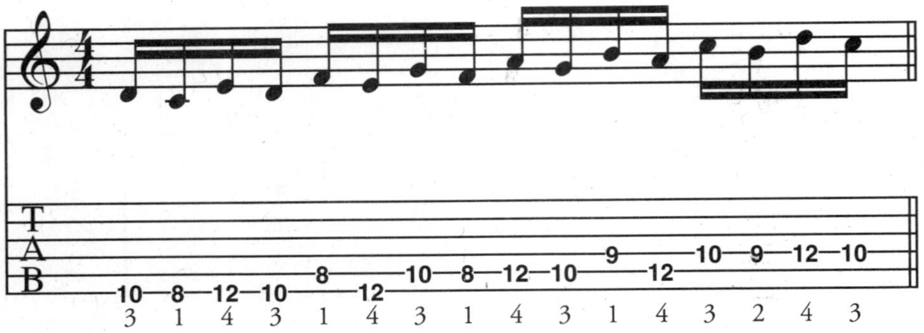

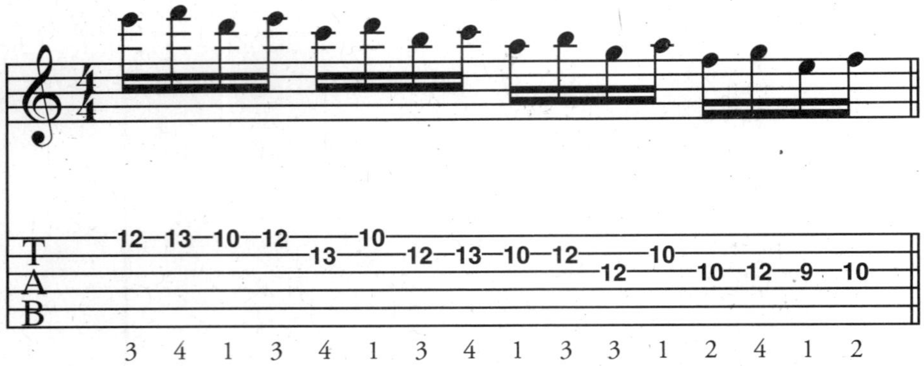

Here, we have simple sequences in 3rds.

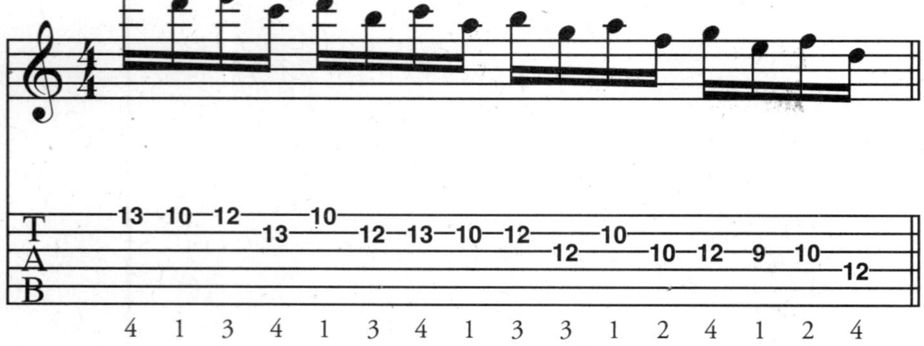

The following examples are patterns of ascending and descending 4ths, 5ths, and 6ths played within the C Ionian three-note-per-string mode. After practicing these sequences, try moving them to the other remaining six scale positions.

Play these patterns slowly and accurately, maybe even singing along to practice your ear training and further develop your pitch/interval recognition.

Hexatonic Scales

The *hexatonic scale* is a great tool for getting around the fretboard. You are probably wondering what hexatonic scales are and how you can use them. Hexatonics are six-note scales. The common major scale (a seven-note scale) is called a *heptatonic* scale. These names are derived from the Greek words for six (*hexa*) and seven (*septa*). We have already looked at another Greek-named scale: the pentatonic scale (*penta* means five). In the next section, we will transform the major scale modes into hexatonics.

Hexatonic Modes

If you use only the first six notes of each of your seven scale positions, or modes, you can easily create a hexatonic mode. Just repeat those six notes one octave higher on the D and G strings, and then one octave higher again on the B and E strings. The result is a hexatonic mode spanning three octaves. These modes are great for playing fast ascending or descending runs. The following diagrams show the seven hexatonic modes of C Major.

Lydian Hexatonic

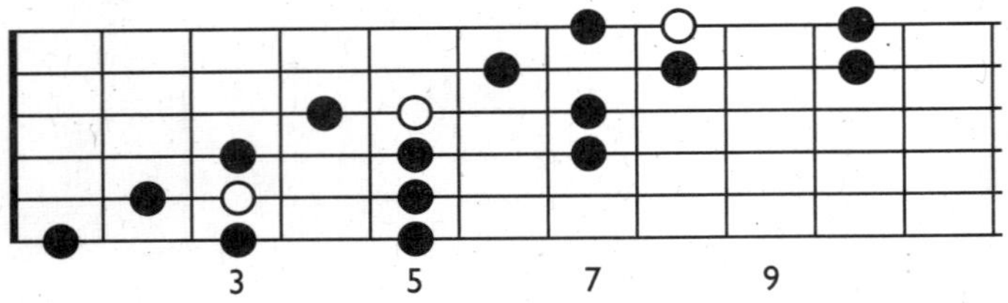

Mixolydian Hexatonic

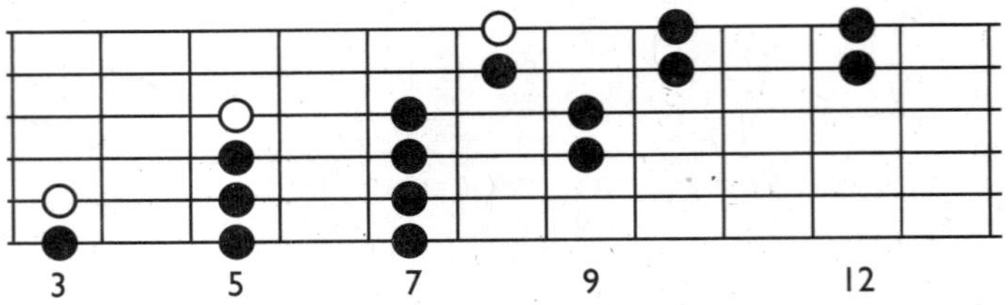

Aeolian Hexatonic

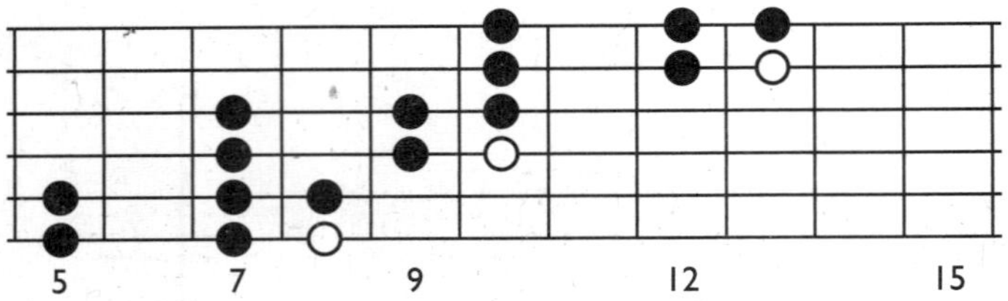

Locrian Hexatonic

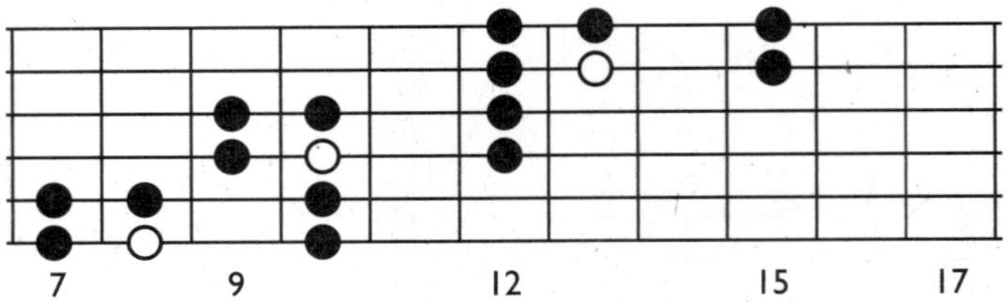

Ionian Hexatonic

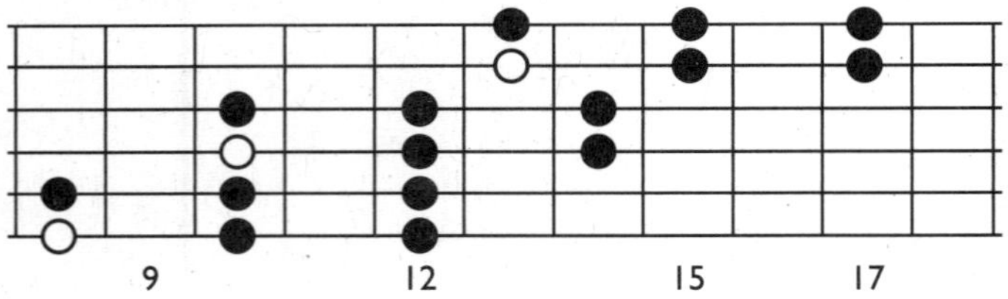

Dorian Hexatonic

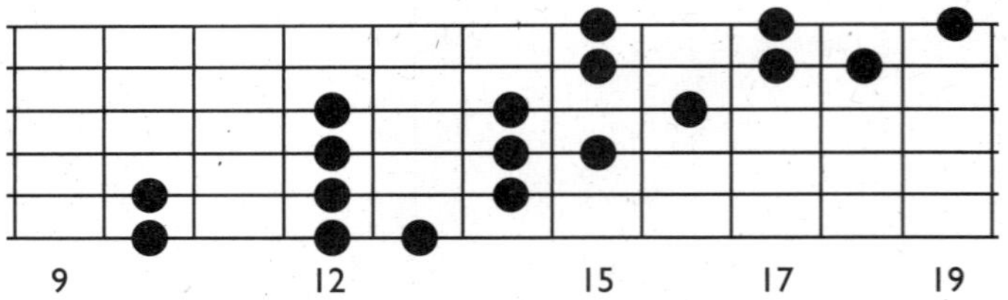

Phrygian Hexatonic

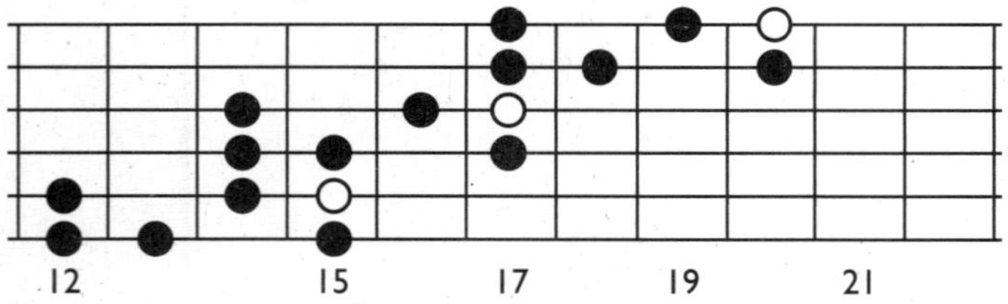

On the next page are a few examples using the hexatonic scales in fast picking runs. More examples on the application of this scale will be covered in later chapters as well.

Below is a fast *sextuplet* run using the A Aeolian Hexatonic mode. Sextuplets consist of six notes in the time of four notes of the same value. For example, below we have groups of six sixteenth notes in the time of four sixteenth notes (one beat). Sextuplets can either be written as one unbroken group of six notes (six sixteenth notes under one beam) or two groups of triplets (two beamed groups of three), as is the case below and throughout most of this book. This lick ends with a slide to the G and a whole-step bend on the 15th fret to A.

3
Track 26.1

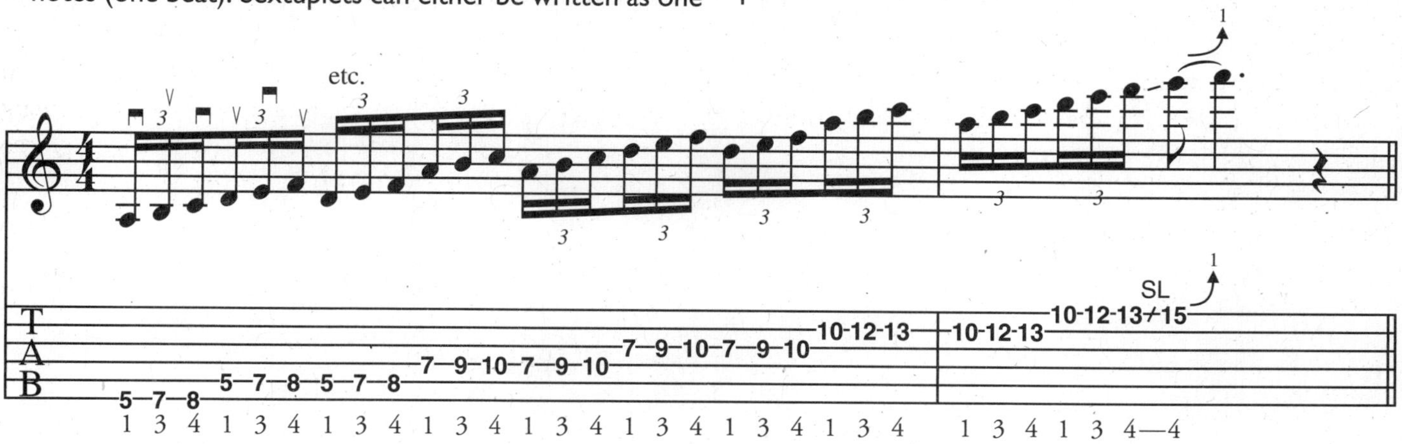

This quick septuplet run is in B♭ Major. It uses the B♭ Ionian Hexatonic mode.

4
Track 26.2

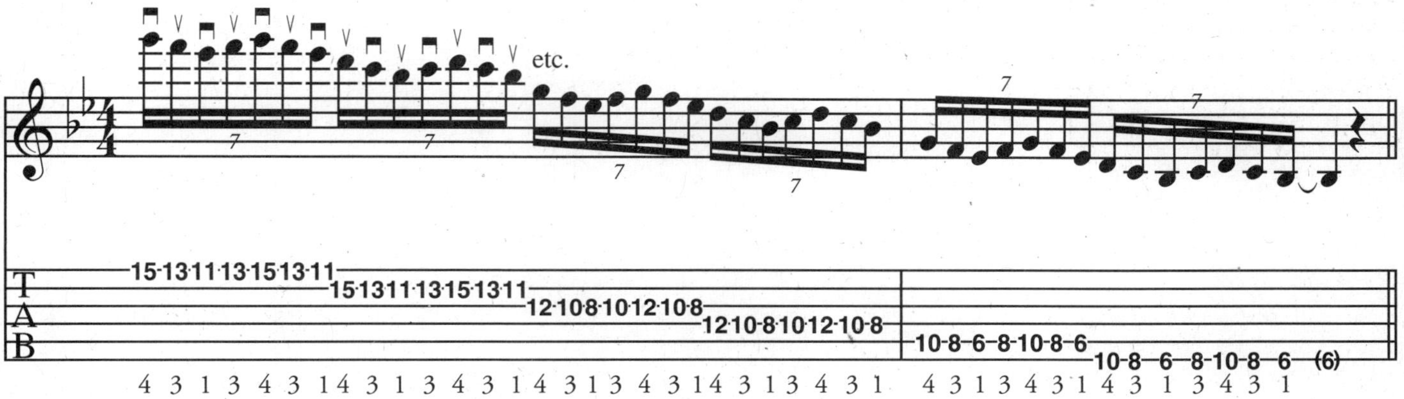

The following example incorporates two different hexatonic scales. It starts off with the B Aeolian Hexatonic and continues with the A Mixolydian Hexatonic.

5
Track 26.3

Music's Phone Number

Do you have music's phone number? No? Okay, let's talk about how you can get it!

Similar to how we broke down the pentatonic scale into five basic shapes (see page 29), the major scale can be broken down as well. This results in seven basic forms, two of which look the same but start on different scale degrees. The forms should be played according to their relative scale position. This means that the first note of Form 1 should be the tonic of the major scale, the first note of Form 2 should be the 2nd degree of the major scale, and so on.

Form 1

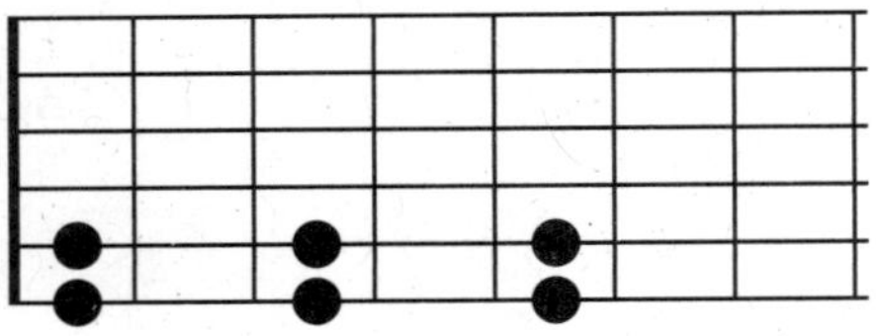

Form 2

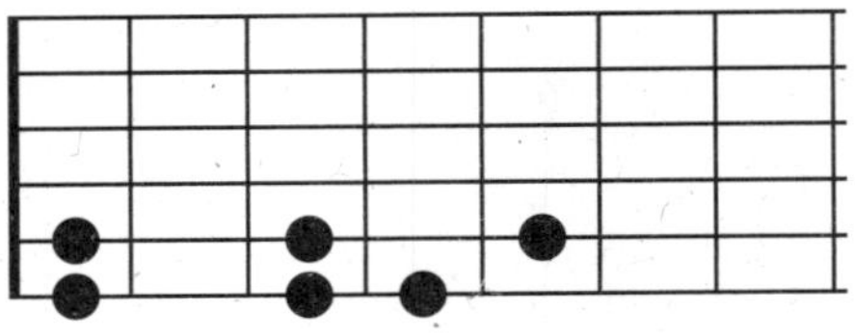

Form 3

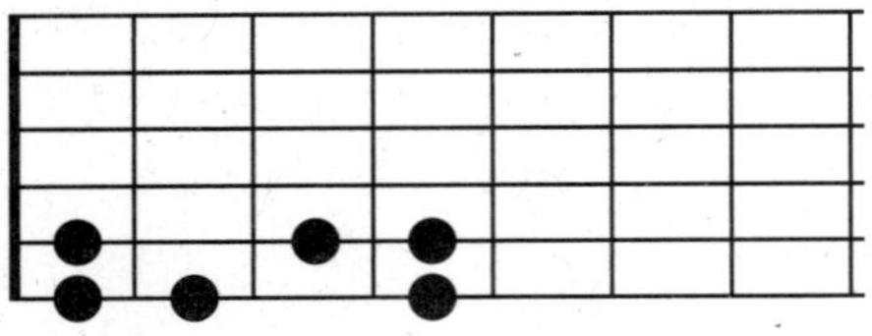

Form 4

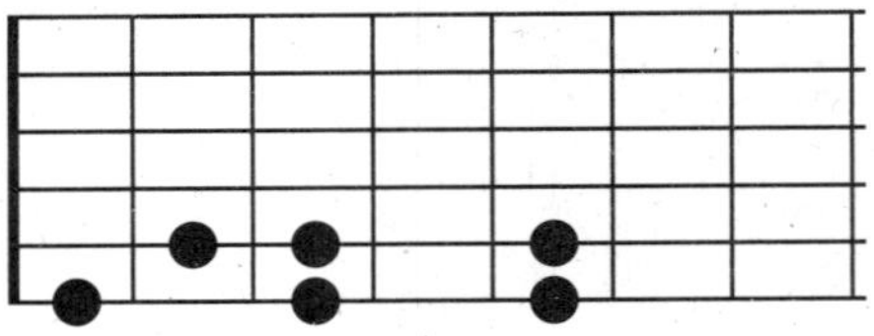

Form 5

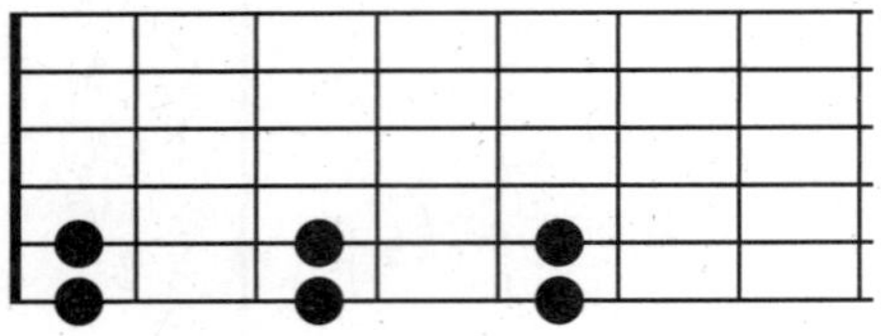

Form 6

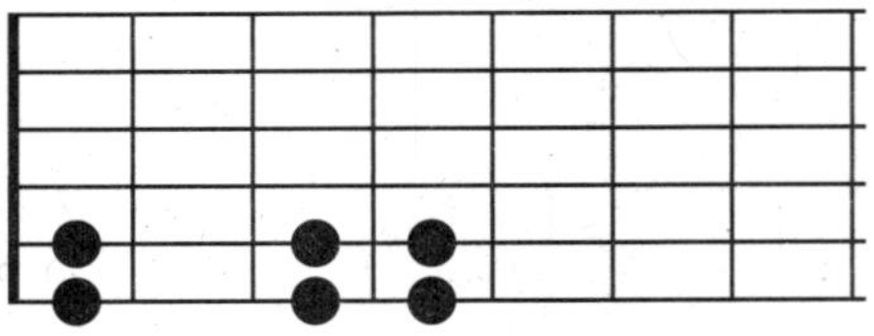

Form 7

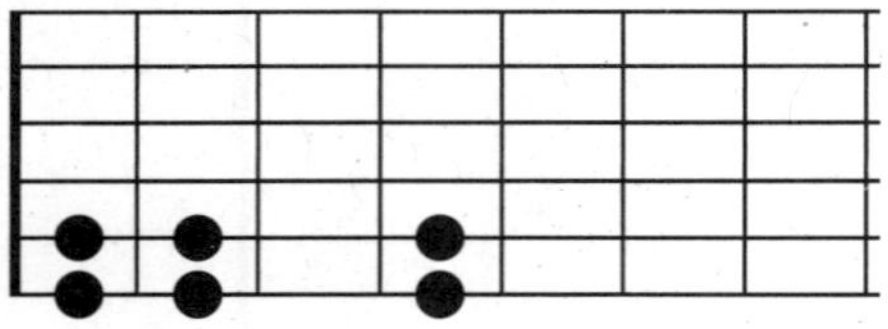

You can use these forms to play horizontally (up and down the fretboard) or vertically (across the strings in one position). Understanding these basic forms will free your playing from typical in-position scale playing.

As mentioned above, the major scale—in particular, the three-note-per string patterns—is made up of five of the basic forms above. Of course, like we did with the five forms of the pentatonic scale, we will have to adjust these forms when playing them on the G and B strings (see Study Tip on page 30).

Playing three notes per string will make you automatically move in 4ths across the strings. In other words, as you go up the strings (6th–5th–4th, etc.), the first note on each new string is a 4th away from the first note on the previous string. This means you will stay in position for most of the time. The exception to this rule is the 7th scale degree: If we were playing this pattern in the key of C, the 7th scale degree (B) is not a perfect 4th; it is an augmented 4th, which means you will have to move one fret up on the fretboard when you cross the strings (see diagram below).

Ionian

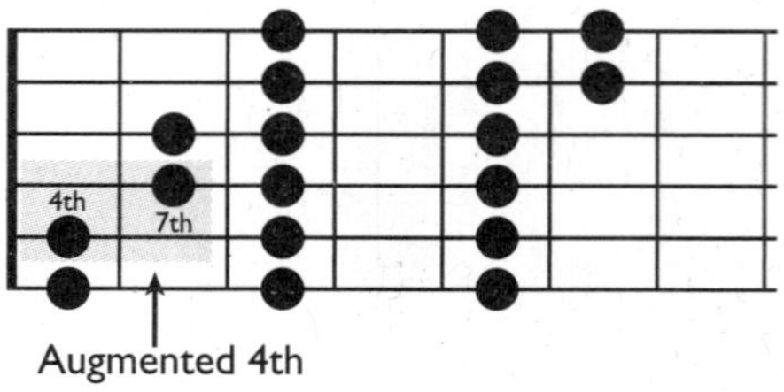

If you isolate the different components of the Ionian mode, from string to string, you will find that it consists of five of the basic forms discussed on the previous page.

Form 1

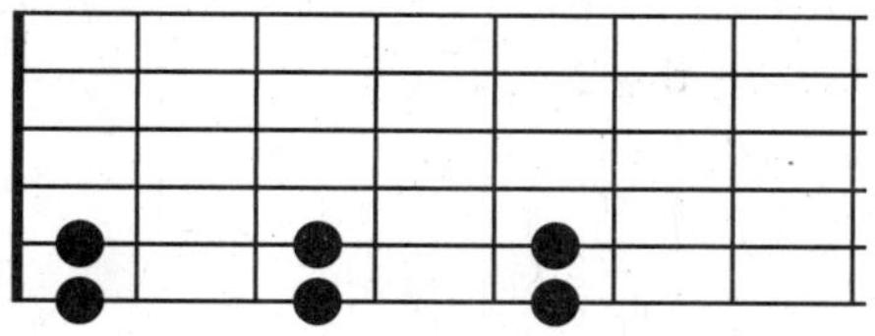

Form 4

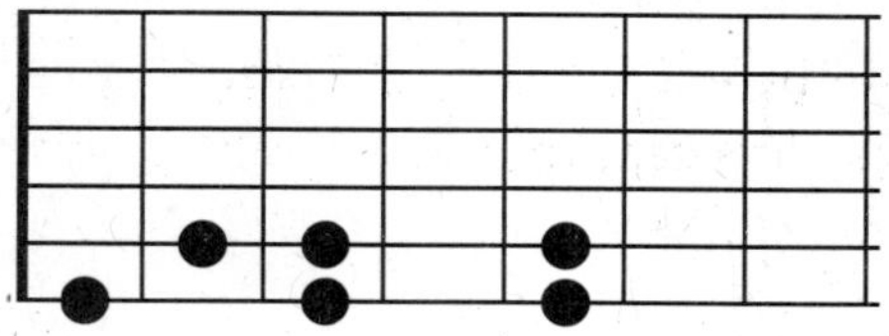

Form 7

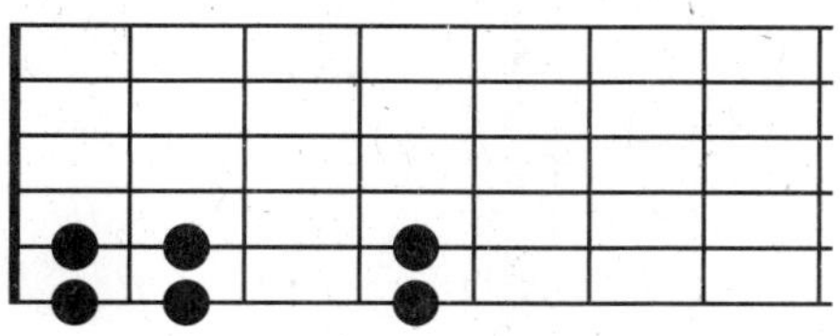

Form 3

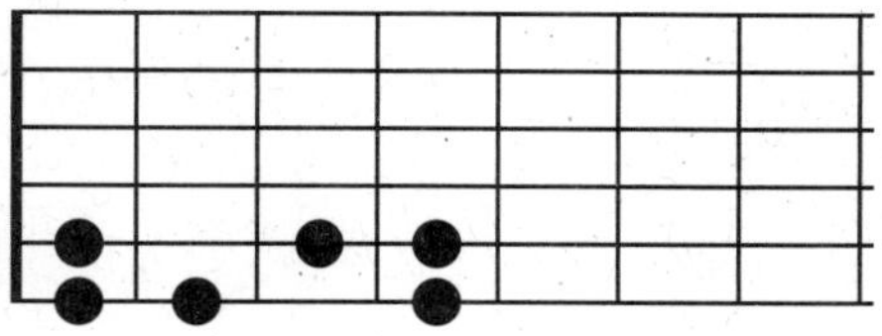

Form 6

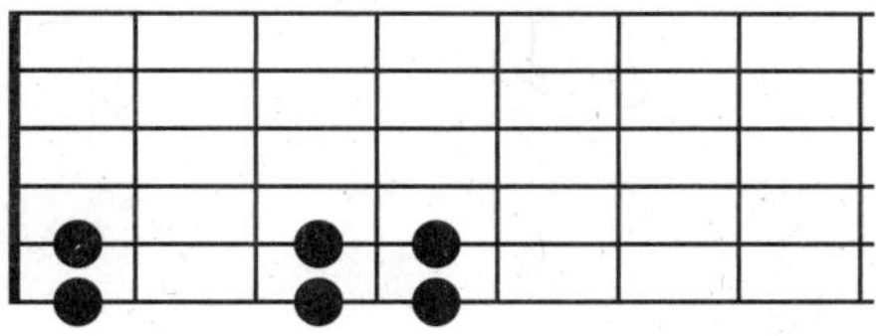

The forms move in intervals of 4ths, similar to the circle of 4ths and 5ths discussed on page 24. Take a look at the remaining six three-note-per-string scales and you will find this circle of 4ths movement. The formula we can derive is: Form 1–Form 4–Form 7–Form 3–Form 6–Form 2–Form 5, or 1–4–7–3–6–2–5. We can refer to this as music's phone number because "dialing into" these numbers will give you greater facility for constructing long scale runs, memorizing notes, intervals, improvisation, and chord progressions.

Licks

Let's apply the basic forms we've been discussing to some licks. Lick 1 below is a scale run in G Minor. Try to label the different forms used in this run. It starts out with Form 6 and continues up on the low-E string to Form 7. Then, it moves across to the A string to Form 3, and so on.

Try to memorize the run before attempting to play it fast, and make sure you use strict alternate picking.

Lick 1

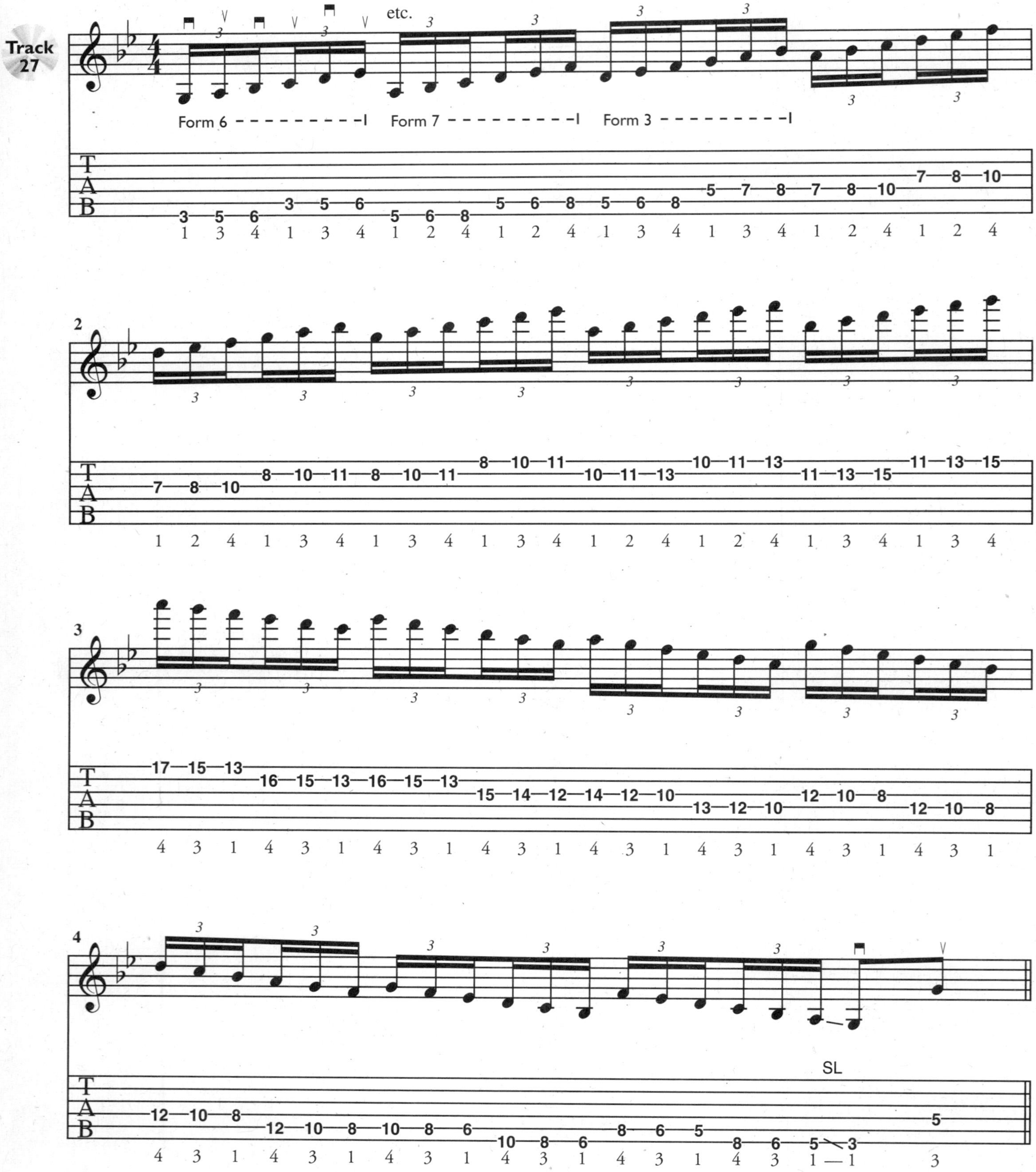

Lick 2 is a string-skipping lick in the style of John Petrucci, guitarist for the progressive metal band Dream Theater. It utilizes alternate picking and a challenging quintuplet rhythm.

Lick 2

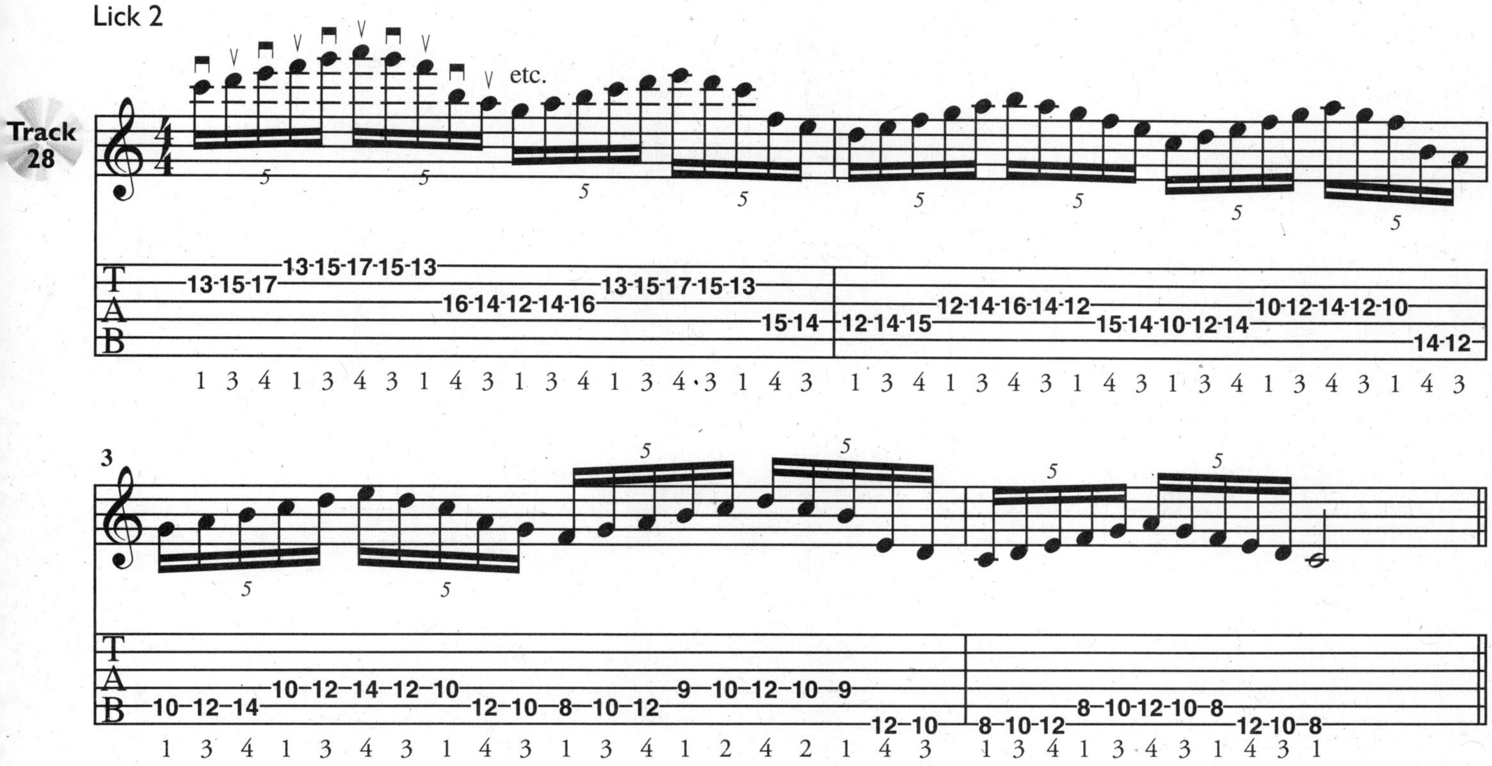

Licks 3 and 4 are fast sixteenth-note picking sequences in the key of B♭. Use a metronome for all of these examples and start out slow.

Lick 3

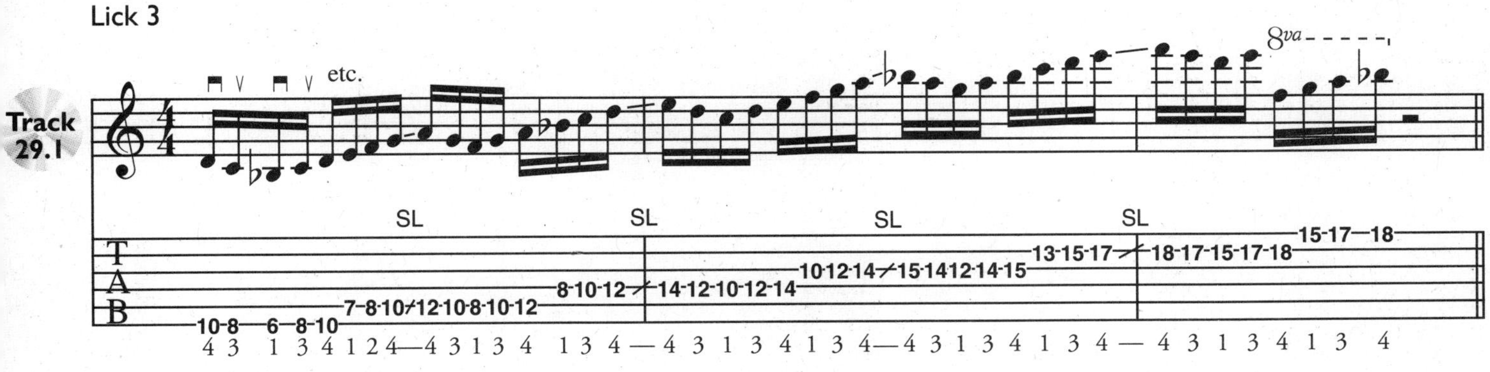

Lick 4

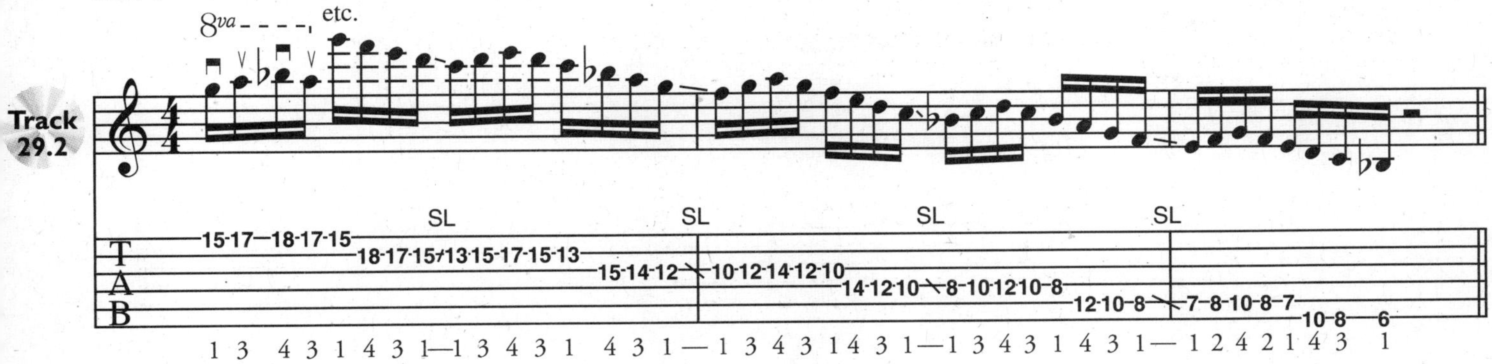

Lick 5 is also a long scale run, utilizing more patterns and covering almost the entire fretboard.

Lick 5

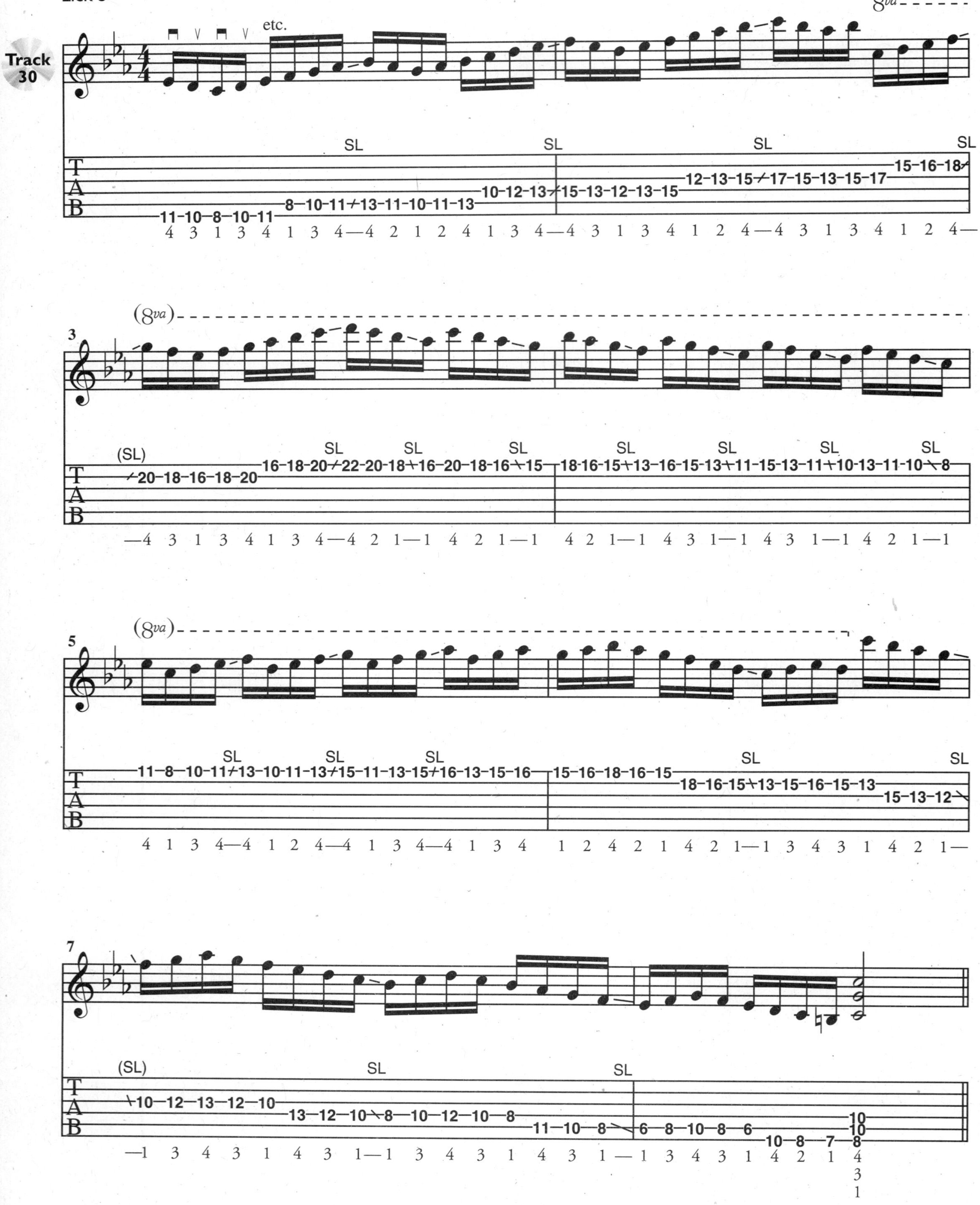

Chapter 8: Sweep Picking

Sweep picking (or just *sweeping*) is a picking technique that utilizes the upward or downward picking direction when playing arpeggios or single notes on adjacent strings. This concept will greatly improve your speed and accuracy when playing arpeggios or other one-note-per-string musical phrases.

Let's take a closer look at this great technique. There are a few things you need to consider when learning and practicing sweeping. Your picking hand needs to be very relaxed and controlled as it moves, or sweeps, across the strings. You will need to hold the pick at a slightly downward angle when sweeping "up" the strings (toward the floor) and at a slightly upward angle when sweeping "down" the strings (toward the ceiling). The pick "falls" across the strings with one continuous stroke, not a strum. This motion needs to be precise and controlled, and the notes should all sound separate but not staccato.

The example below concentrates on your picking hand technique. No fretting-hand action is required, aside from a light *muting* of the strings (gently place a left-hand finger on the strings without fretting them). Additionally, add some light *palm muting* with your picking hand. This is done by placing the side of your palm just slightly on the strings where they meet the *bridge*. (A guitar's bridge supports the strings and anchors them to its body.)

The first example is perhaps the most challenging one, as you sweep across only two strings; this is tricky and should be practiced very slowly with a metronome. The next example is a three-string sweeping exercise, which can be extended to four, five, or all six strings as well.

1 Track 31.1

2 Track 31.2

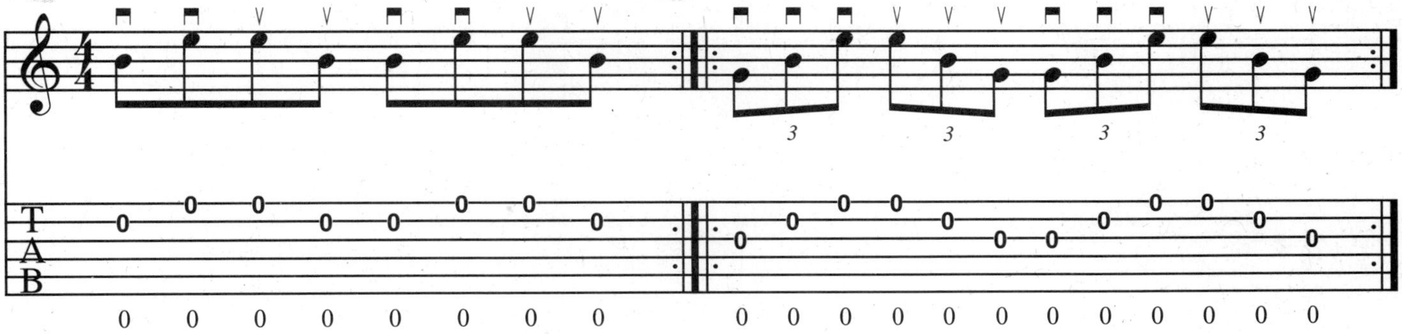

Sweeping on two strings can be a very interesting and intensive learning experience. There are countless musical ideas you can play on two strings using this technique, including those involving intervals and pedal tones. The example below shows a simple C Major scale harmonized in 5ths on the top two strings. Try to move this to the other strings as well, and, of course, try other intervals such as unisons, 2nds, 3rds, 4ths, 5ths, 6ths, and so on.

3 Track 31.3

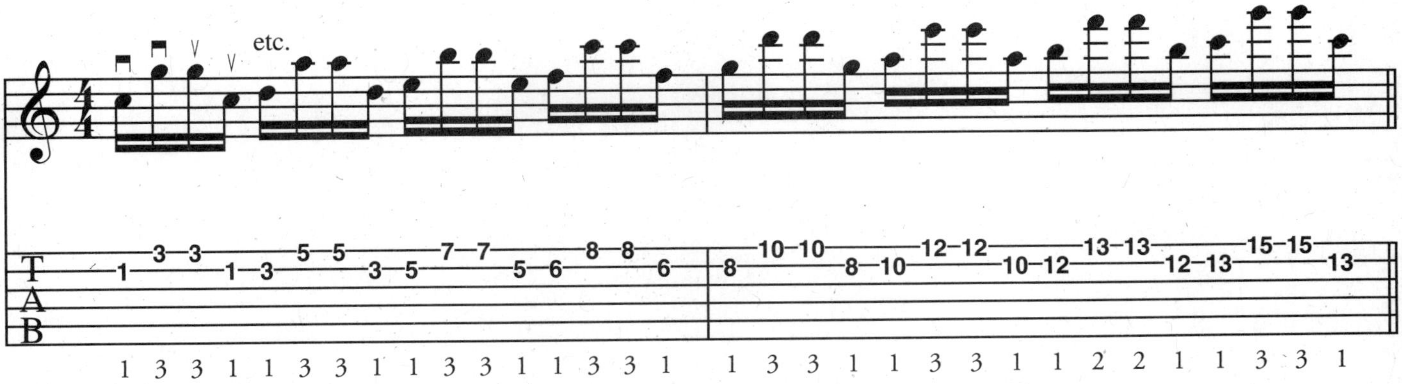

This next etude in B Minor showcases the two-string sweeping idea. It uses simple triad structures with the addition of *passing tones* (notes that connect one chord tone to another). For example, in the first measure below, we are using the notes of the B Minor triad (B–D–F♯) and adding an E, which is in between the D and F♯.

Try to develop more intervallic sweeping ideas. Because this forces you to look at scales and intervals differently, it will broaden your understanding of the fretboard.

Sweeping is primarily used in the context of arpeggio playing. The easiest way to play a triadic arpeggio is on two strings. The diagrams below show the four basic types of triad (major, minor, diminished, and augmented) on the top two strings. The shapes will remain the same when you move them to the other remaining string sets (4th-3rd and 6th-5th). The only exception is the string set of G-B (3rd-2nd), in which the top part of the shape will be moved one fret higher.

Major

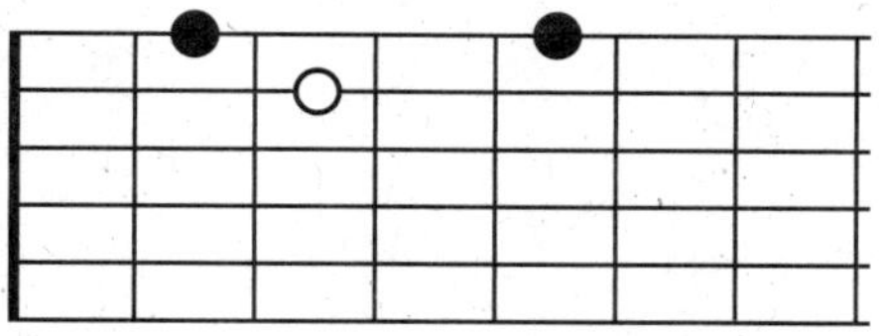

Minor

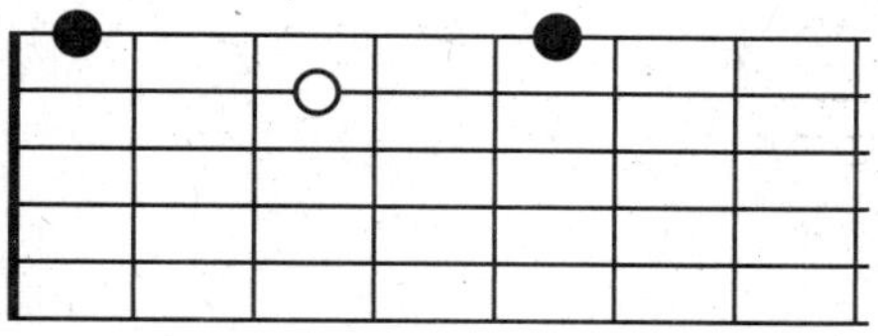

Diminished

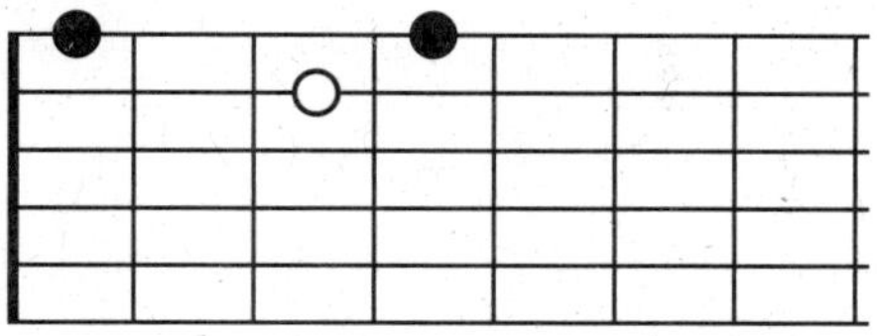

Augmented

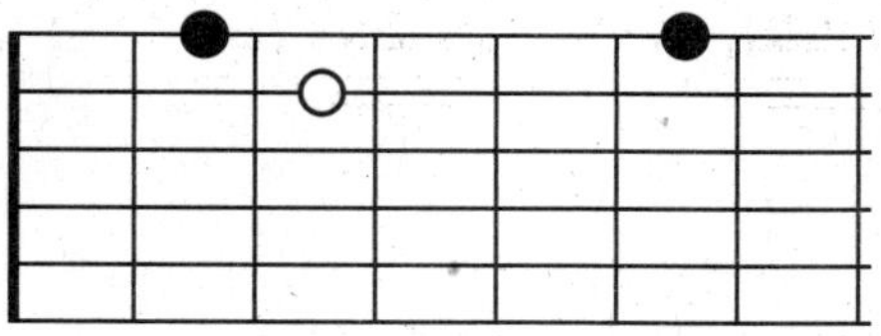

The example below demonstrates the different ascending and descending sweep-picking variations you can use for these arpeggios. Learn these patterns and move them up and down the fretboard and across the strings using the major, minor, diminished, and augmented forms.

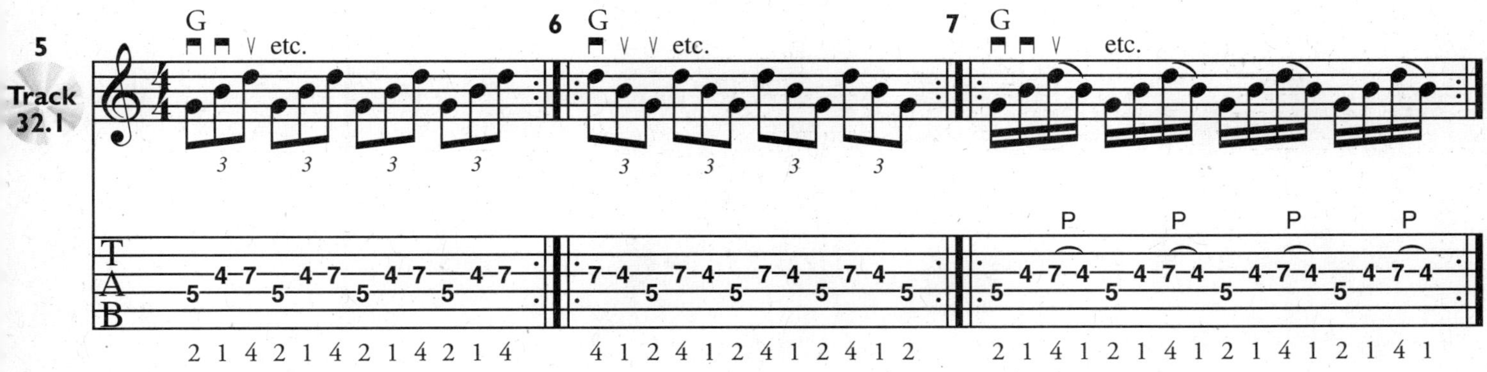

The best way to practice your technique is to combine it with music theory. You can practice sweep picking while simultaneously learning the diatonic triads of a scale. Example 8 below shows the triads in the key of E♭ Major.

Practice this example slowly, paying close attention to the correct sweeping technique and the diatonic triads. Furthermore, move the triads to the next string sets as well.

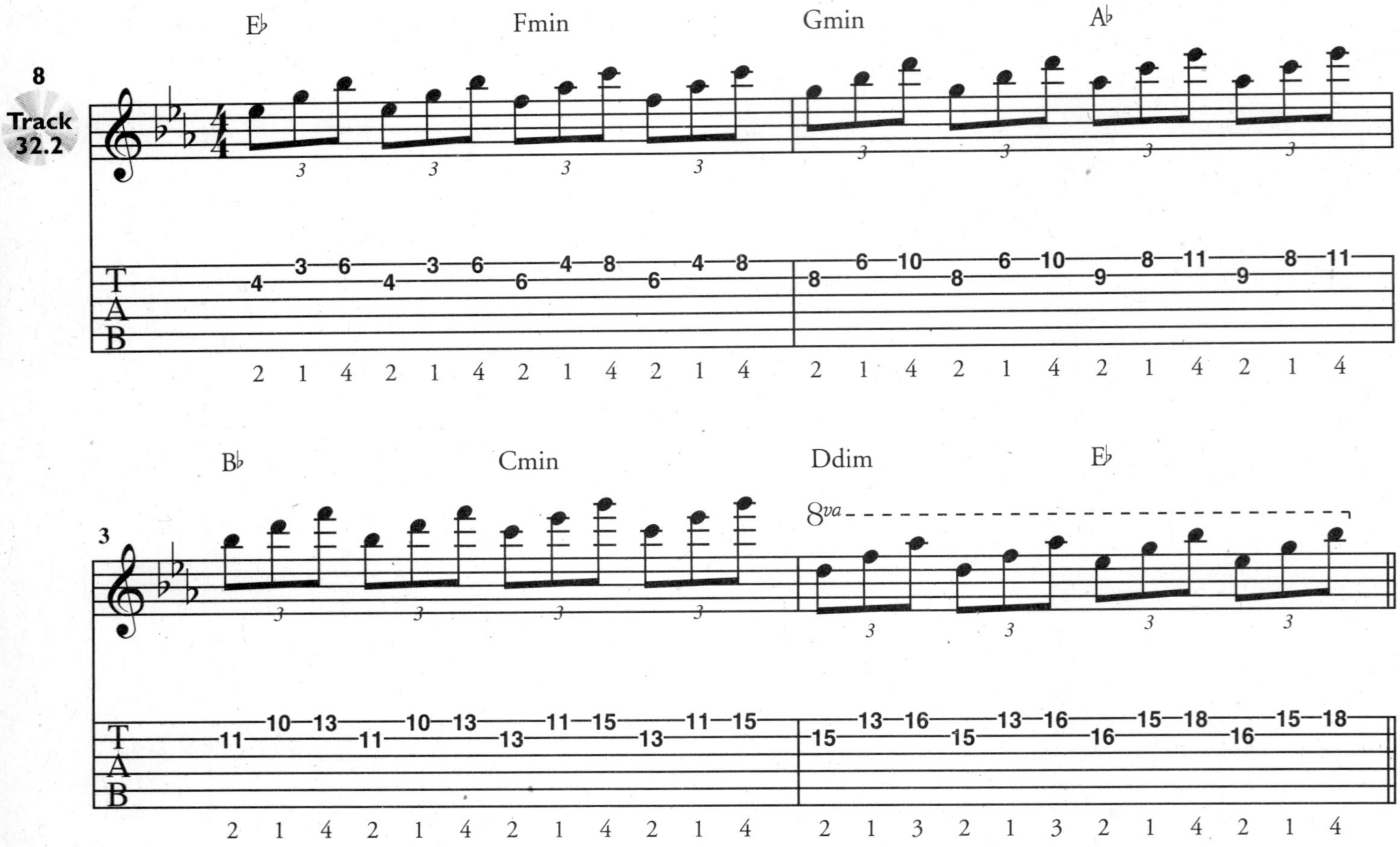

Another great way to work on your technique and theory is to play diatonic triads across the strings, combining ascending and descending movements. Example 9 is a simple lick in C Major featuring two-string arpeggios.

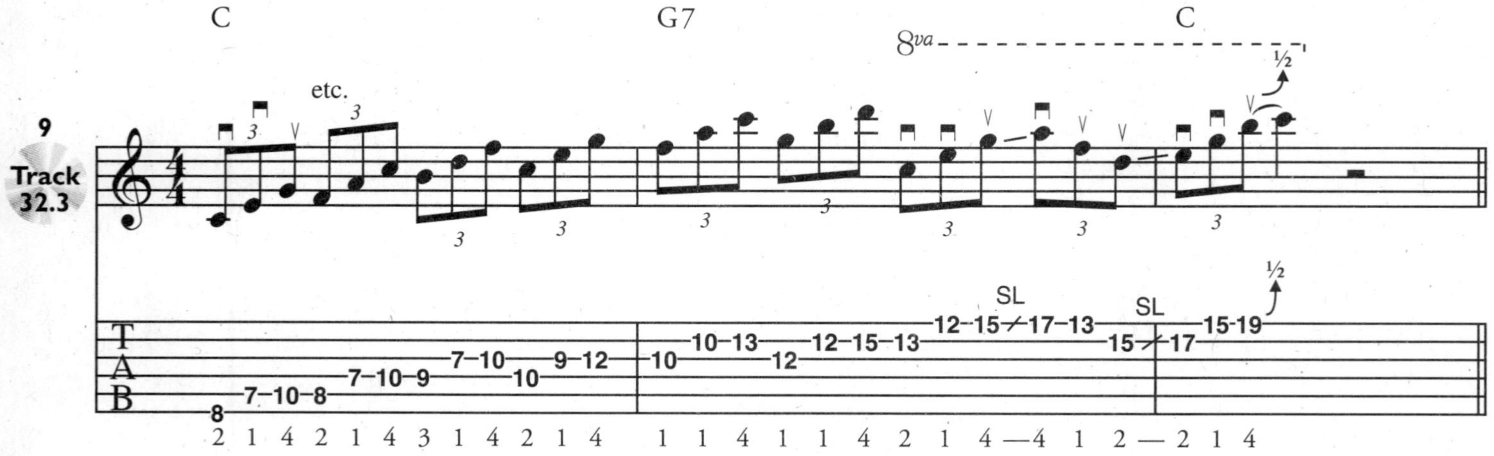

Three-String Sweeping

The basic sweeping motion can be extended to three or more strings. Example 10 is a three-string sweep on a C Major arpeggio. Make sure you lift your left-hand fingers from the fretboard once the note has been played in order to avoid notes ringing out together.

10

Track 33.1

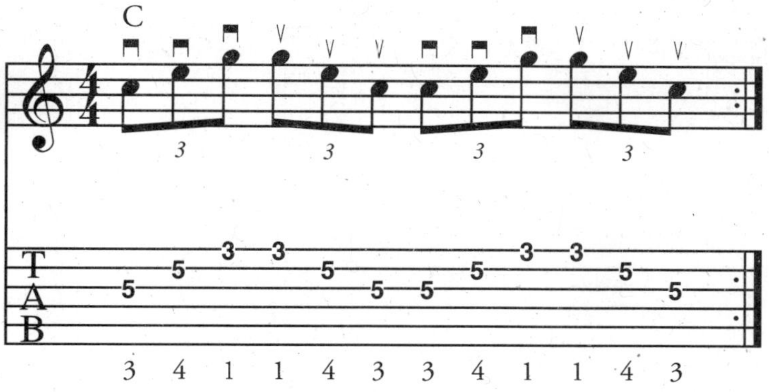

Similar to the previous example, you can practice sweeping and your diatonic triads at the same time.

11

Track 33.2

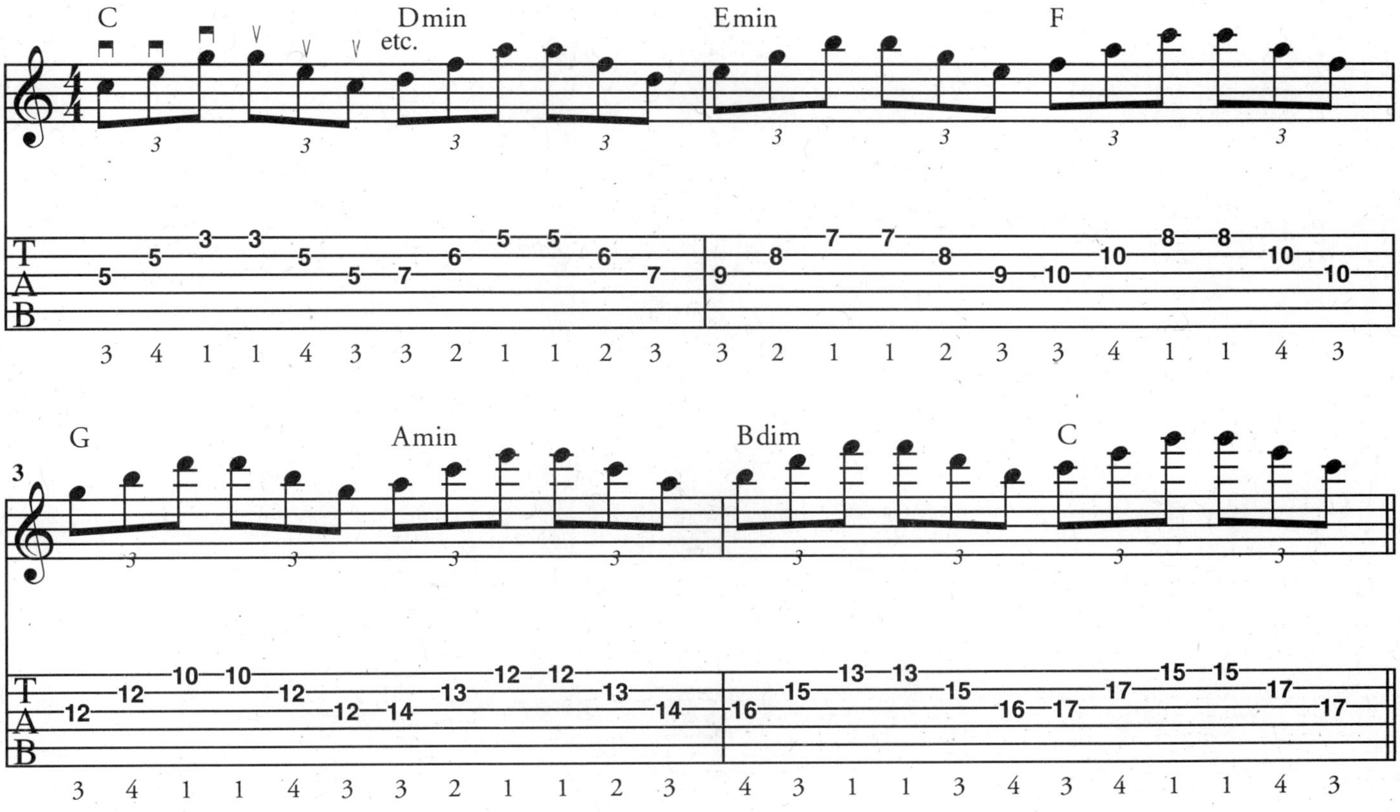

The next example is a variation of the previous idea, but it does not have any doubled notes on the low and high strings. The arpeggios ascend and descend from triad to triad. This will require a good knowledge of your triads and shapes.

12
Track 33.3

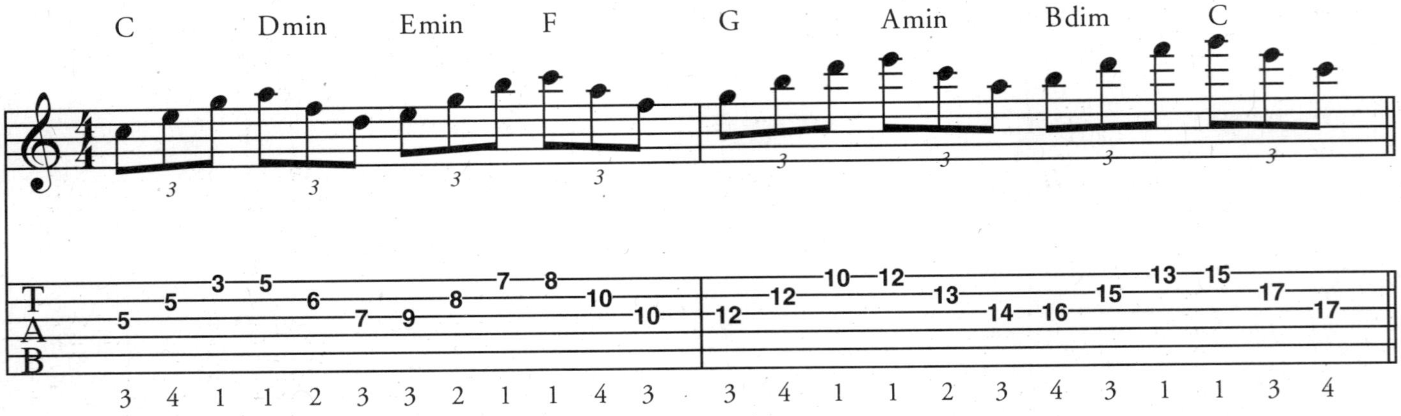

The basic triad shapes can be extended and also combined with their *inversions*. An inversion is a chord that has another chord tone, instead of its root, in the bass. If a triad has the 3rd as its lowest note, it is in *1st inversion*. If a triad has a 5th as its lowest note, it is in *2nd inversion*.

Example 13 is a cascading A Minor arpeggio in two octaves, and Example 14 is the same in A Major.

13
Track 33.4

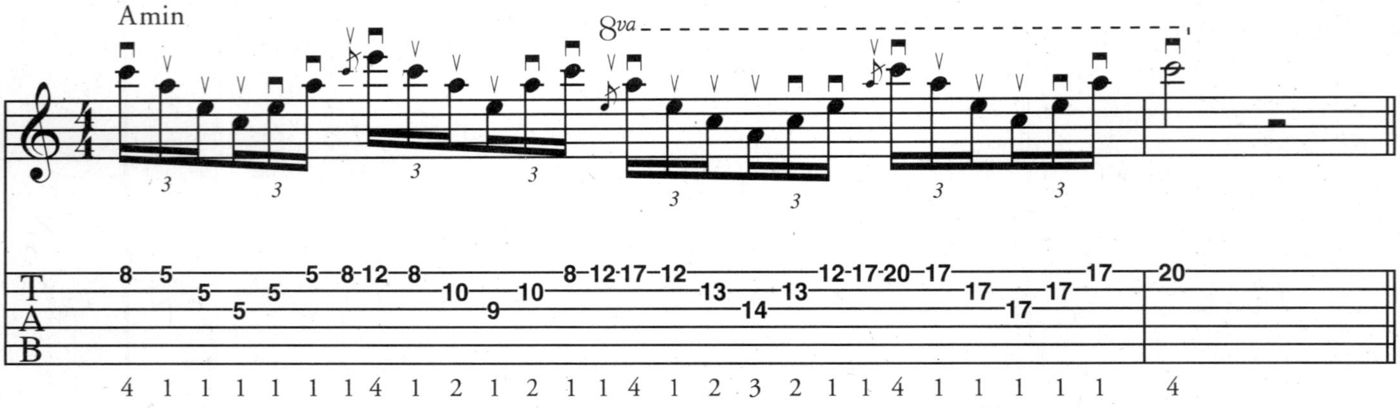

14
Track 33.5

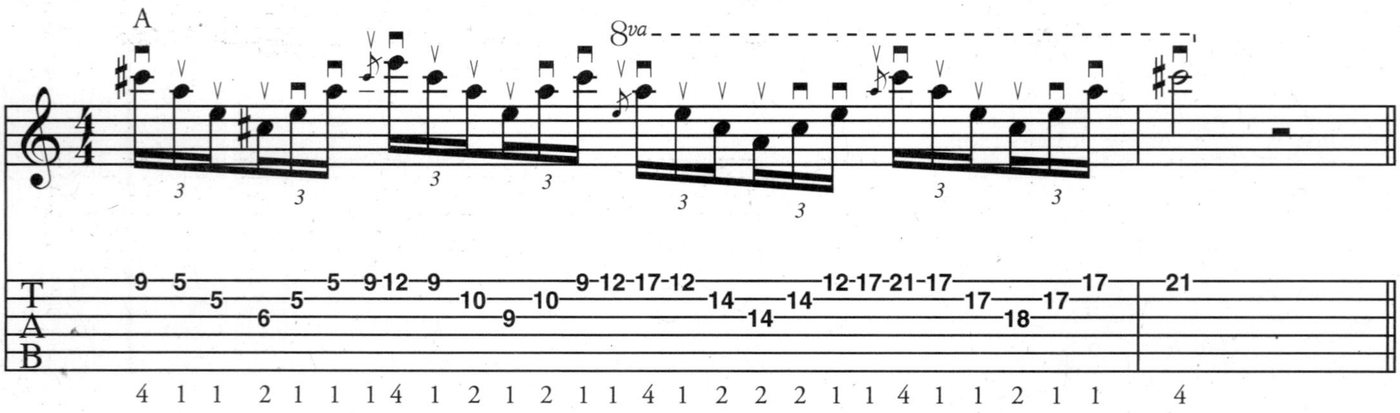

Example 15 shows a fully diminished G♯ arpeggio run across the strings. Try to extend it and practice it in different positions. The sequence can be played continuously by moving the arpeggio shape up or down the fretboard in minor 3rds.

15
Track 33.6

Four-String Sweeping

Now, let's extend our sweeping to four-string arpeggios, while also looking at a couple of different ways to play the top or bottom string of an arpeggio shape.

Example 16 shows the "traditional" way of changing the sweep direction by utilizing hammer-ons and pull-offs. This can be tricky as you have to combine two opposite techniques (picking and legato) to make a smooth transition from an ascending to a descending picking direction, or vice versa. This will require a lot of precise muting and picking-hand skips.

Then, there is strict sweep picking with a combination of alternate picking when changing directions, as illustrated in Example 17. Play both ideas and decide for yourself which is easier and more beneficial to you.

16
Track 34.1

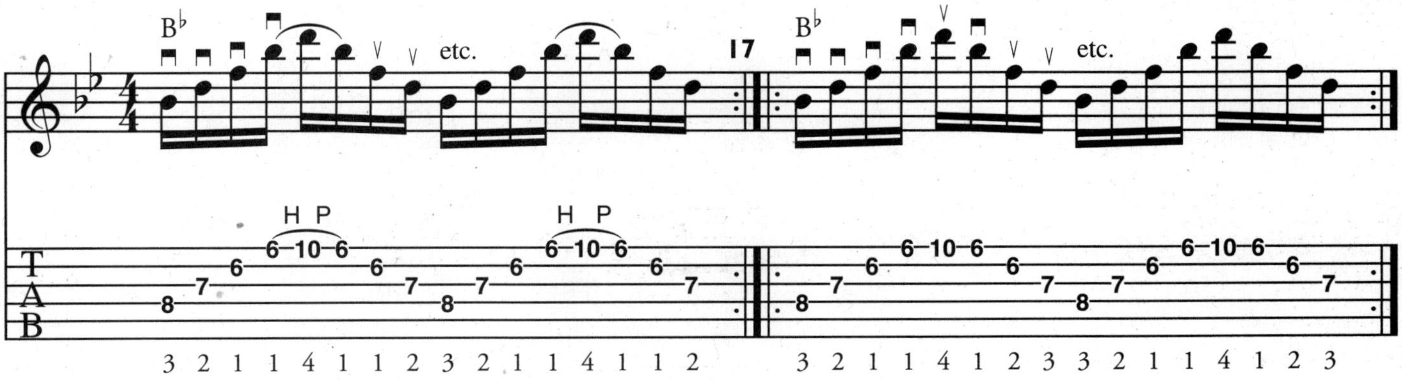

The example below shows the diatonic triads of G Major across the top four strings. Try playing this idea on other string-sets as well (like the 5th, 4th, 3rd, and 2nd strings).

Note: The D/F♯ chord (consisting of F♯–A–D) is substituted for F♯dim (F♯–A–C) in measure 7. This can be done because the chords are so similar (only the C and D notes are different), and it is desirable sometimes to vary the tonality of a progression.

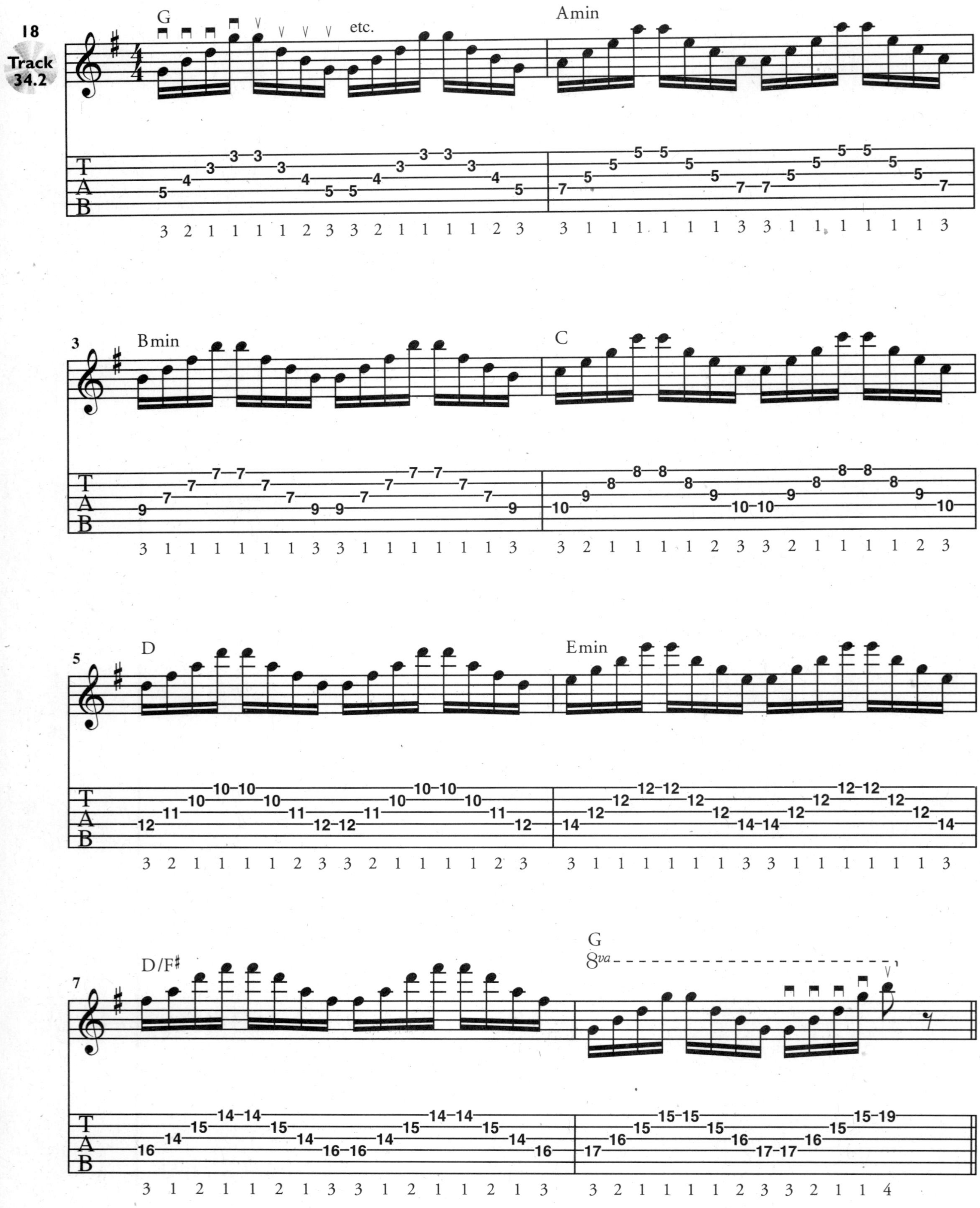

The following example shows the diatonic triads of B♭ Major with added chord tones on the top string. Notice the same type of chord substitution in measure 4 (F/A for Adim) as with the previous example. On your own, try writing similar chord progressions of sweep arpeggios to practice.

19
Track 34.3

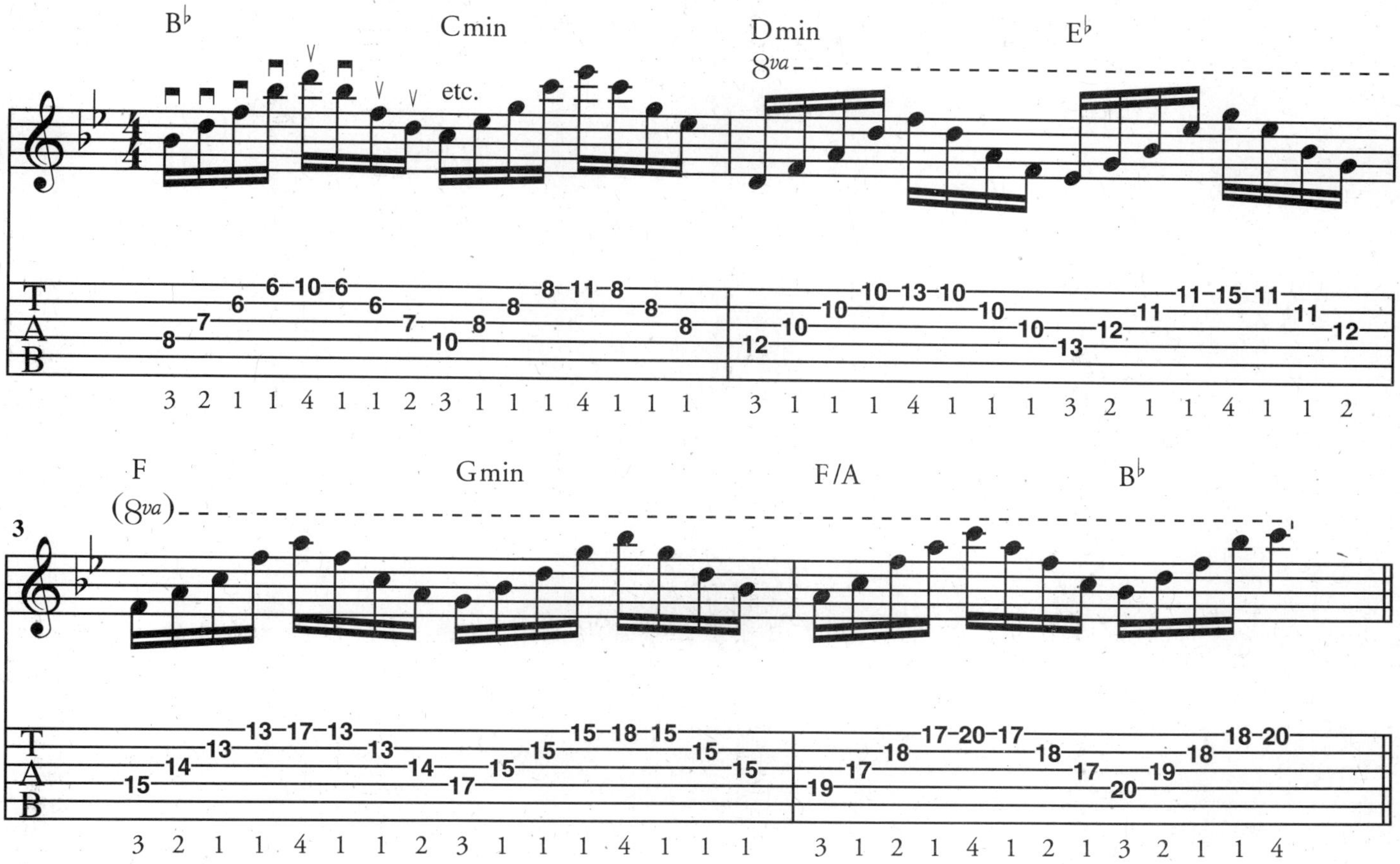

Below is a short arpeggio sequence in D Minor that combines alternate picking with sweep picking.

20
Track 34.4

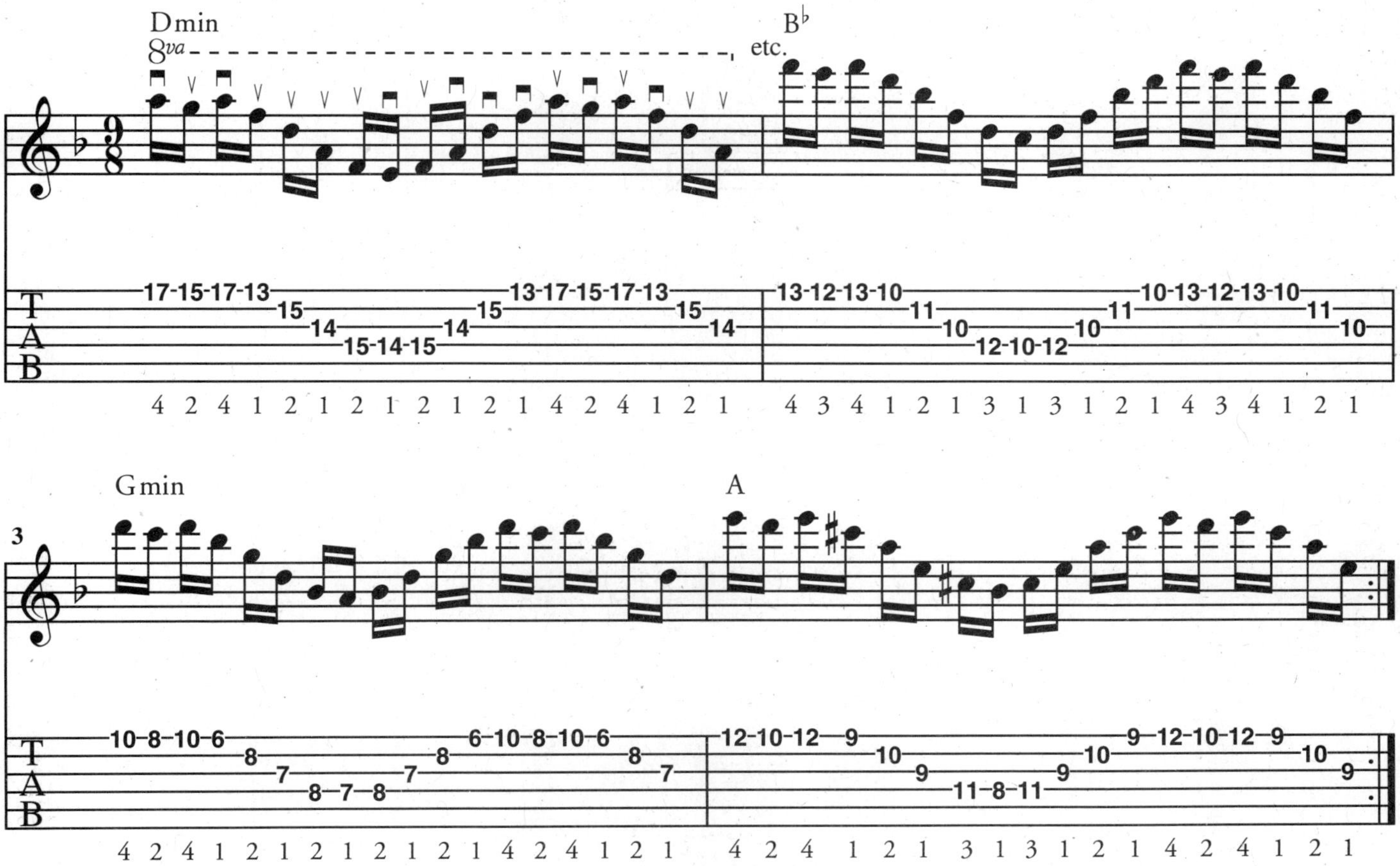

All Across the Fretboard

Sweeping across even more strings can be quite difficult, but with practice and patience, you will make great improvements. The first step is to learn all the different arpeggio shapes. The diagrams below show the different shapes for major, minor, diminished, and augmented triad arpeggios in root position, 1st inversion, and 2nd inversion. Some of the five-string shapes can also be extended to the low-E string but, generally, they are played on five strings only.

Major Triad

Root Position

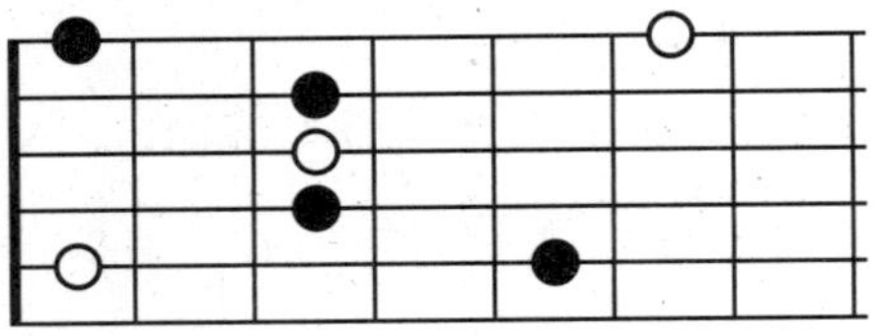

1st Inversion

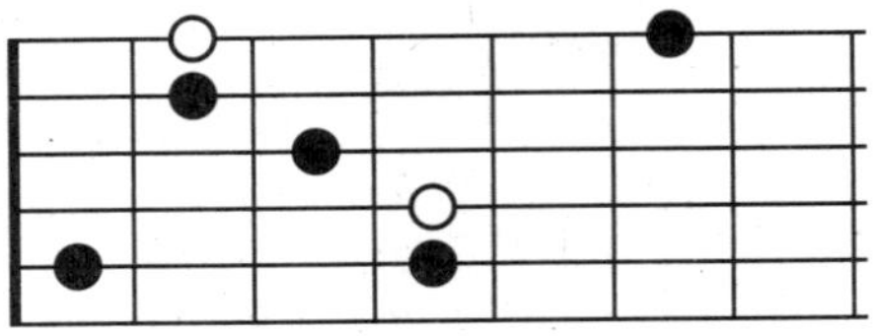

2nd Inversion

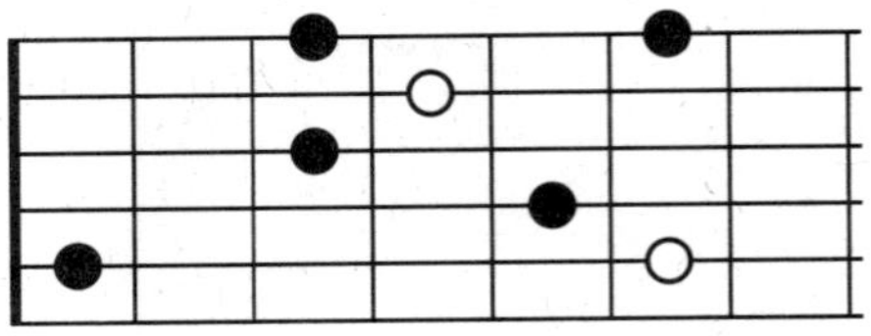

Minor Triad

Root Position

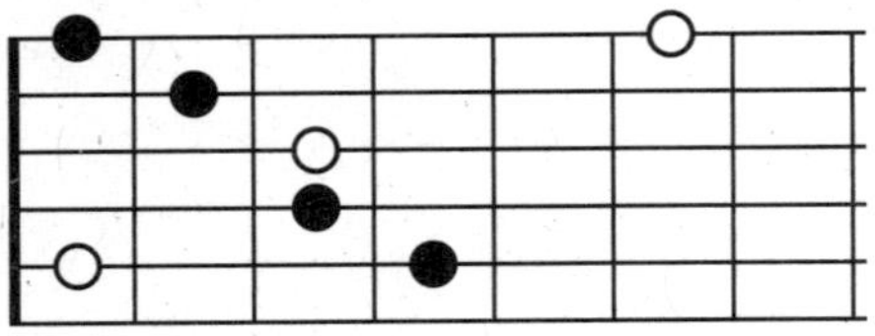

1st Inversion

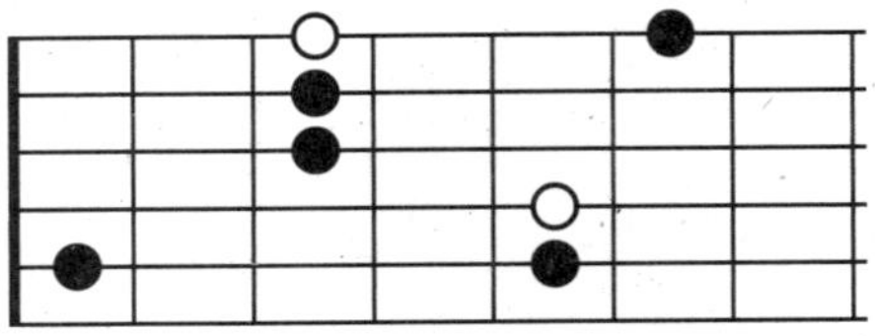

2nd Inversion

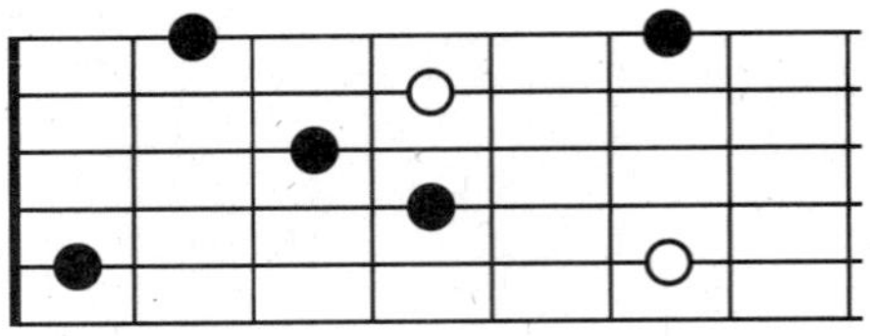

Diminished Triad

2nd Inversion

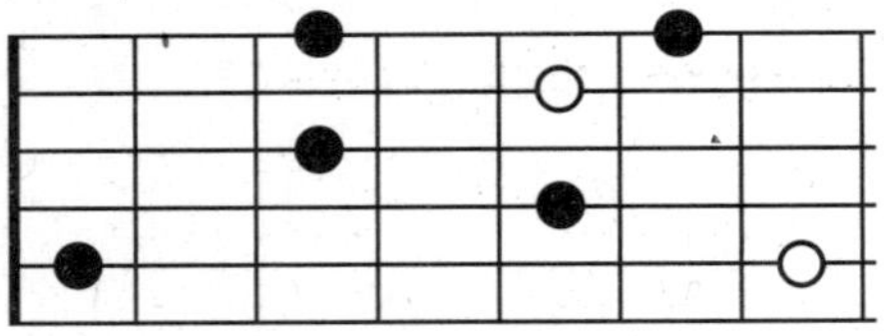

Augmented Triad

2nd Inversion

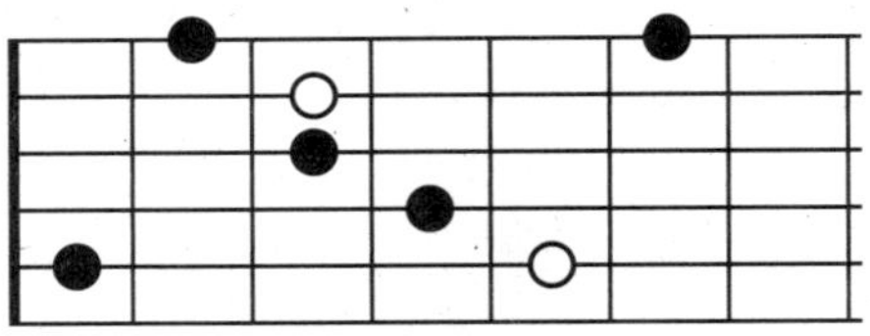

Try to practice these shapes slowly and accurately. Furthermore, practice the arpeggios by playing the diatonic ascending or descending triads of all 12 keys as previously discussed.

The two examples below are simple sweep-picking patterns that will help you with your picking.

21
Track 35.1

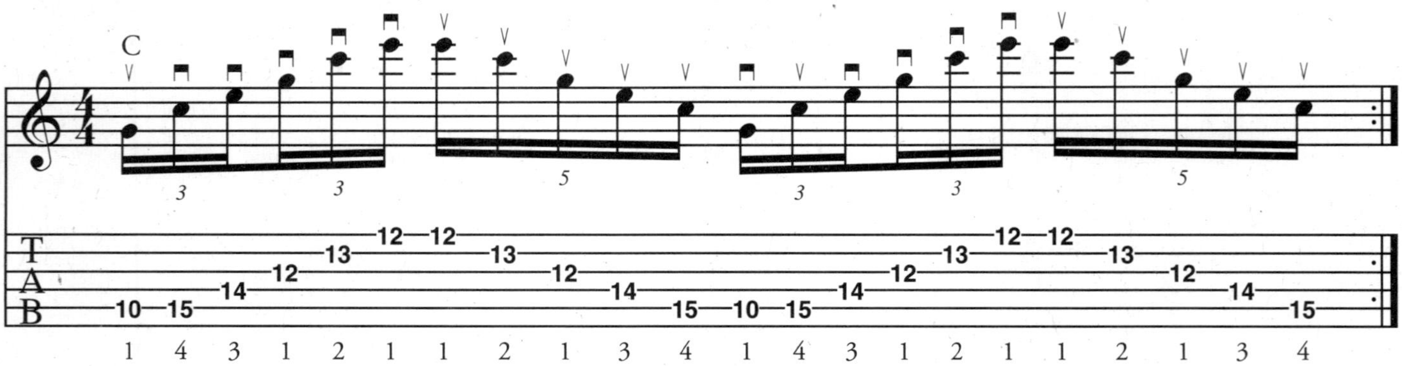

21A
Track 35.2

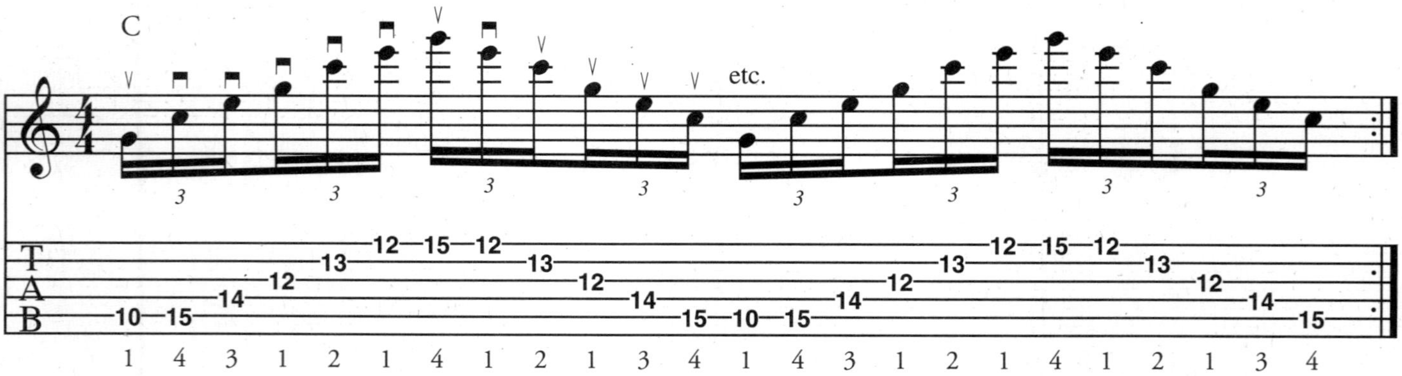

In order to understand and utilize all these shapes, you should try to combine the different major, minor, diminished, and augmented shapes into longer phrases.

The example below is an arpeggio section taken from one of my songs, "The Lightspeeder," in D Minor.

22

Track 35.3

The Lightspeeder

(Excerpt)

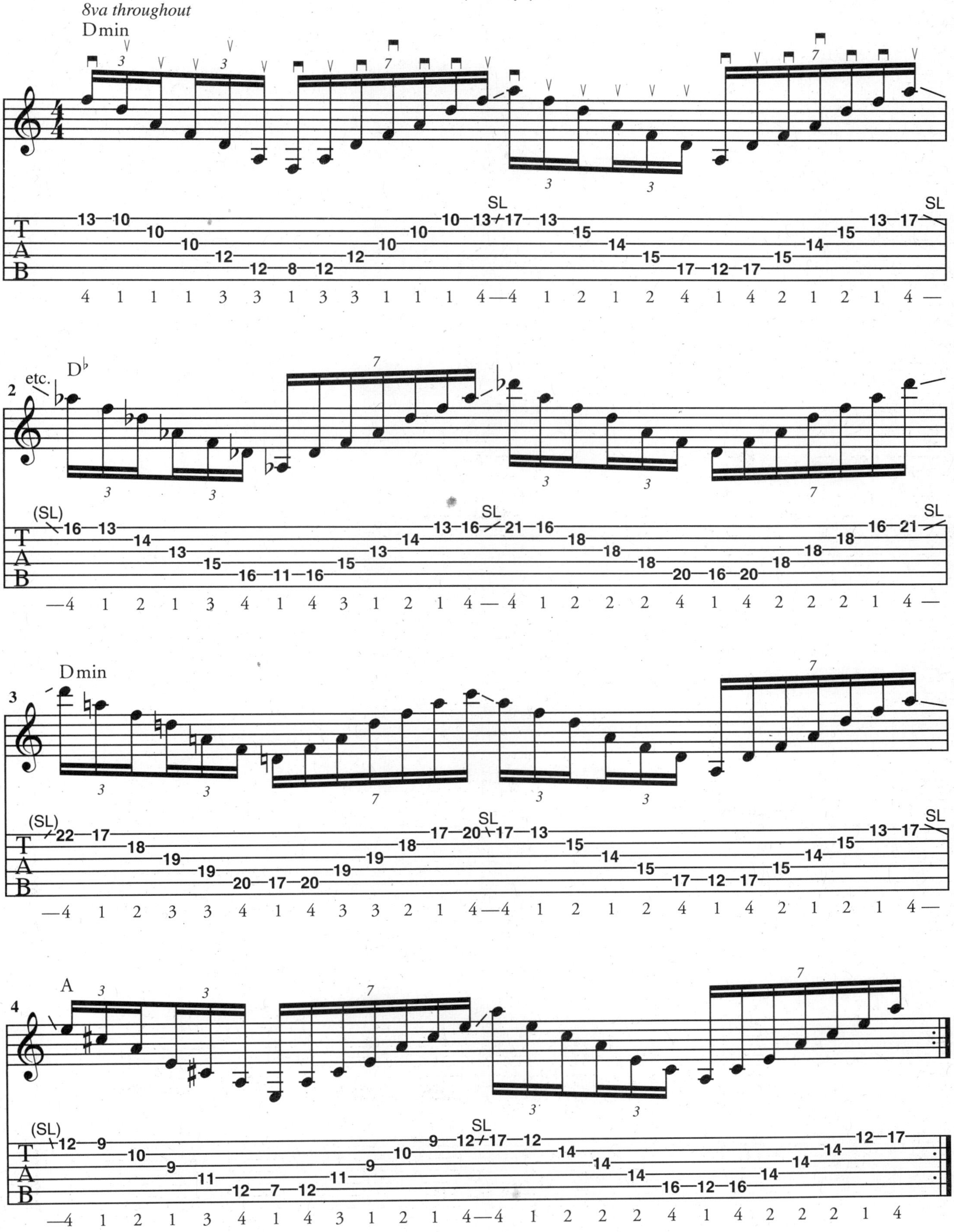

In the example below, we are combining parts of three different shapes (from page 66) to create a three-octave C Minor sweep arpeggio.

23
Track 35.4

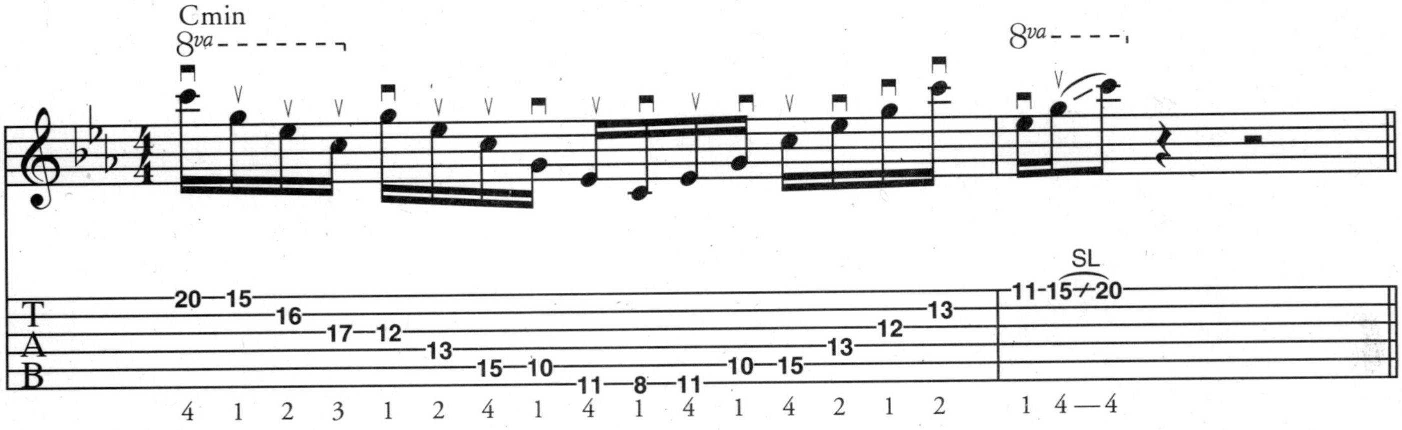

Example 24 is a lick based on a D Major arpeggio (2nd inversion) that combines tapping (see Chapter 10) and sweeping.

24
Track 35.5

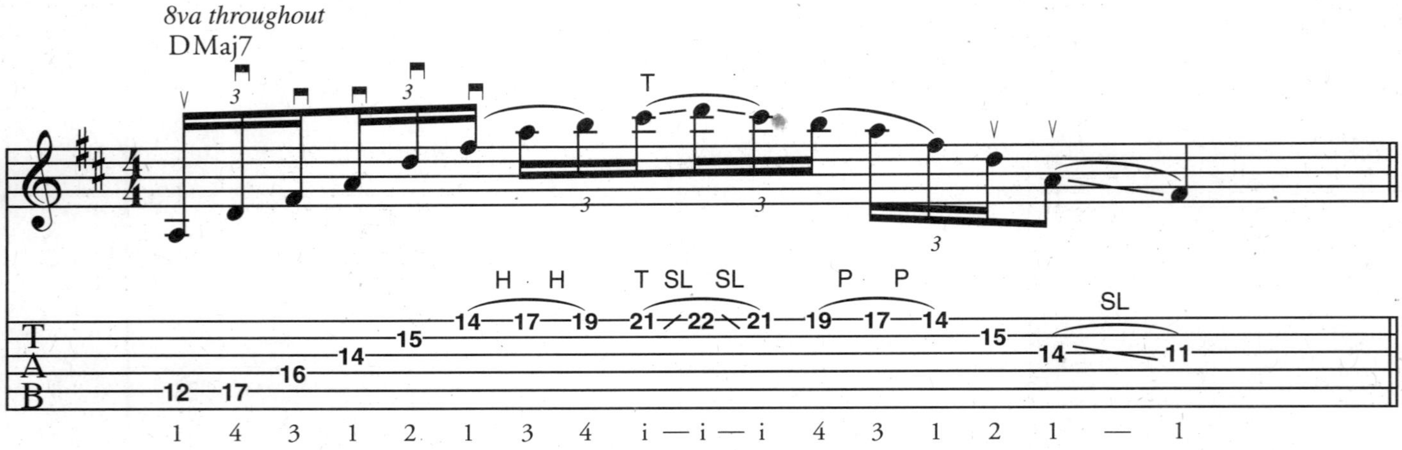

Sweeping 7th Chord Arpeggios

Let's go a step further and apply the sweep-picking technique to 7th chord arpeggios. The diagrams below show the basic root-position 7th chord arpeggios. Practice them by playing the diatonic 7th chord arpeggios of all 12 keys in ascending or descending order. For example: CMaj7, Dmin7, Emin7, FMaj7, etc.

Major 7

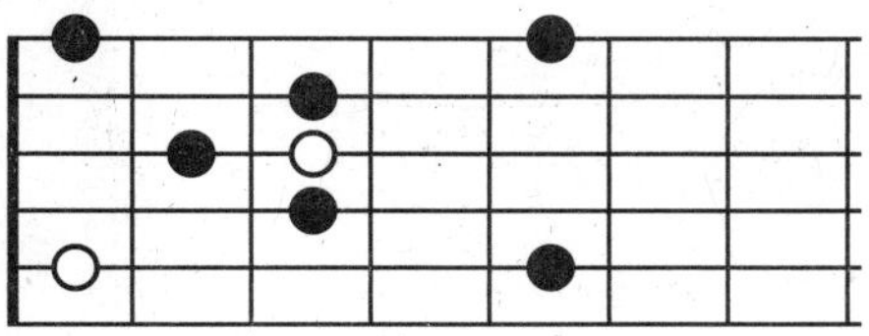

Dominant 7

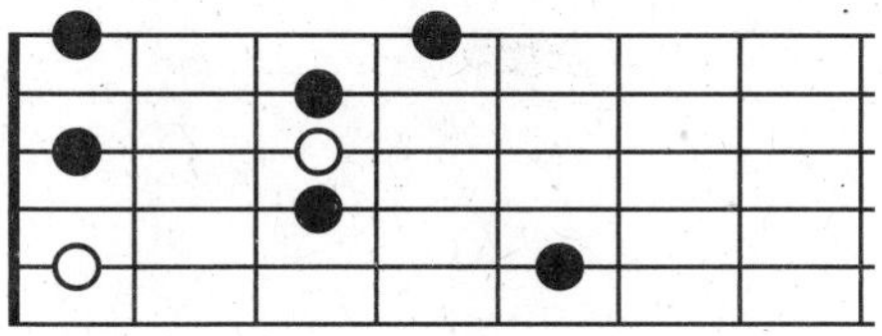

Minor 7

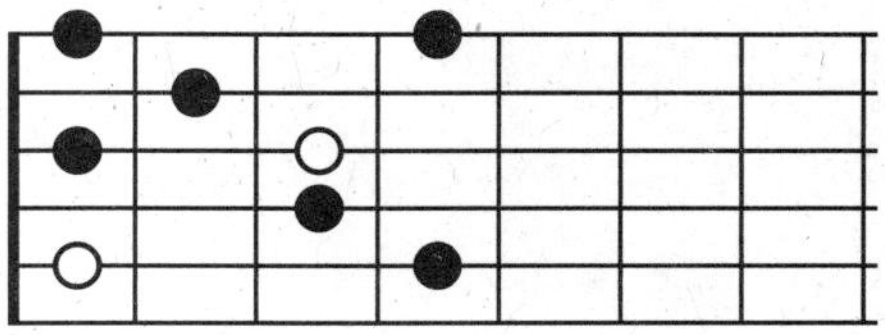

Minor 7♭5

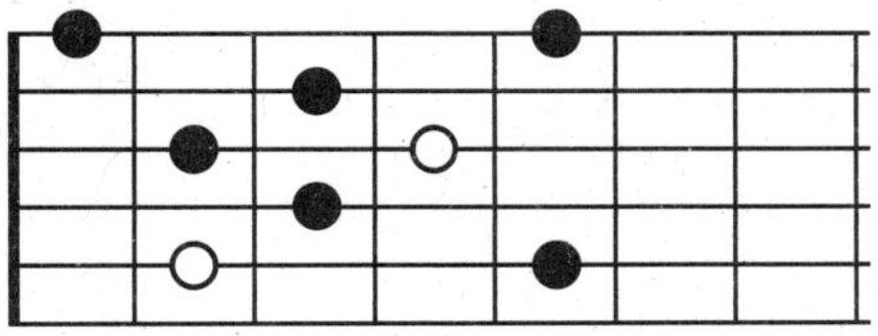

Diminished 7

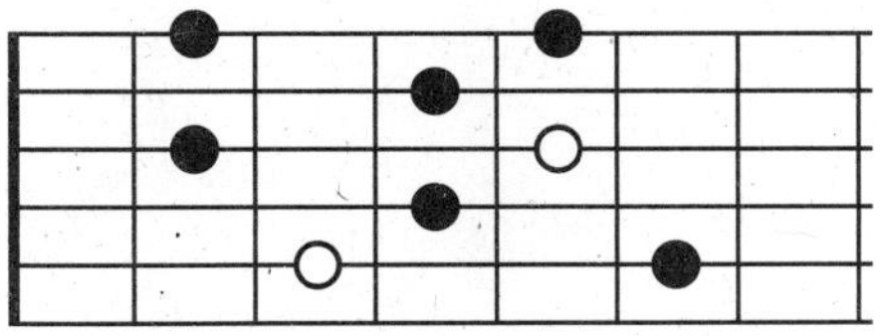

Examples 25 and 26 illustrate the upper and lower octave of the Major 7 arpeggio. Pay close attention to the picking pattern. The first note is played with an upstroke only the first time through the sequence (to make it easier to start the lick). On subsequent repeats, this note should be played with a downstroke.

25
Track 36.1

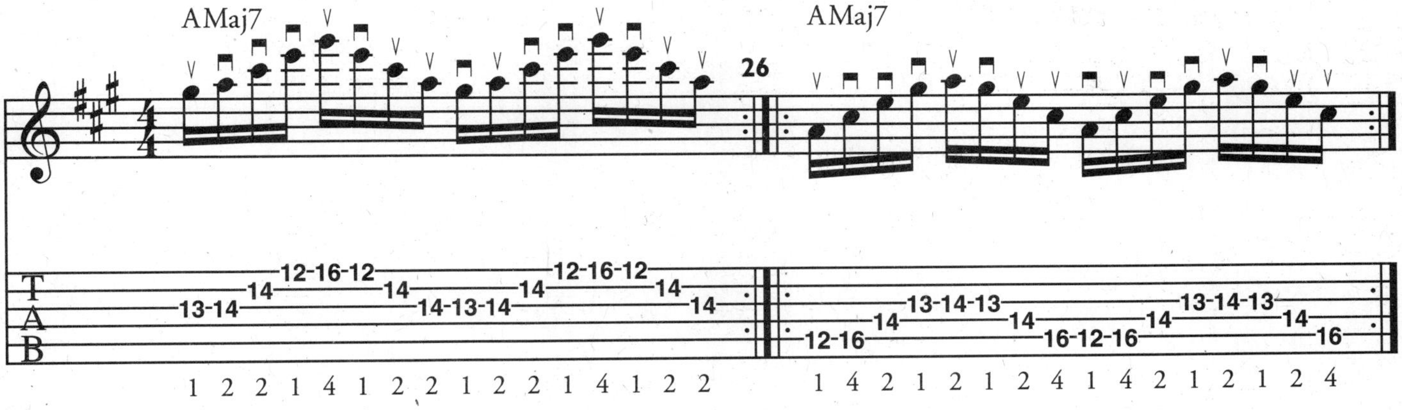

Our next step is to combine both forms and create a two-octave shape as shown below. Watch out for the $\frac{6}{4}$ time signature (six beats per measure with the quarter note receiving one beat). After you play the example below as written, try applying the concept by playing the diatonic arpeggios ascending and descending, or by creating chord progressions of your own.

27
Track 36.2

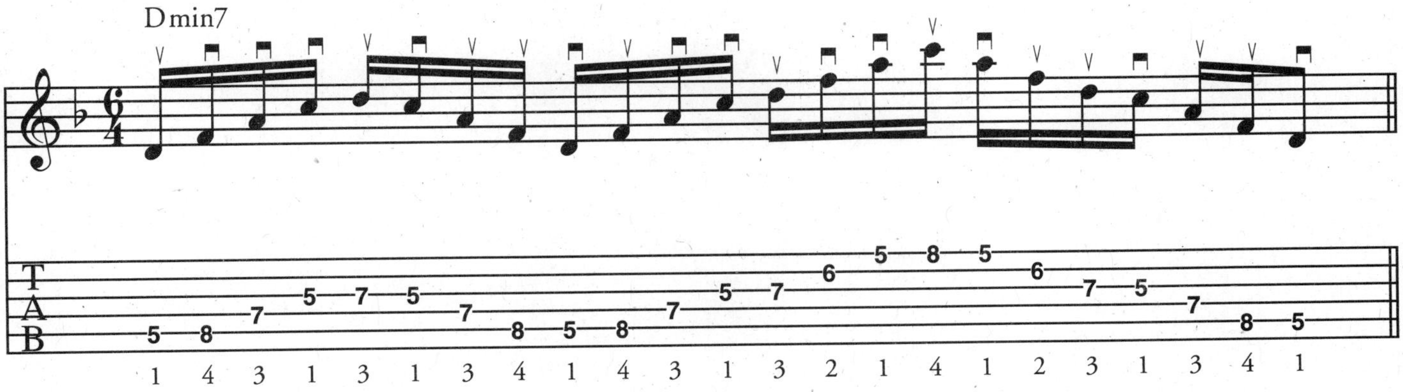

The next examples use 7th chord arpeggios in different musical situations. Example 28 is a B♭dim arpeggio played over a C7♭9 chord resolving to an Fmin chord.

28
Track 36.3

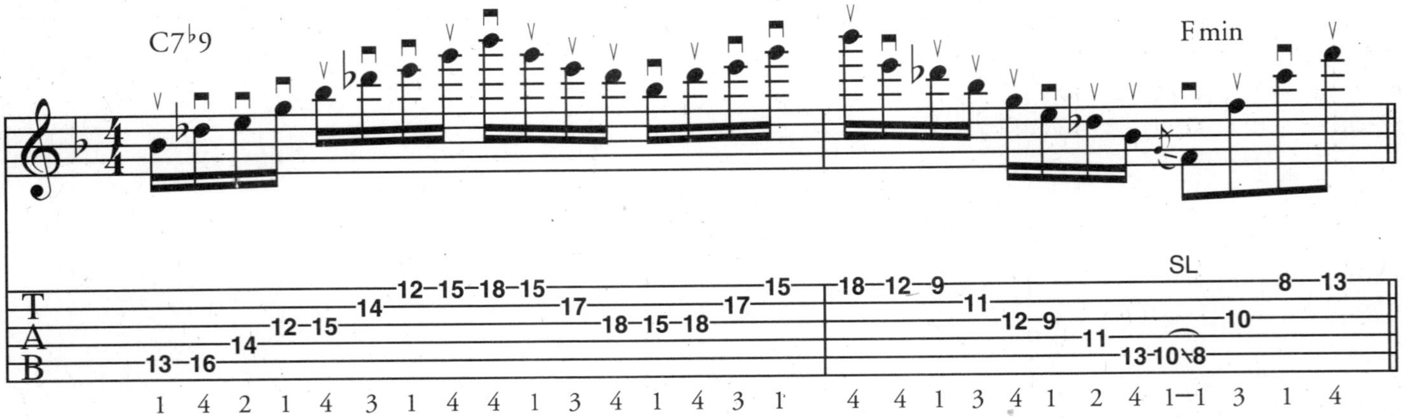

Example 29 combines GMaj7 and Bmin7 arpeggios to create an extended GMaj9 sound. The formula for a GMaj9 chord is: 1–3–5–7–9. The 7 (A) of Bmin7 is the 9 of GMaj9.

29
Track 36.4

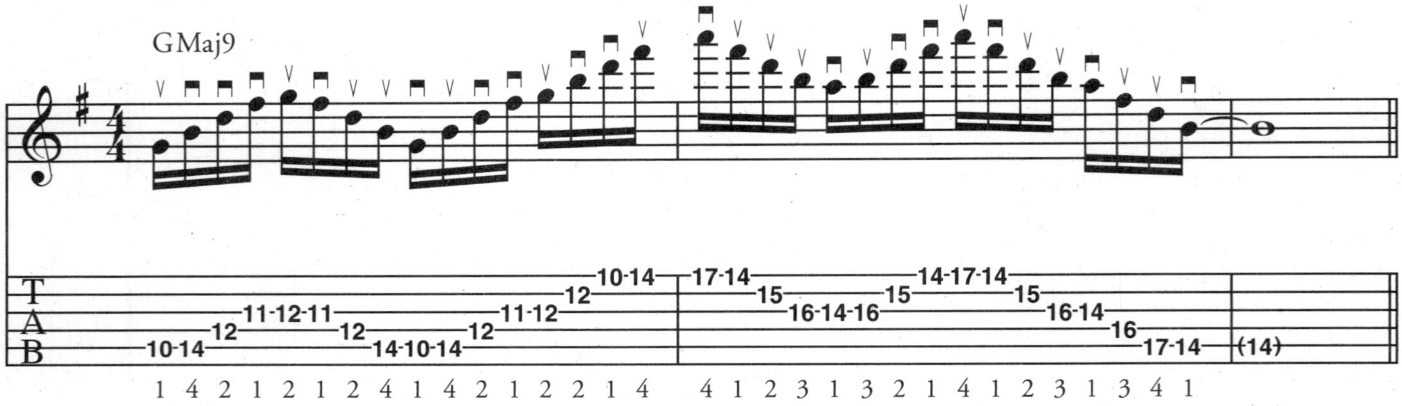

Example 30 simply adds a 9 to an EMaj7 chord to produce an EMaj9. Pay close attention to the added note on beat 3 and the slight change of picking.

30
Track 36.5

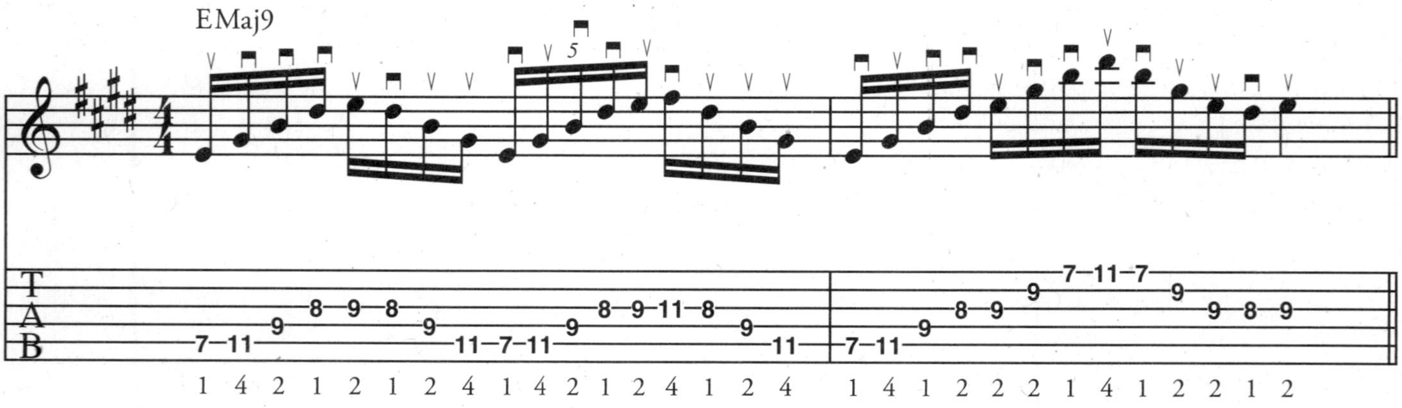

Chapter 9: Open-Voiced Arpeggios

Let's look at a different approach to the common triad. This chapter will show you how to use *open-voiced triads* to develop new sounds and ideas without sounding repetitive.

C Major Triad (Closed Voicing)

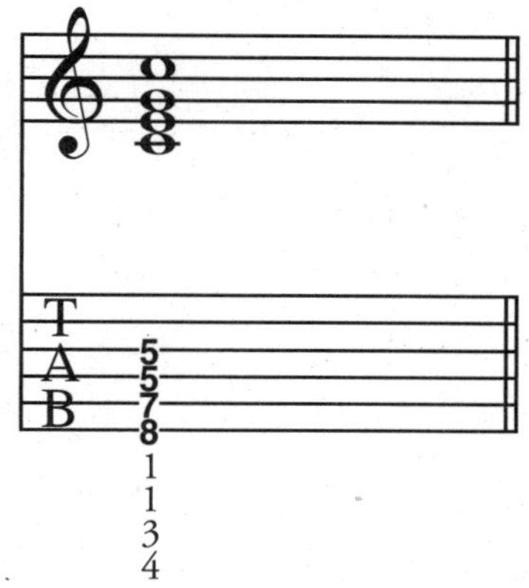

What is an open-voiced triad? Let's take a look at the example to the right. This is a simple C Major triad in a *closed voicing*. Closed voicing means that the notes of the basic triad, or arpeggio, are all within one octave. As you can see, the triad spans from the root note C to the C note one octave higher. This closed-voicing arpeggio produces a distinct, typical sound used by many guitarists. The chord formula is: 1–3–5–8(1)

C Major Triad (Open Voicing)

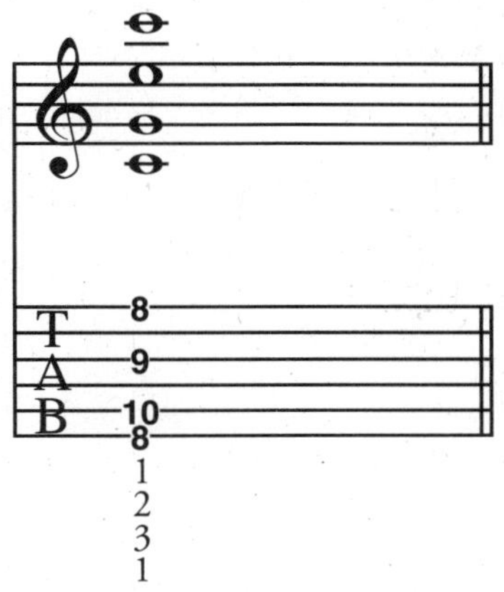

Open voicing means that the range of the triad is beyond one or, sometimes, even two octaves. Take a look at the example to the right and play it on your guitar.

What has changed? You probably noticed that this voicing uses different strings and sounds much brighter and "wider." The concept is quite simple but very effective. Start with the root note of your triad, chord, or arpeggio (in this case, it is C), then skip the next chord tone, E, and play the G. Next, skip the C and play the E. And, finally, skip the G and play the C. The final formula for your chord is: 1–5–3–8(1).

Notice how this voicing actually ranges over two octaves—from the root note C to the C note two octaves higher. This is a great way to make a predictable chord progression or arpeggio sequence new and refreshing.

Now, let's take a look at all the different open-voiced triad arpeggios and their inversions.

Below is an open-voiced C Major triad in root position, first inversion, and second inversion. Play all forms slowly, making sure to avoid all string noise. This may not be so easy, as you have to skip over strings and will not be able to barre strings. Use your picking hand for muting, and be very precise with your fretting hand. Alternate picking should be used throughout the arpeggios. There is an extra note on the high-E string, which will allow your alternate picking to remain even.

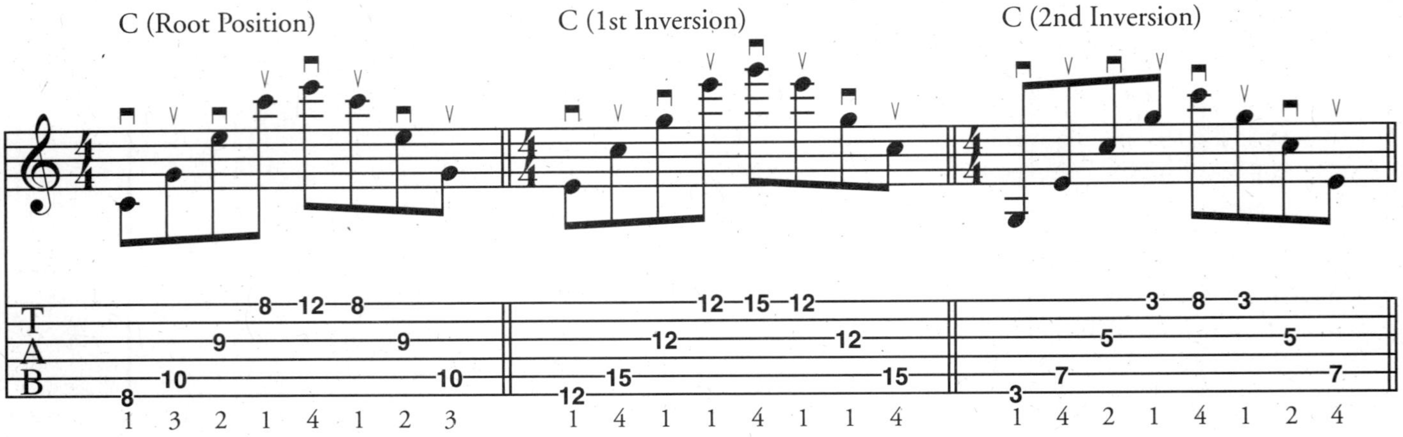

Next up are the C Minor forms.

Again, you should be using alternate picking for all examples. Try also to smoothly connect the different inversions. Following are the C Augmented forms.

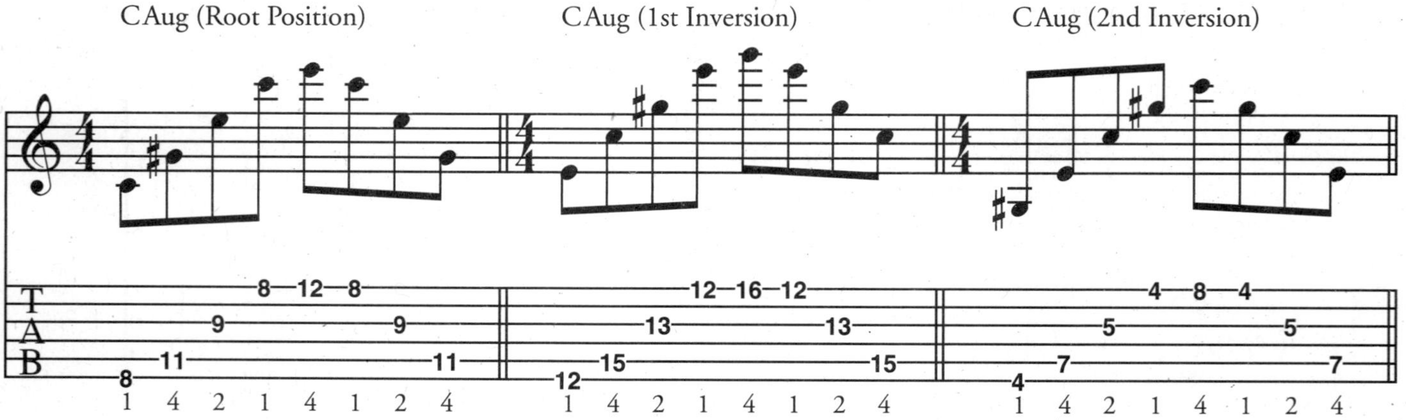

You may have noticed that the shapes for all the augmented chords are the same. Why is this? Well, it has to do with the symmetrical intervallic structure of the augmented chord. It consists of three major 3rd intervals, which divide the octave into three even parts. Thus, if you invert the augmented triad, the intervallic distance from root note to 3rd or augmented 5th is always the same. This is really cool because, technically, you only have to learn one shape and move it in major 3rds up or down the neck.

Below are the C Diminished forms.

The diminished triad has a similar structure to the augmented triad, with the exception that it is based on minor 3rds. If you divide the octave into four equal parts, the intervallic distance from one note to the next is a minor 3rd. However, a triad has only three notes: 1–♭3–♭5. Missing is the last interval, the ♭♭7, that would complete the symmetrical structure of the octave when divided into minor 3rds, or four equal parts. Because of this, when playing diminished triads, each chord shape is very different from the one that precedes it. But, if you play a fully diminished chord with all four notes (1–♭3–♭5–♭♭7), you could use one of the above shapes and just move it in intervals of minor 3rds up and down the neck, just like you did with the augmented arpeggios.

Now, let the fun begin. After learning all the basic shapes and ideas, let's start using our new knowledge to make some really awesome music and guitar licks.

The first lick starts out with an open-voiced C Major arpeggio and then adds some skips and slides to make it more interesting.

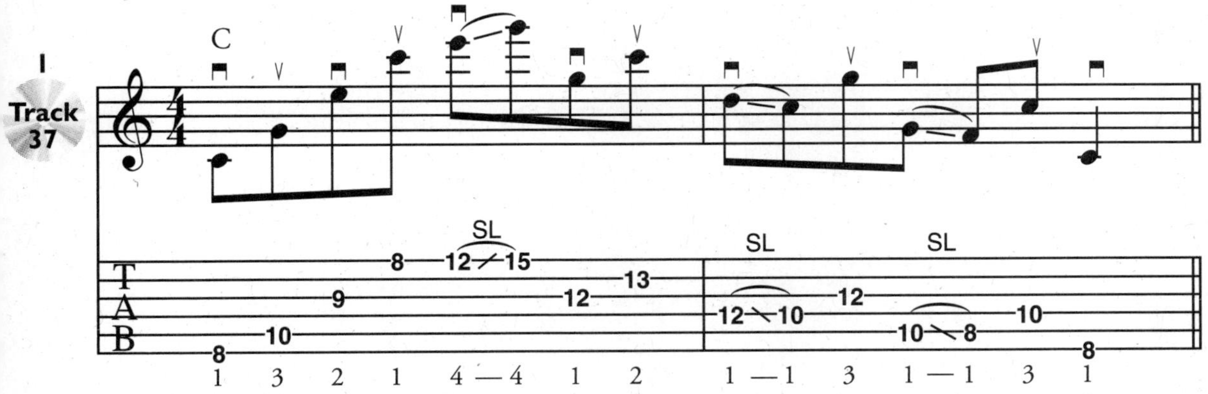

The next lick is another example of this cool style of playing. After the open-voiced arpeggio on beat 1, there is a large skip where we slide all the way up with the pinky from the 12th to the 24th fret. Then, we are using slides and skips of 5ths and 4ths to descend. Finally, we skip up a 5th and end up on a sustained note preceded by a bend. Check it out.

2
Track 38

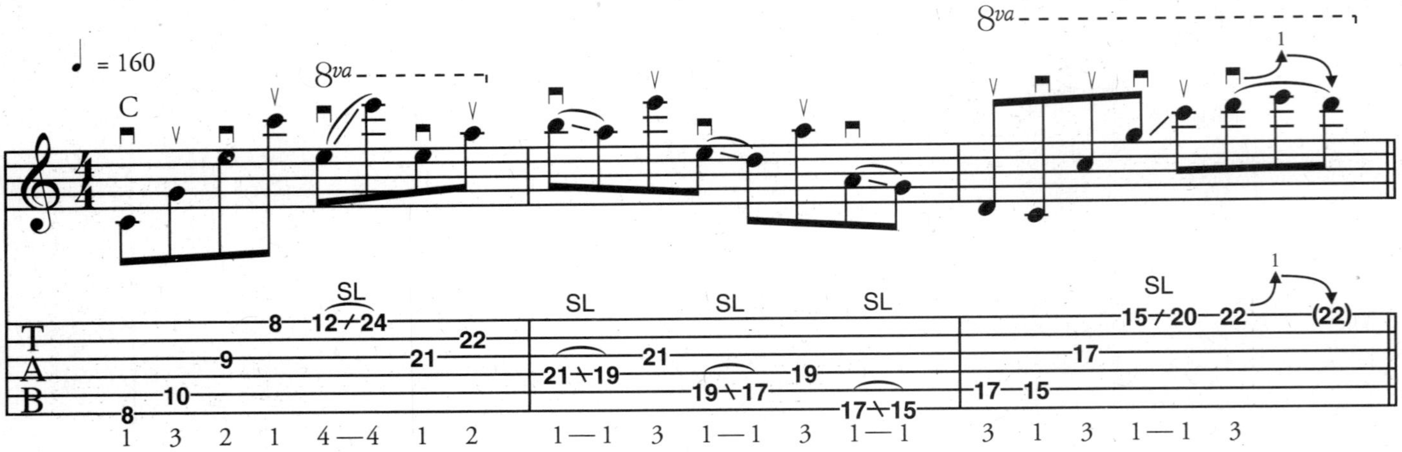

Now, let's take a look at some longer phrases that will utilize the entire fretboard.

The following lick is based on an easy chord progression in B♭ Major: B♭–D–Gmin–E♭–F (I–V/vi–vi–IV–V). The example uses pedal-tone licks and intervallic string skipping. Practice the example slowly, making sure to play each note loudly and clearly. This is a great melodic tool and a sophisticated alternative for playing common chord progressions.

3
Track 39

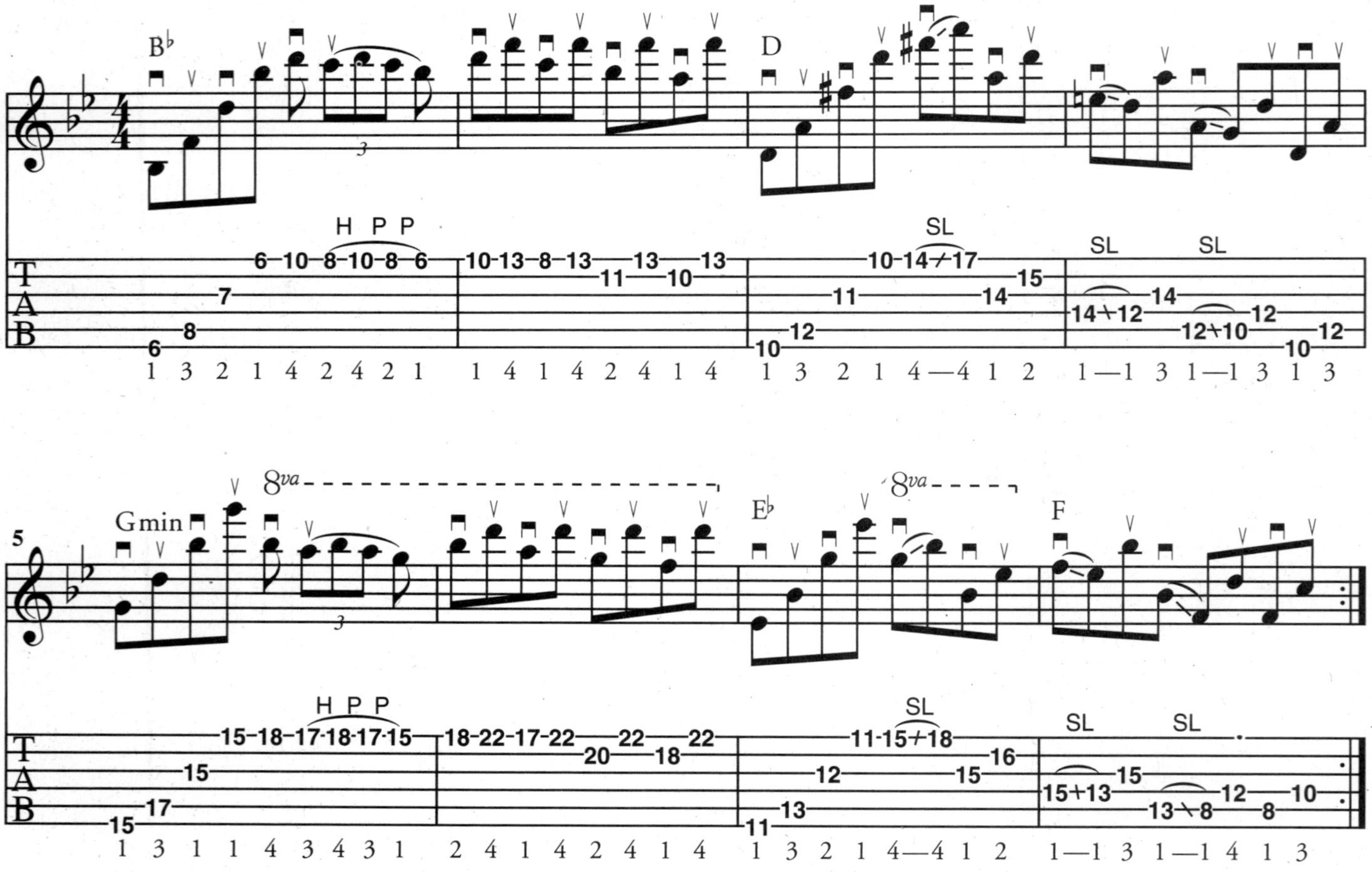

The next etude is based on two chords: D Major and A♭ Major. It uses skips and slides similar to the previous examples and is a really great exercise for covering a lot of ground. Take this lick slowly at first, as the slides and connections can be very tricky. Listen to Track 40 and try to emulate the smoothness before attempting to play the lick at full speed.

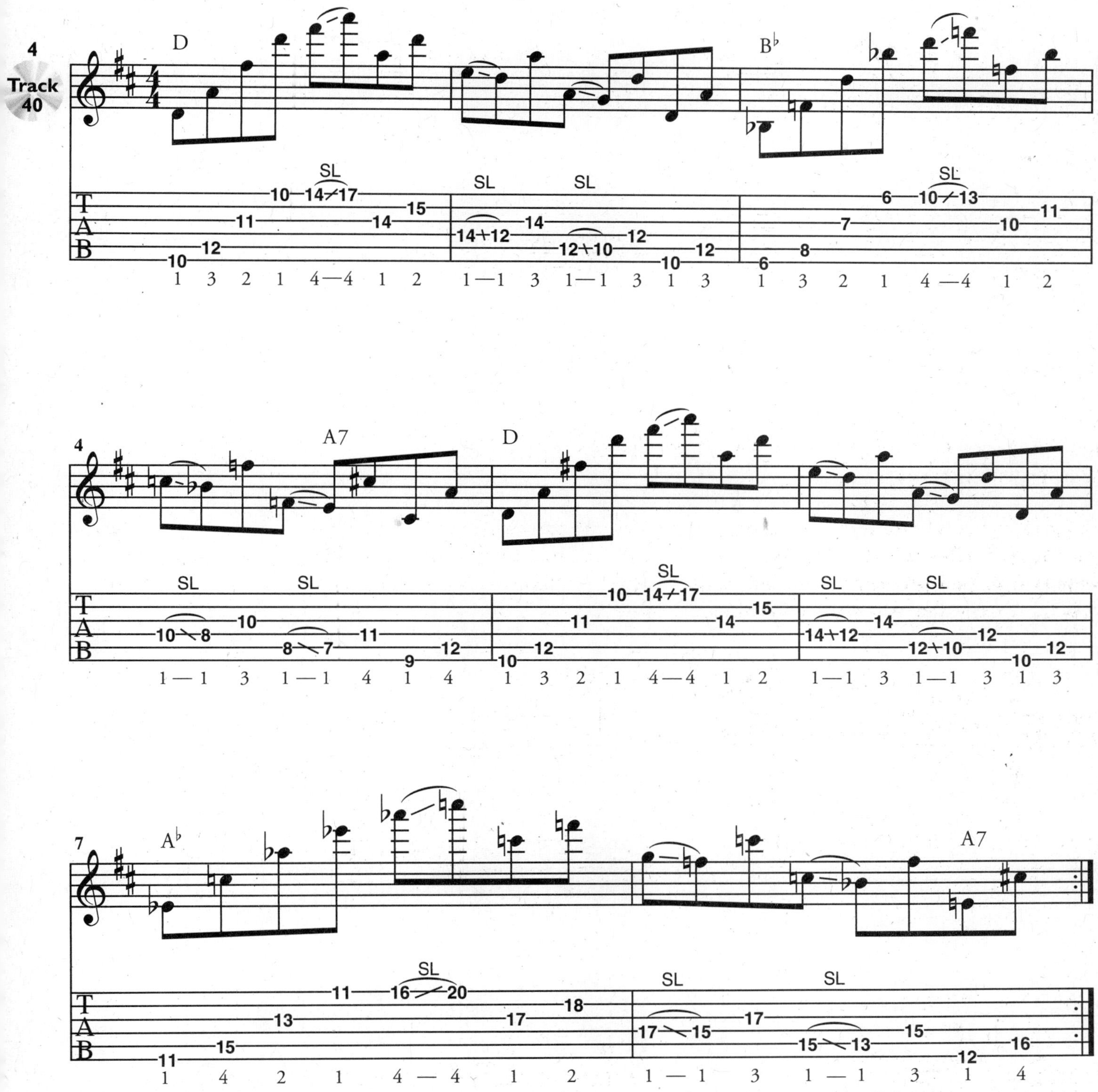

The next etude uses all types of major, minor, and diminished arpeggios and their inversions. The chord progression is based on a simple D Minor sequence: Dmin–B♭–Bdim–C (i–♭VI–vi°–♭VII). What is challenging about this example is the range of the progression and making smooth connections between the arpeggio inversions. For the most part, the pinky finger should be used on the high-E string to connect one arpeggio form to the next. This ensures a fluid sound and a good connection.

Open-voiced arpeggios are great for bringing more variety into your solo playing or rhythm accompaniments. Consider rewriting some of your own licks and ideas using this concept. Maybe even write a whole song using this idea!

Chapter 10: Tapping

Tapping is a guitar technique utilizing fingers of both the fretting and picking hands. This style of playing was first made popular by Eddie Van Halen in the late 1970s and has been developed further by such guitarists as Steve Lynch, Jennifer Batten, and Stanley Jordan. The idea is pretty simple: picking-hand fingers are used to play, or *tap,* additional notes on the guitar. Some of the basic patterns and movements are shown in the examples below. Use the index finger (i) of the picking hand to play the notes indicated with a T.

There are two ways you can tap:

1. Tap the note, by hammering your finger onto the string, then pull your finger downward toward the floor.
2. Tap the note and flex your finger inward towards your palm.

As a general rule, rest your thumb on the side of the fretboard to stabilize the tapping hand.

Basic Minor Pentatonic Tapping

Examples 1 and 2 show a basic ascending or descending triplet pattern based on the A Minor Pentatonic scale. Example 1 requires you to use the *hammer-on-from-nowhere* technique with your left hand. To execute this technique, hammer a left-hand finger onto the appropriate note, causing that note to sound. Hammer-ons-from-nowhere are indicated in both the standard notation and TAB with an H.

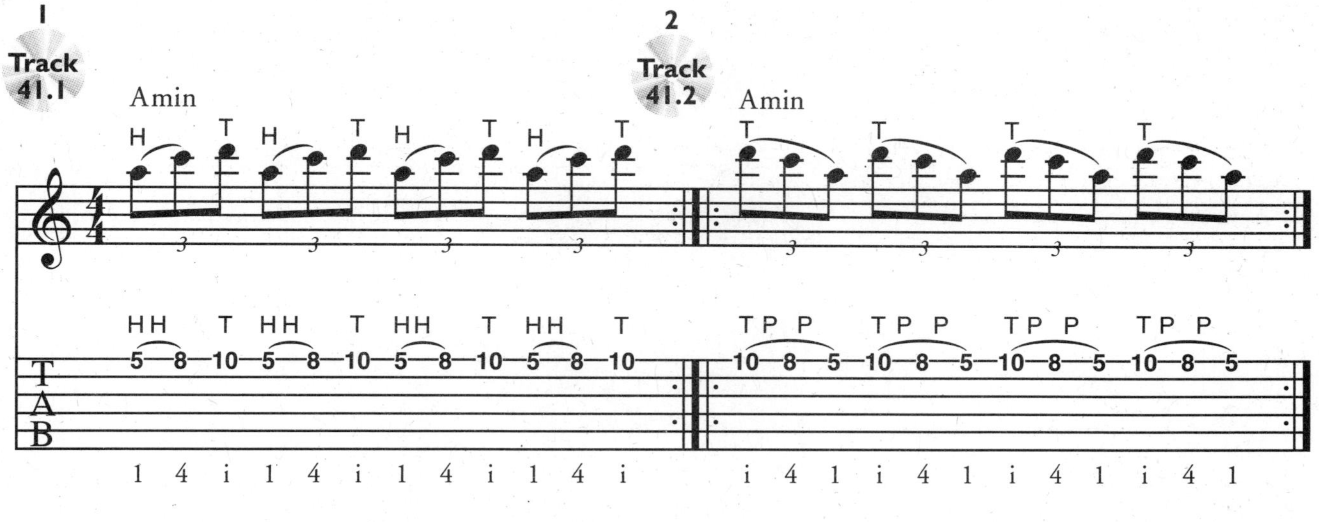

Examples 3 and 4 are common eighth-note tapping patterns based on the A Minor Pentatonic scale.

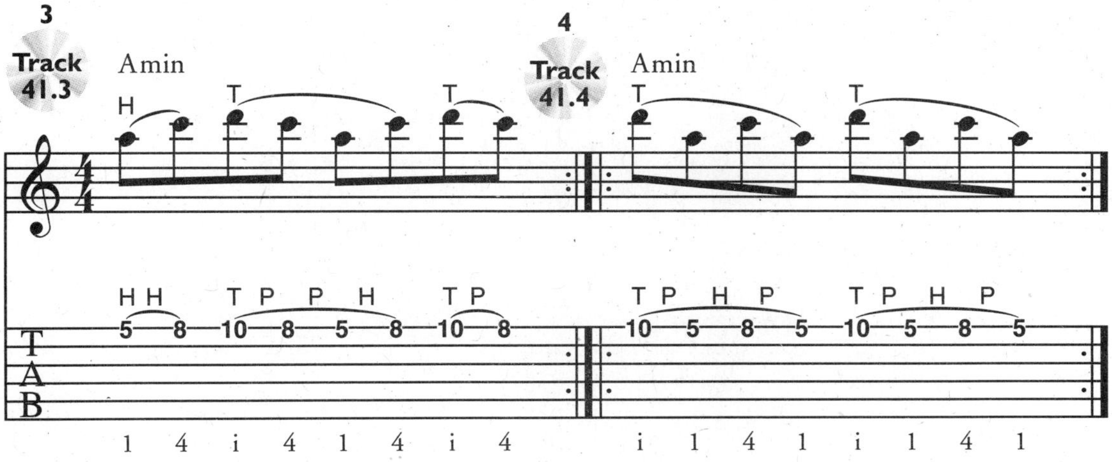

Extend the patterns to two strings as in Example 5 below.

5

Track 42.1

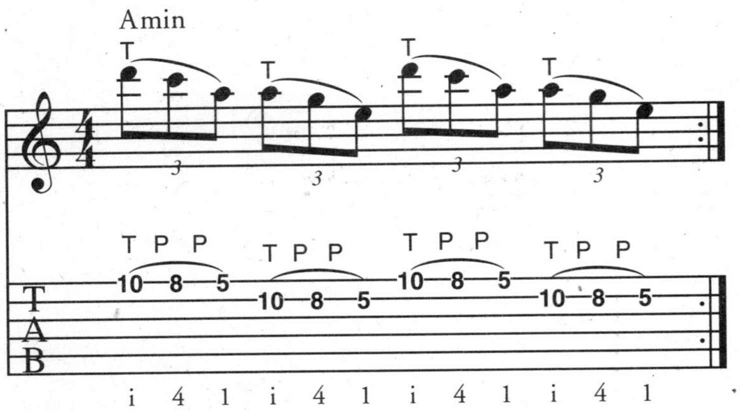

Adjacent Pentatonic Position Tapping

Now, apply the basic ideas from the previous section to all six strings. To get the right notes for your tapping hand, simply combine the neighboring pentatonic scale forms (creating a kind of *double pentatonic*), and tap the third note on each string (shown as gray dots in the diagram to the right).

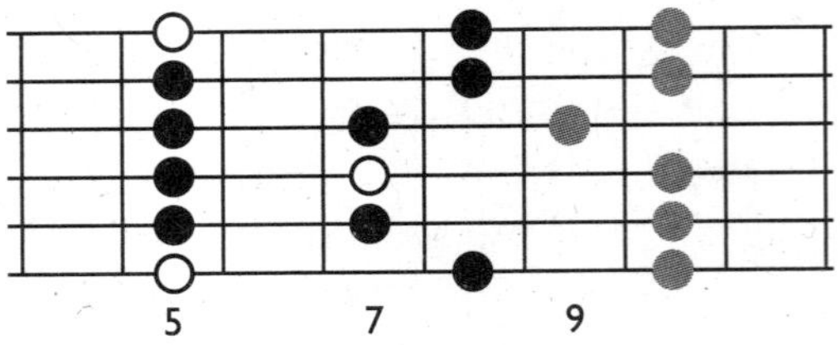

Now, try to build other double pentatonic scales using the remaining pentatonic positions (see page 25), and practice these basic patterns on all six strings. Below are a couple of ascending and descending tapping licks.

6

Track 42.2

7

Track 42.3

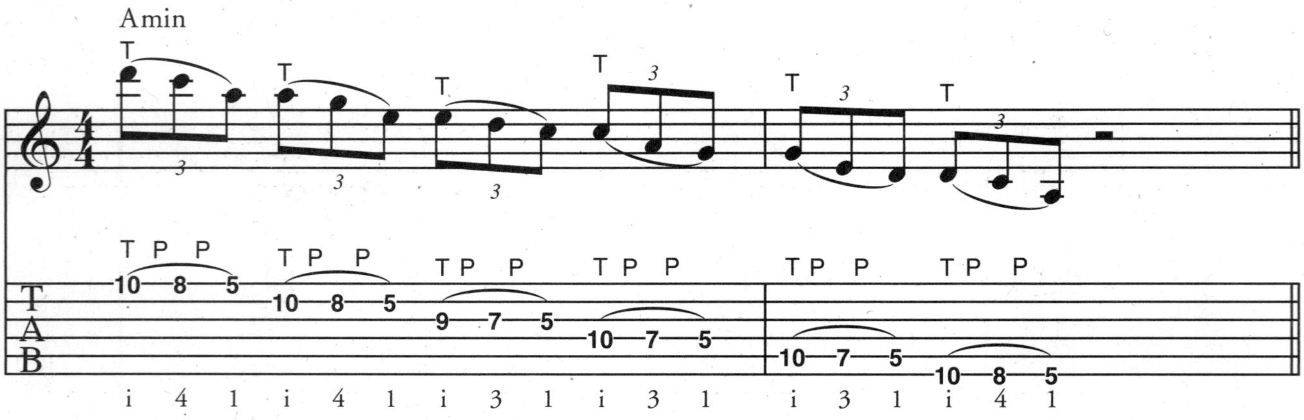

The pentatonic scale can also be played horizontally on two strings. Following is an example played on the B and E strings.

8

Track 42.4

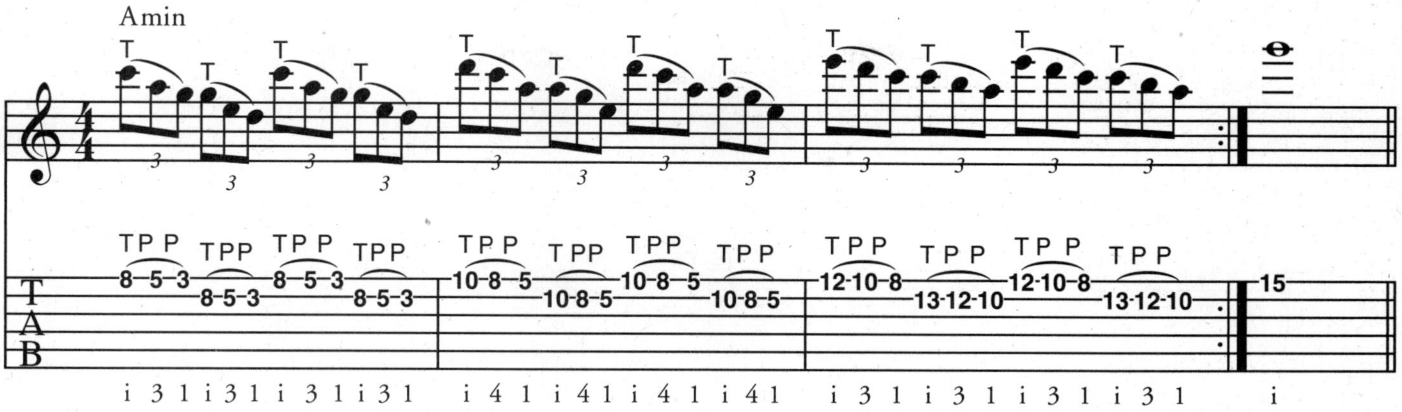

The next example is an ascending tapping pattern using the A Minor Pentatonic scale on the D and G strings. The run continues to the B and E strings and ends on the 20th fret. Hold this note with your tapping finger and add a little vibrato.

9

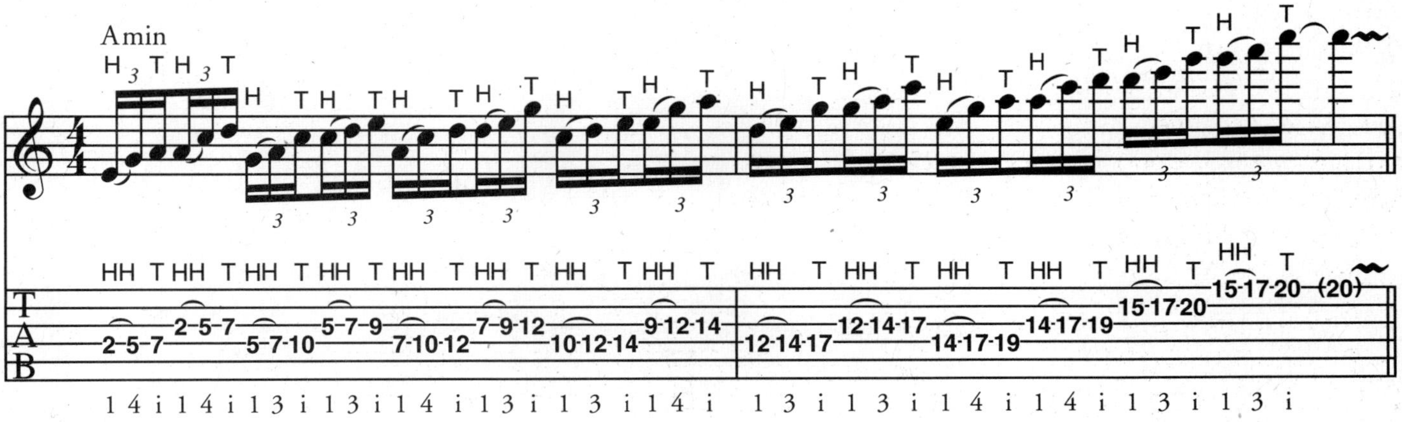

Pentatonic Licks

Generally, once you learn an idea, or a new scale or sound, you should organize it into some basic sequences and patterns so you can practice the technique while also developing musical vocabulary and licks. The following examples are scale sequences and patterns you can use to create long tapping runs. Remember to practice all the examples with the remaining pentatonic positions and in all keys. Example 10 is a simple descending run.

10

Track 43.1

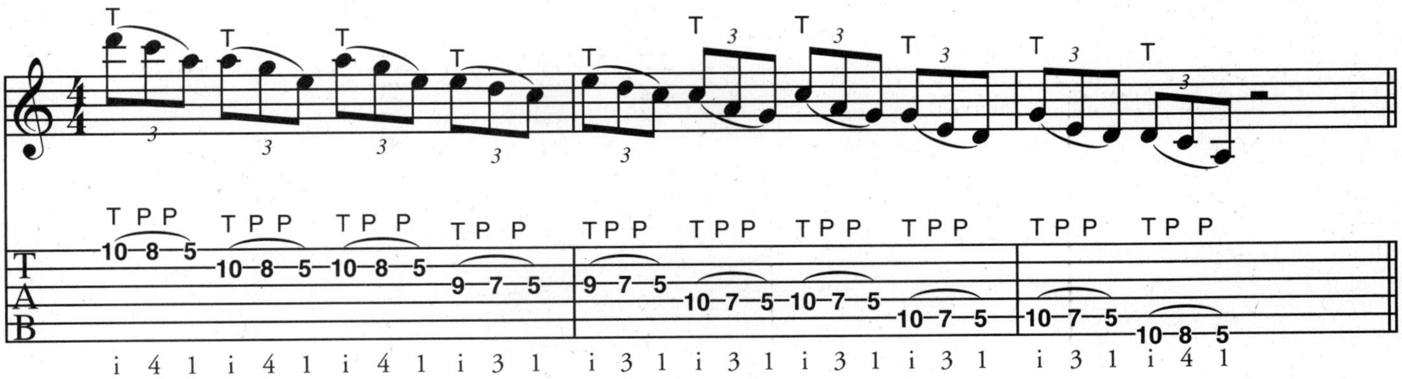

The triplet run below is in groups of nine descending notes. To clarify these groups for you, they are bracketed in the music. This lick has a very interesting sound. Reverse the idea and play it as an ascending run as well.

11
Track 43.2

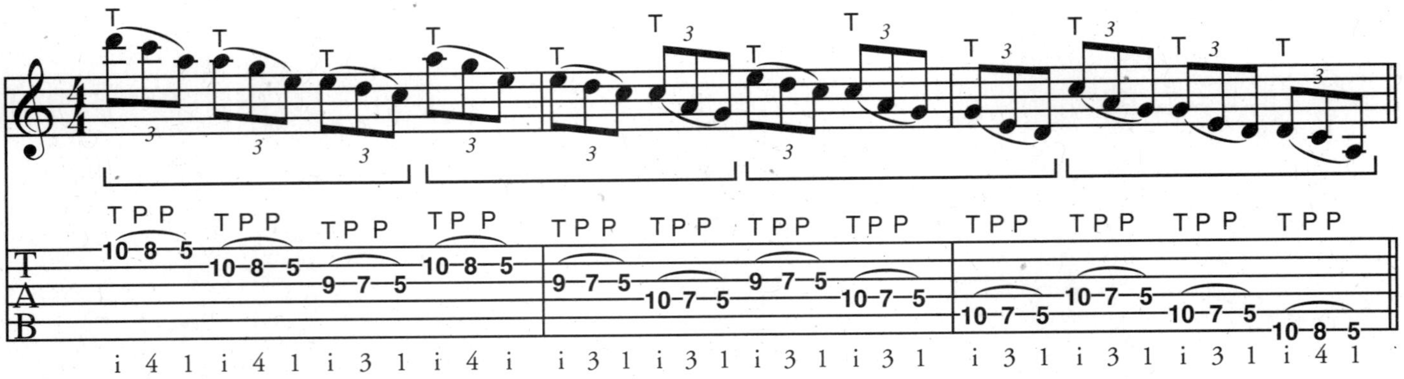

The following extended pentatonic run is very unconventional, as it is features ascending four-note groups but also a lot of doubled notes. This will definitely turn some heads.

12
Track 43.3

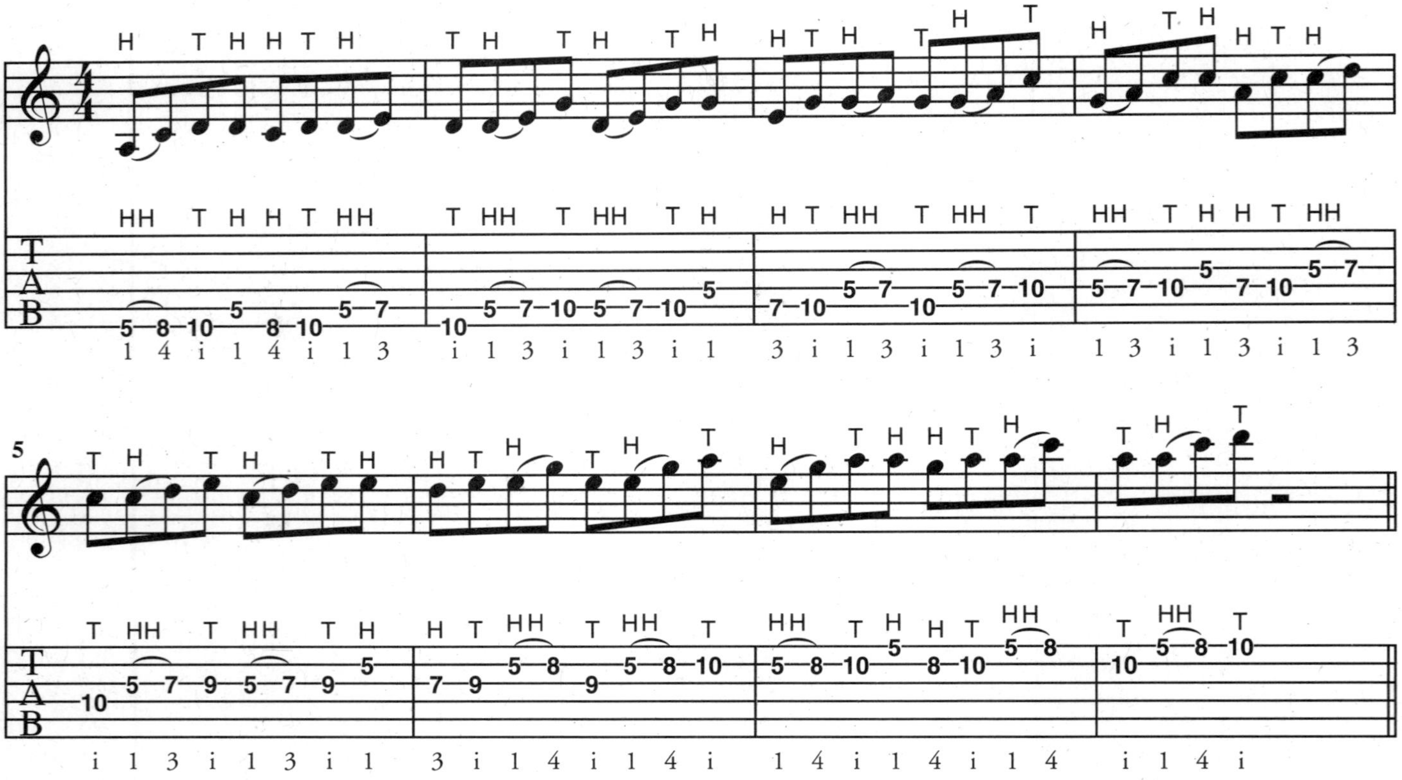

This descending triplet run below is in the style of guitarist Greg Howe and requires a lot of coordination, as you tap the second note right after your fretting hand frets it. Practice the lick slowly and make sure all the notes are accurate.

13
Track 43.4

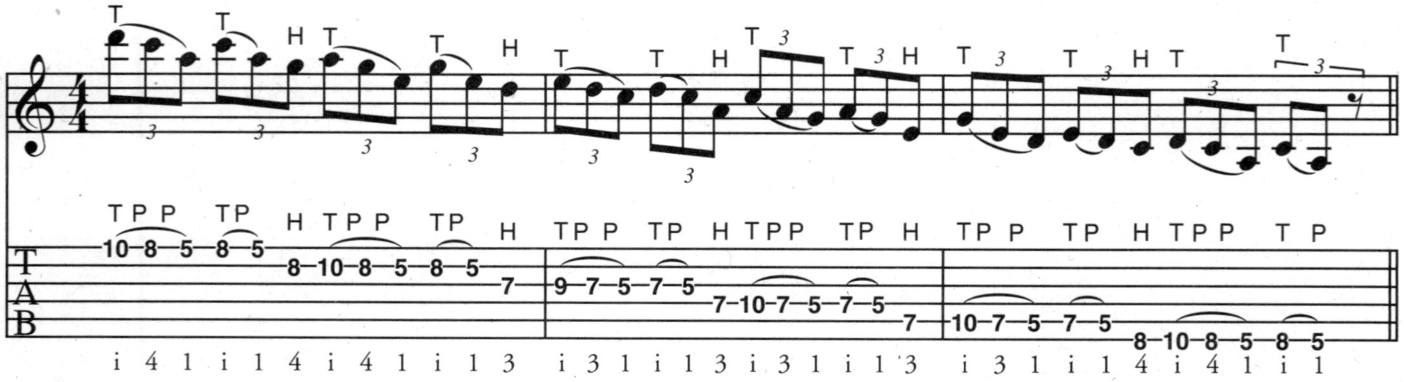

Mirrored Pentatonic Tapping

The term *mirrored pentatonic tapping* refers to the use of two pentatonic scales within a key. Within a major or minor key, there are actually three pentatonic scales that can be used for soloing. In a major key, you can use the scales starting on the 2nd, 3rd, and 6th scale degrees; in a minor key, you can use the scales starting on the 1st, 4th, and 5th scale degrees.

In C Major, you could use the following:

- D Minor Pentatonic (2nd scale degree in C Major) D–F–G–A–C
- E Minor Pentatonic (3rd scale degree in C Major) E–G–A–B–D
- A Minor Pentatonic (6th scale degree in C Major; relative minor pentatonic) A–C–D–E–G

In A Minor, you could use:

- A Minor Pentatonic (1st scale degree in A Minor) A–C–D–E–G
- D Minor Pentatonic (4th scale degree in A Minor) D–F–G–A–C
- E Minor Pentatonic (5th scale degree in A Minor) E–G–A–B–D

As you can see, the pentatonic scales are the same either in C Major or its relative minor key A. Also, all the notes of any of the scales are within the C Major scale. This is a great way to add variety to your pentatonic soloing.

When playing mirrored pentatonics, one scale is played by the left hand while the other scale is played by the right hand. In the diagram to the right, A Minor Pentatonic is played by the left hand and D Minor Pentatonic is played by the right. Both scales are in root position.

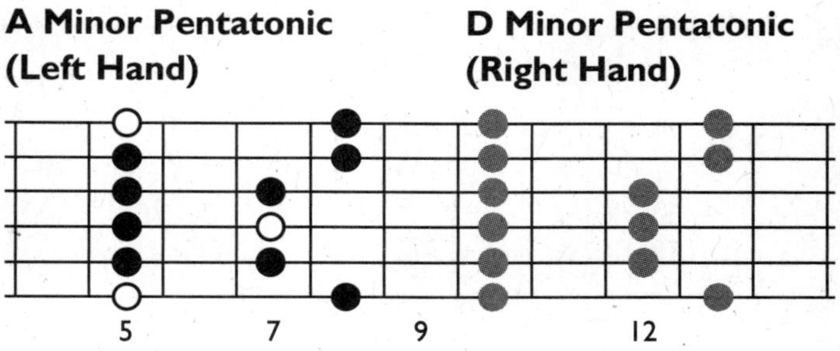

The lick below shows a descending, linear combination of the A Minor and D Minor Pentatonic scales.

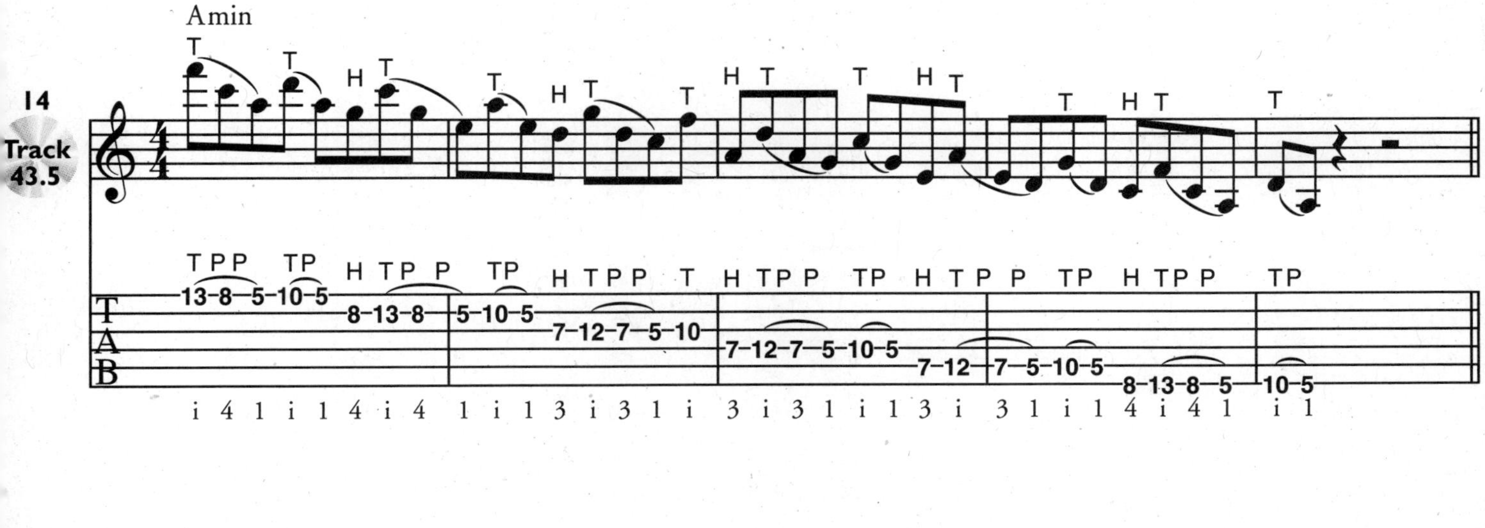

The following lick is an ascending variation of Example 14. Practice the other pentatonic positions in a similar way.

15
Track 44.1

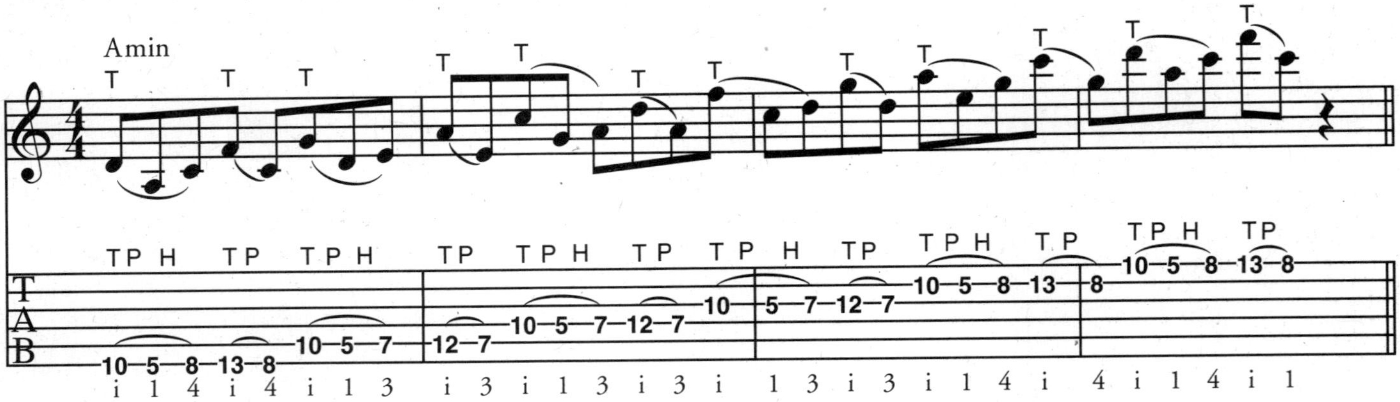

The next possible combination is A Minor Pentatonic and E Minor Pentatonic.

A Minor Pentatonic (Left Hand)

E Minor Pentatonic (Right Hand)

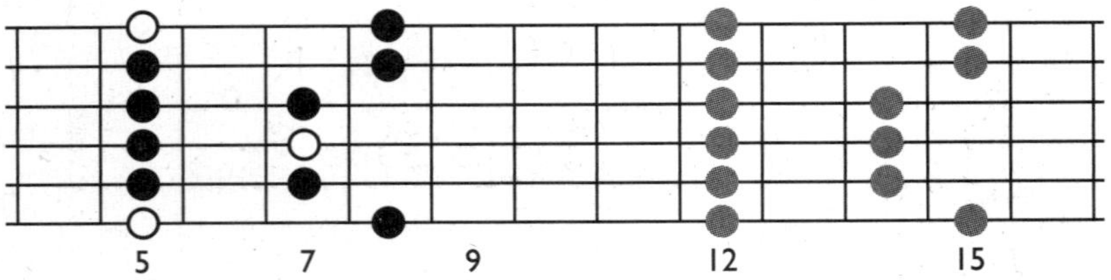

Don't forget to use the previous licks with this new combination, as all licks and ideas will work together perfectly. Continue to practice the licks with the remaining positions.

Example 16 is an ascending intervallic idea moving in 4ths from string to string. This lick has a very "angular" and modern sound.

16
Track 44.2

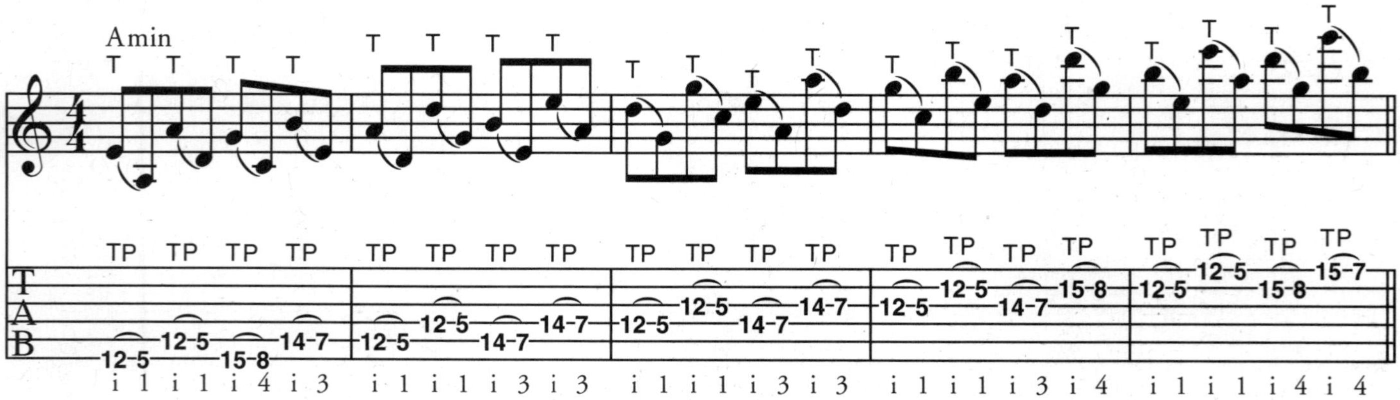

Below is the descending version of Example 16.

17
Track 44.3

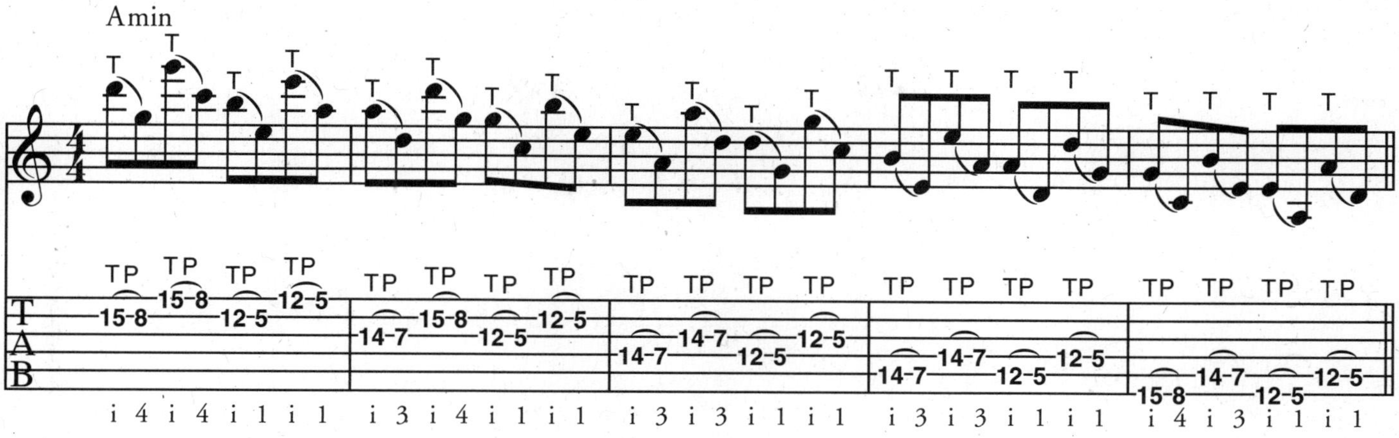

You can also use two fingers of your right hand for tapping. T2 indicates a tap performed with the right-hand middle finger (m). This will take practice; take it slowly at first. (For more on this topic, see Multi-Finger Tapping on page 88.)

18
Track 44.4

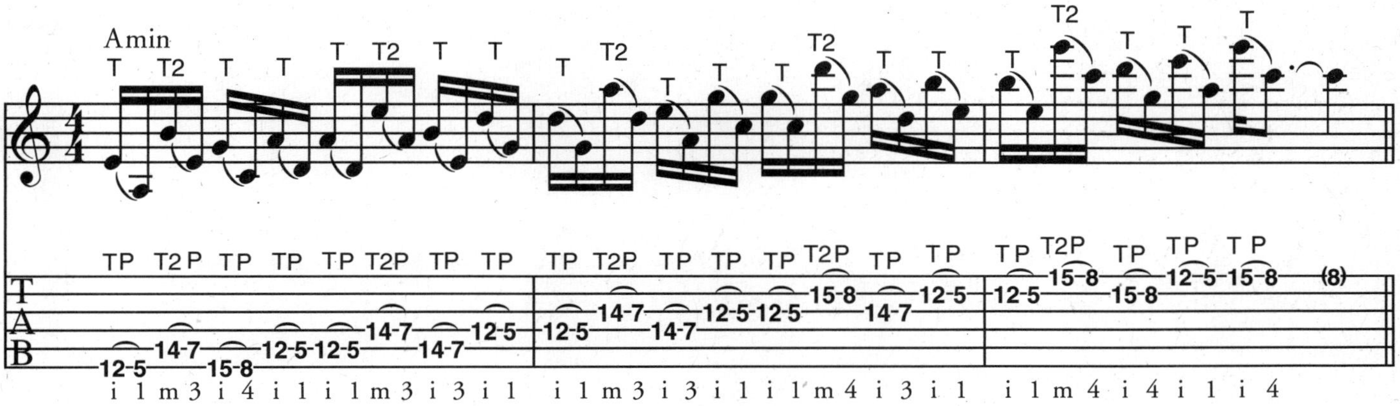

Try to vary your intervals while maintaining similar finger movements. For instance, in the example below, the basic intervallic movement is in 5ths, but 3rds, 7ths, and octaves are also present—all the while, maintaining the same finger motions. After playing this example as written, try to work out the ascending version, or look for variations and combinations. This is a great way to get some really outrageous sounds.

19
Track 44.5

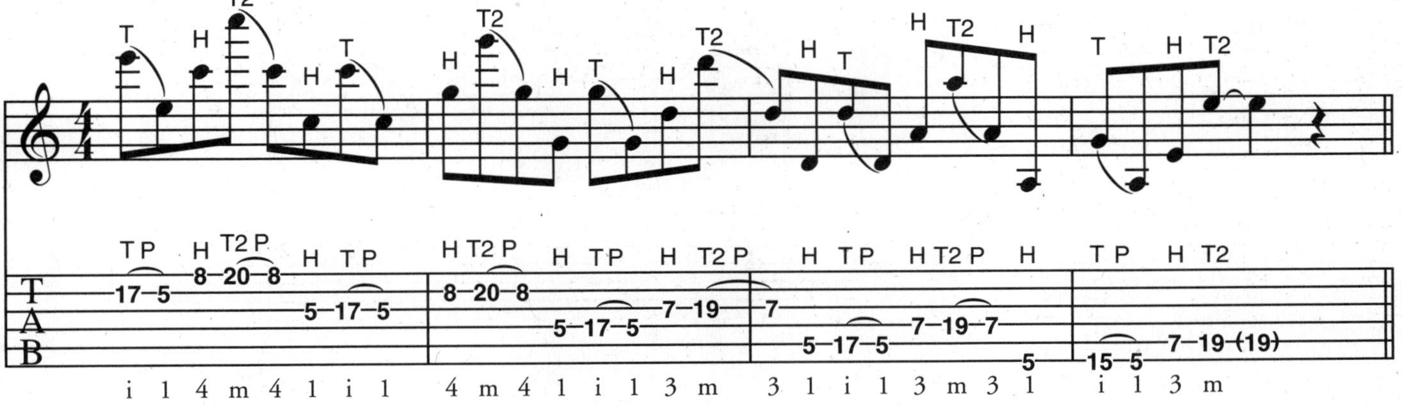

Octave Tapping

The next lick is a string-skipping lick with the pentatonic scale doubled at the octave. Check out the diagram below.

A Minor Pentatonic (Left Hand) **A Minor Pentatonic (Right Hand)**

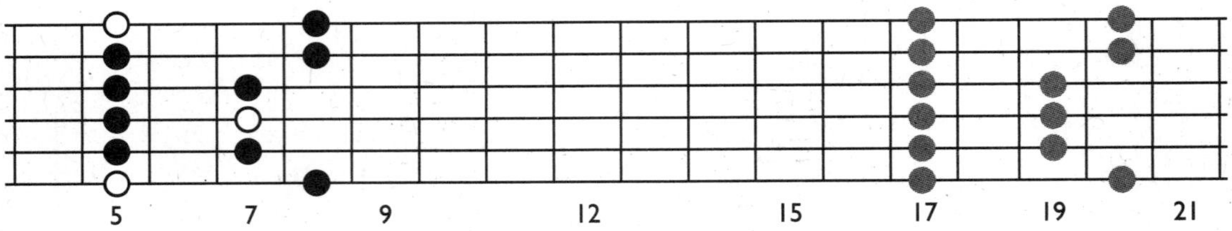

This is a really fresh and interesting sound. Here, you are basically doubling the same notes one octave higher. Apply this idea to previous licks and patterns, and have fun exploring this new sound.

20
Track 44.6

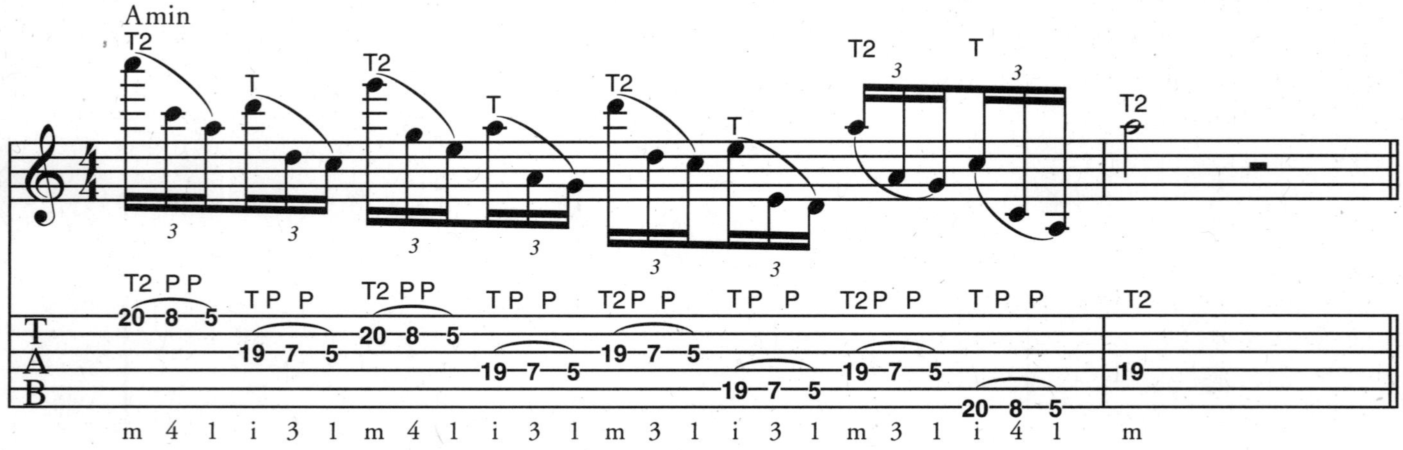

2+1 Tapping

Another great way to play three-note-per-string scales, or other scalar lines, is to divide the notes between your fretting and tapping hand. One way of doing this is: two notes with your fretting hand and one tapped note. The following two examples show the C Major scale played with this technique.

C Major Scale (Ascending)

21
Track 45.1

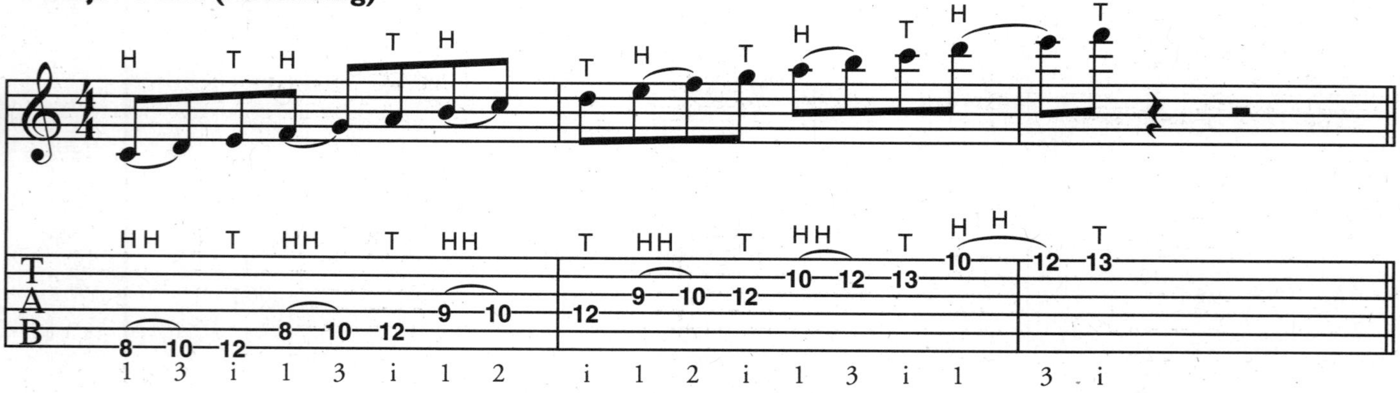

C Major Scale (Descending)

22
Track 45.2

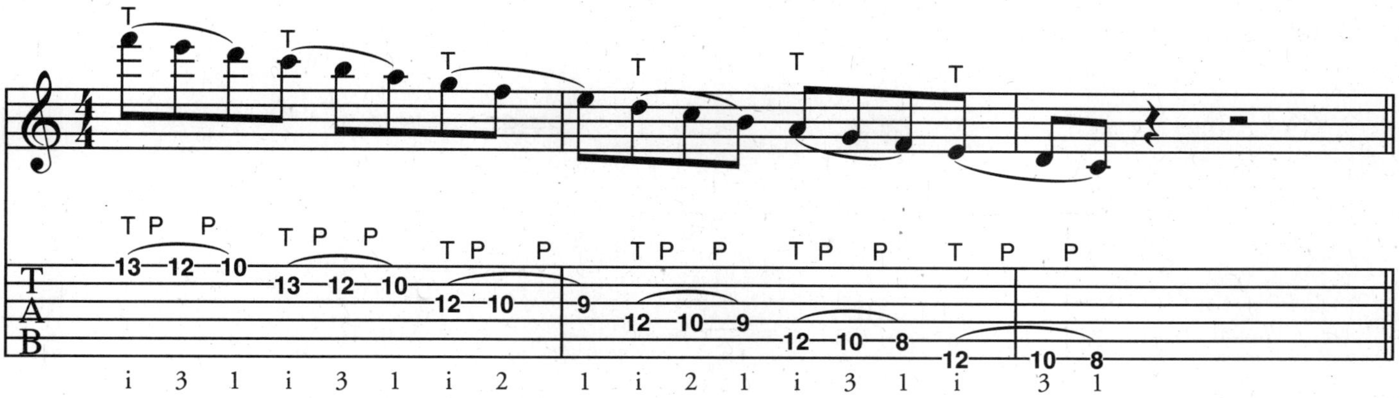

Apply this idea to all the other three-note-per-string scales, such as the remaining six positions of the major scale, the harmonic and melodic minor scales (see pages 97 and 104), and more. It will open up many new and interesting possibilities for licks.

Following are some chops-building exercises and scale patterns to help you develop this technique.

The example below is a simple four-note ascending scale sequence—similar to the one you have already practiced with alternate picking (see Chapter 7, page 44).

23
Track 45.3

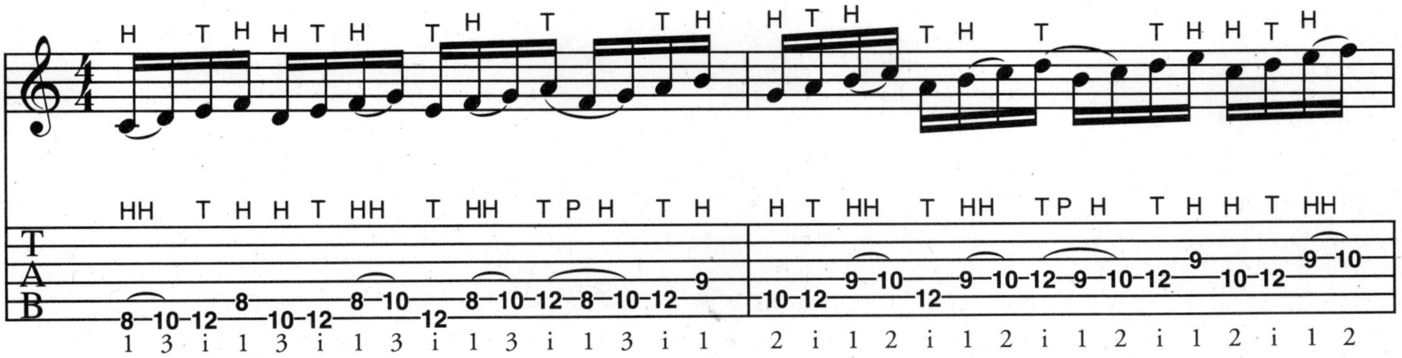

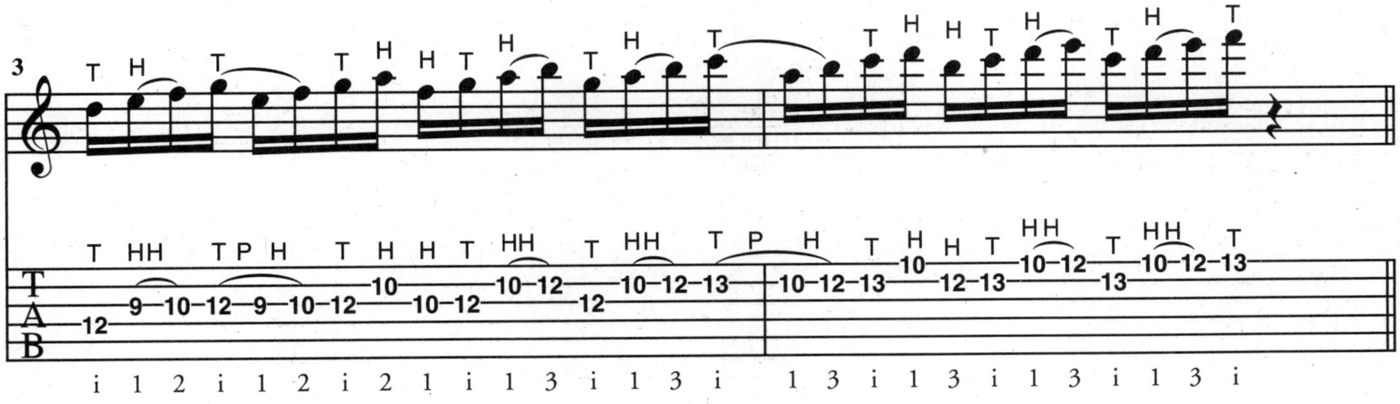

The next example is a variation of the previous one and combines five- and four-note groupings of sixteenth notes. This one has a really unique and unpredictable sound.

24
Track 45.4

And now, we have a descending triplet run that is very interesting.

25
Track 45.5

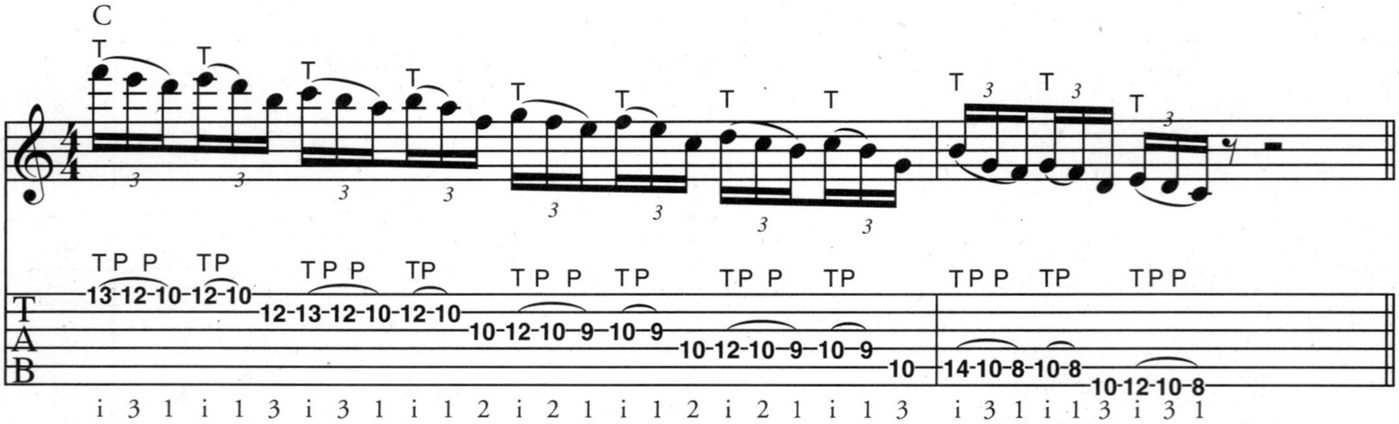

As always, apply these concepts to all the other scales. This will build up your technique and musical vocabulary.

The following licks will demonstrate the 2+1 technique and, hopefully, inspire you to write more licks in this style.

Below is a single-string tapping lick in the style of master shredder Paul Gilbert, who is known for his work with Mr. Big, Racer X, and G3.

26
Track 46.1

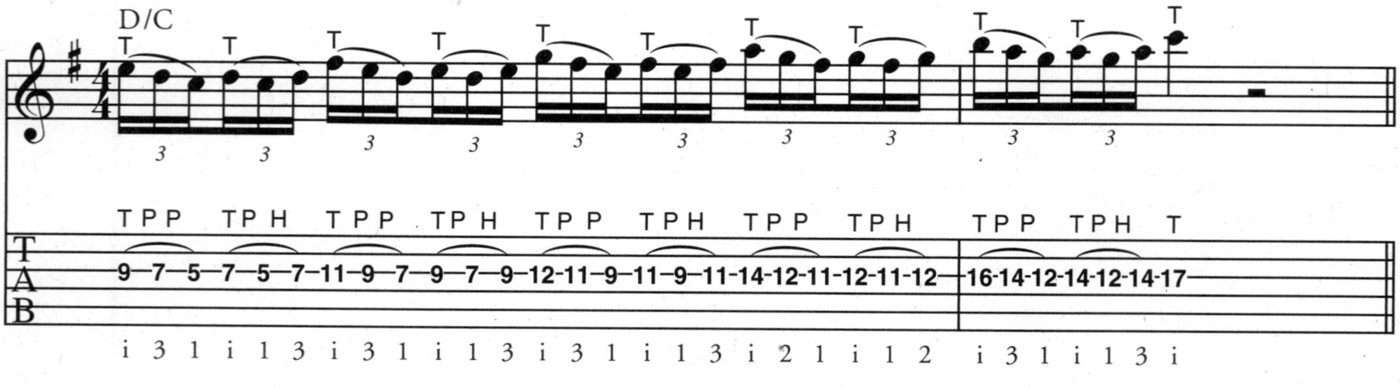

Following is a rapid sextuplet run in B♭ with nine-note groupings (see brackets in the music).

27
Track 46.2

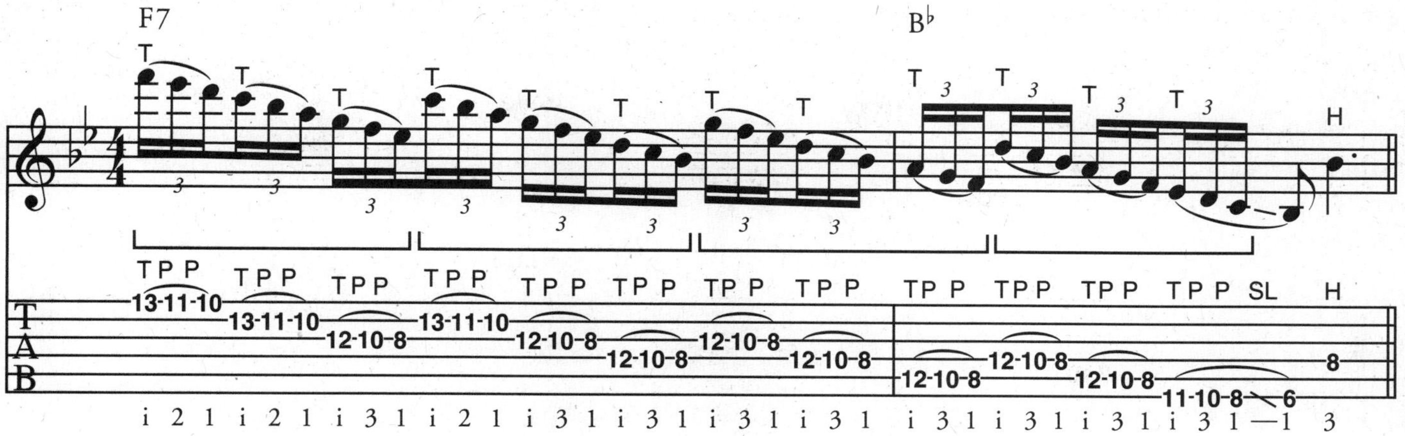

The lick below is based on the *whole tone scale* (a scale consisting entirely of whole steps) played over an Aaug7 chord. This is truly an otherworldly sound.

28
Track 46.3

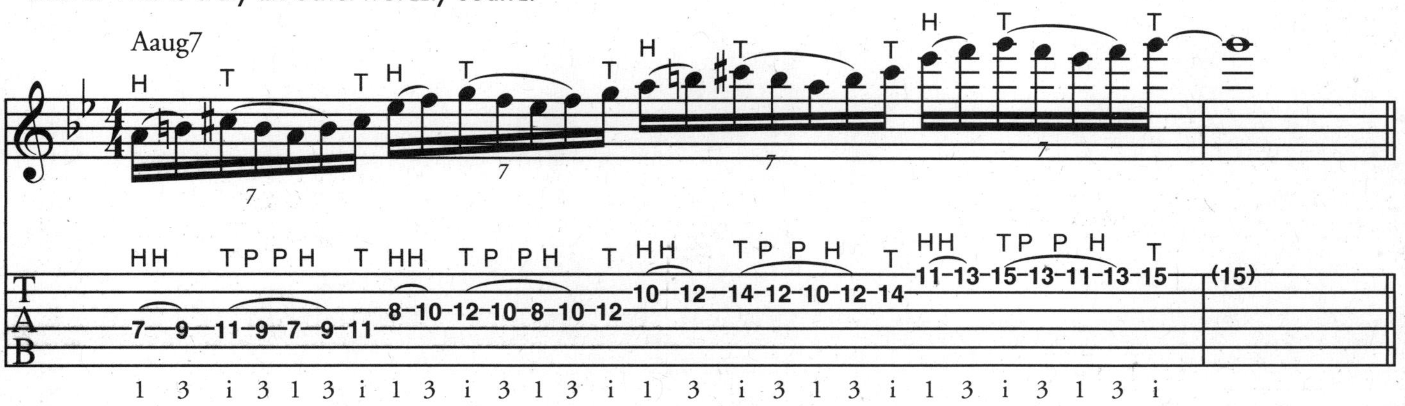

Our final lick of this section uses only a scale fragment of three notes, which moves in octaves on the 5th, 3rd, and 1st strings. By using this technique, you can cover a lot of notes and fretboard very quickly. The notes don't necessarily have to be all within a certain interval range. Try using larger intervals; this will yield some amazing sounds.

29
Track 46.4

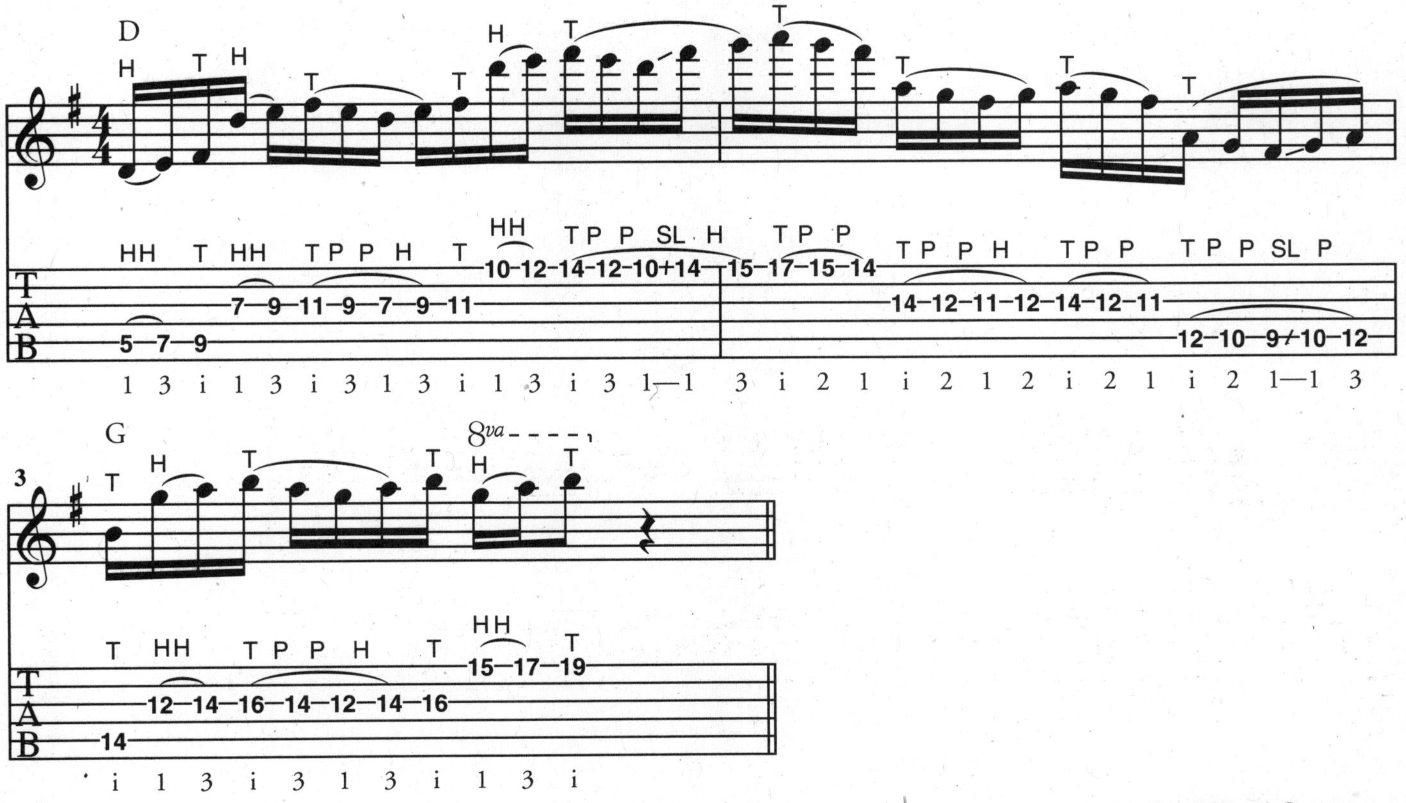

Multi-Finger Tapping

Let's expand the tapping-hand technique to use more than one finger. (We have already touched on this technique on pages 83–84.) The exercises below will train all your four right-hand fingers for *multi-finger tapping*. Make sure you are practicing this on all strings and in any position possible. Be very patient, as it will take time to develop the necessary strength and coordination in your tapping hand. Note that the letter a indicates the right-hand 3rd finger and c, the right-hand pinky.

The example below is a simple tapping-hand hammer-on and pull-off exercise. Practice it slowly and use a metronome for more accuracy.

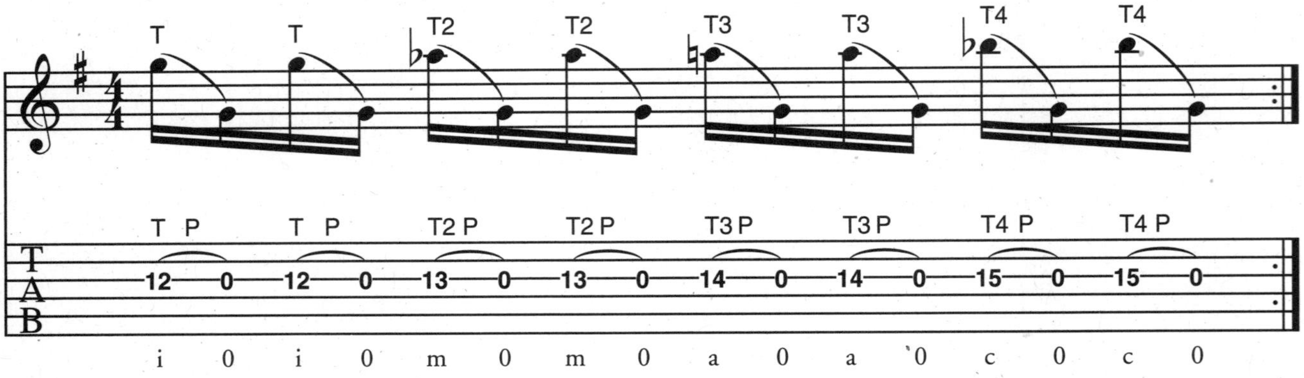

The example below is a chromatic fretting- and tapping-hand exercise. Play all of the notes with hammer-ons and pull-offs. Strive for a smooth sound and move the exercise to all strings and all positions for better results.

Let's take a closer look at the different possibilities for playing scales and scale fragments with multi-finger tapping. Remember, there are many different ways to do this; use these examples as springboards for your own creativity.

The following example is a four-note-per-string C Major scale played with a 3+1 model. This means you play three notes with your fretting hand and your picking hand taps one note. You can use pretty much any finger you feel comfortable with to tap.

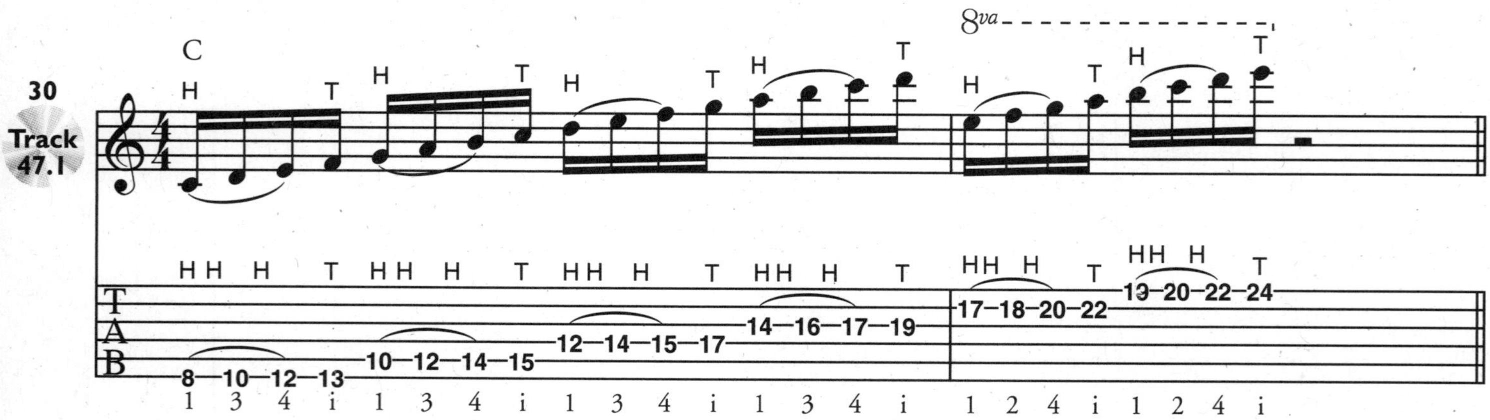

Another way to play the same scale is to use a 2+2 finger approach, like in the example below. Also, try different tap-finger combinations, such as 2+3 or 3+4.

31
Track 47.2

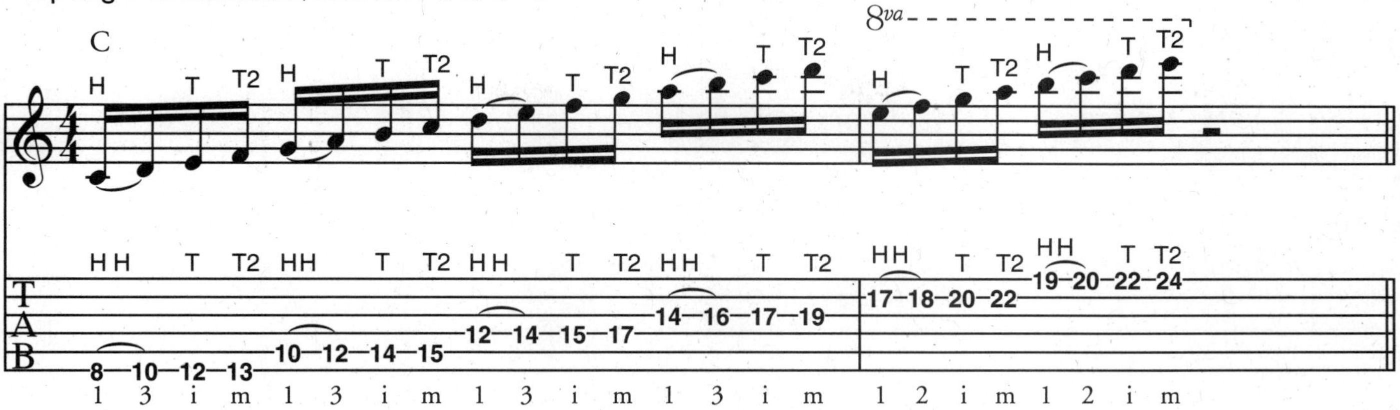

You can also expand the number of notes per string and utilize string skipping. The following example uses a 3+3 finger approach. There are many possible combinations and ideas you can use; be sure to explore more on your own.

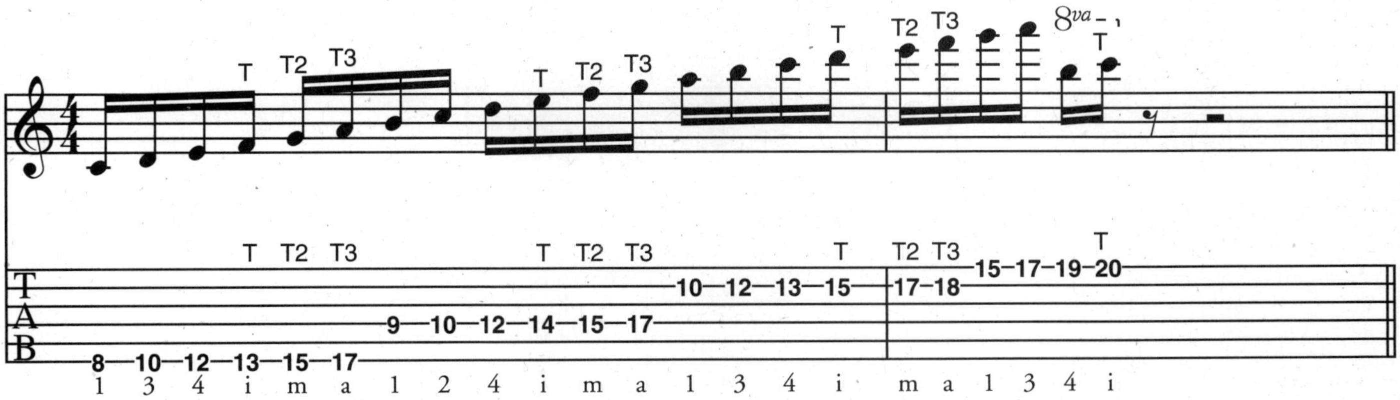

The next example utilizes different techniques, such as *tap-slides* and larger intervallic skips played with tapping. To execute a tap slide, tap a note with a right-hand finger and slide to another note on the same string.

32
Track 47.3

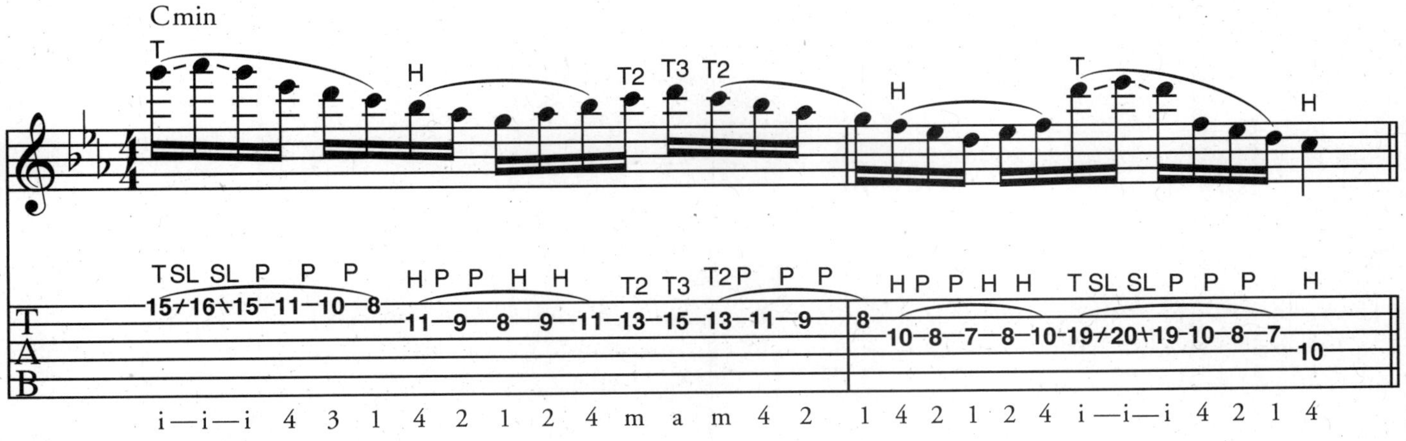

The following example mixes hammer-ons with multi-finger tapping.

33
Track 47.4

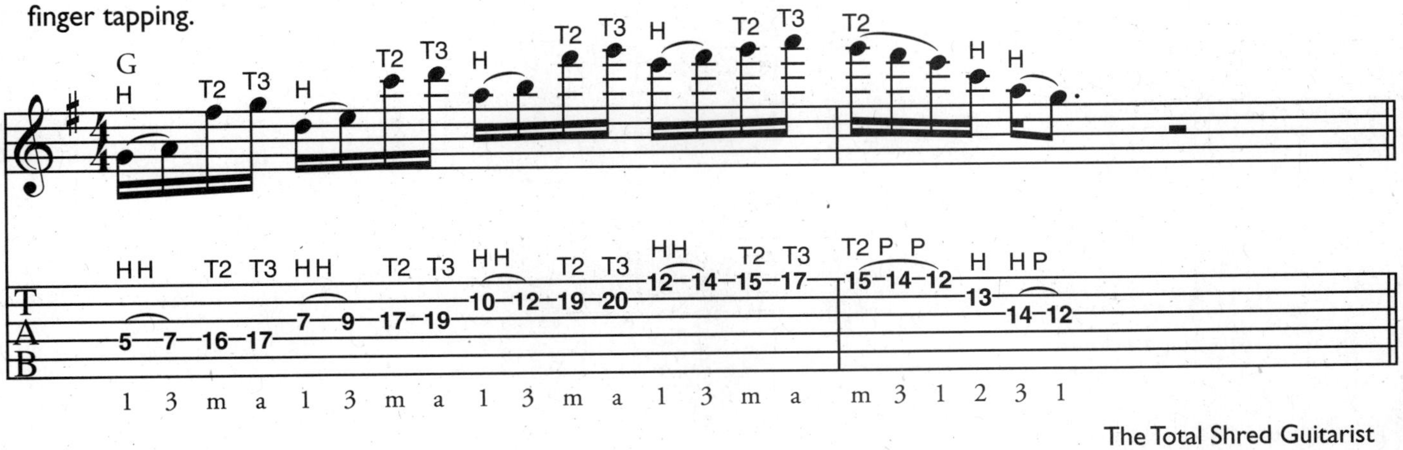

Tapping Arpeggios

Using the tapping technique to play arpeggios is a great way to bring new sounds to your playing. Let's start with the basic triads in root position. The diagrams below show the four basic triads: major, minor, diminished, and augmented.

G Major

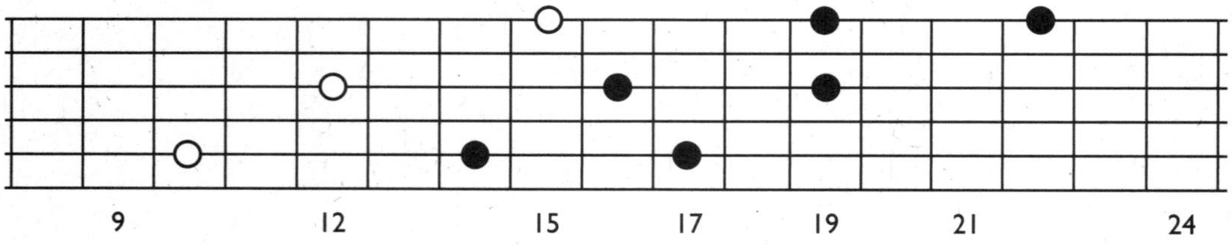

G Minor

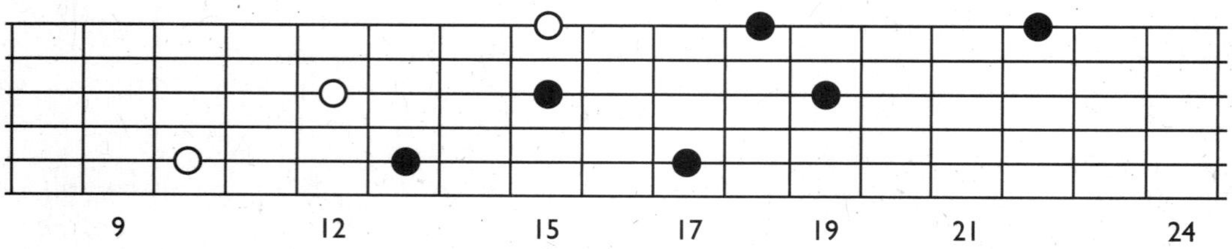

G Diminished

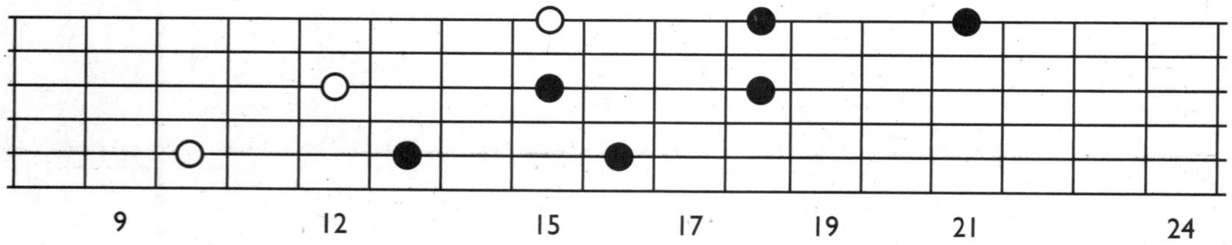

G Augmented

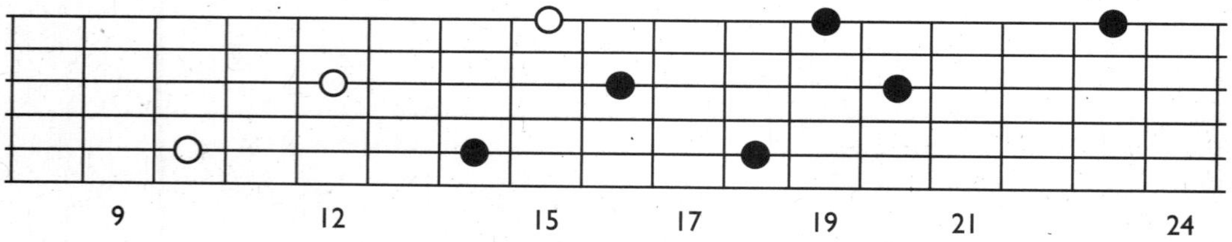

As you can see, the basic three notes of the triad are just being "copied" from the A string to the G string to the E string. You can also start the same arpeggios on the low-E string and move it to the D string and B string. Practice the different arpeggios and use them to harmonize all major, minor, and other scales. To get you started with some more interesting ideas and patterns, below are some common arpeggio sequences. Practice them slowly and make sure that all notes are played accurately and sound clean. This first example is an ascending four-note sequence.

34

Track 48.1

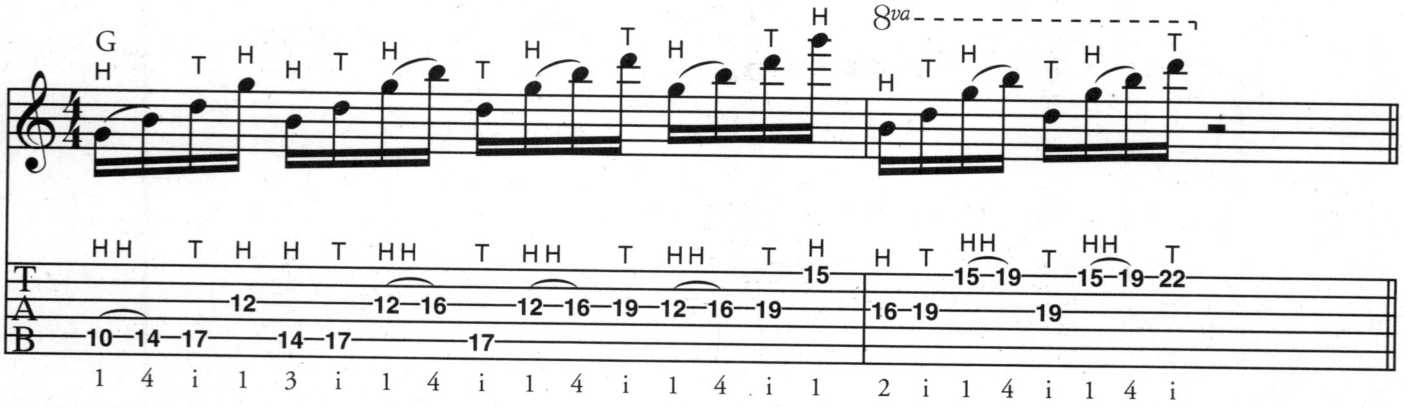

The following two examples are simple sextuplet runs. These are very common and will always sound great. Make sure you practice all the examples with all arpeggio types and on both three-string sets (A–G–E and E–D–B).

35
Track 48.2

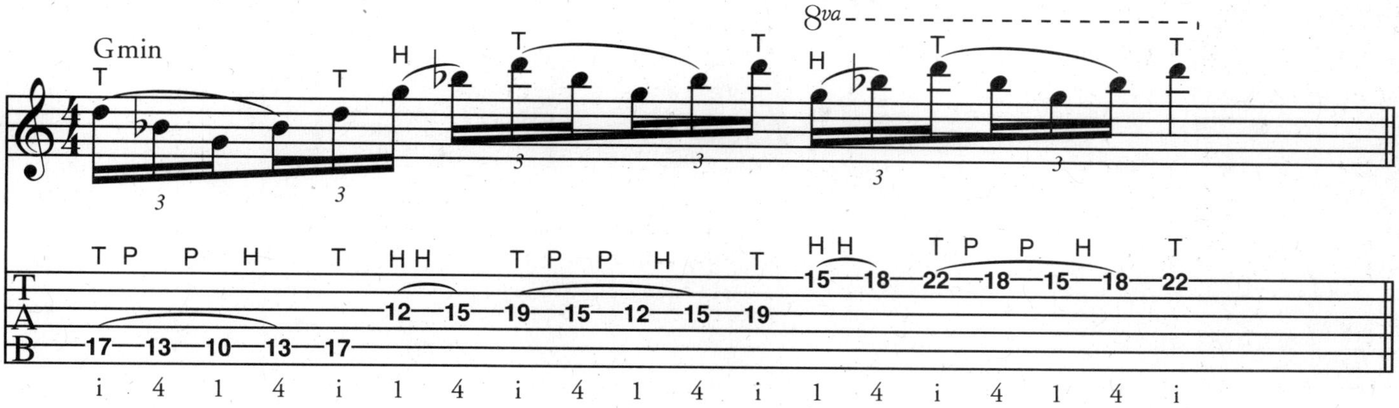

36
Track 48.3

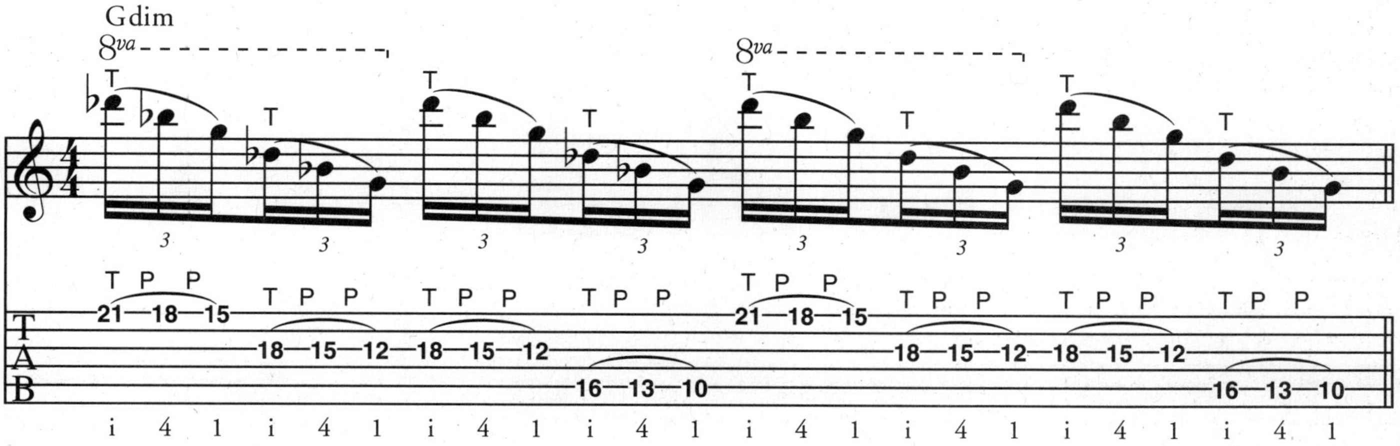

Now, it's time to actually come up with some musical licks and ideas.

The lick below is in F Minor. First, you start off with a sextuplet arpeggio run, ending on the C on the 20th fret. You will use this note to pivot to the next arpeggio, C Major, which is played in descending three-note groupings.

37
Track 48.4

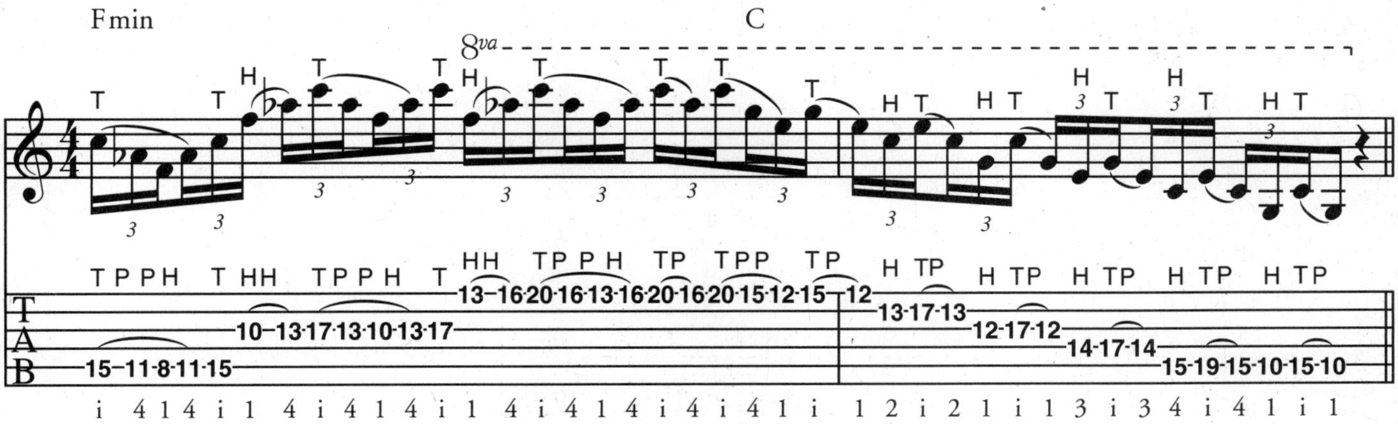

The next lick utilizes odd ascending groupings of five and four notes. After the ascent and descent of the G♯ Diminished 7th arpeggio (anticipating the 7th chord arpeggios in the next section), it resolves to an A Minor arpeggio in a four-note sequence.

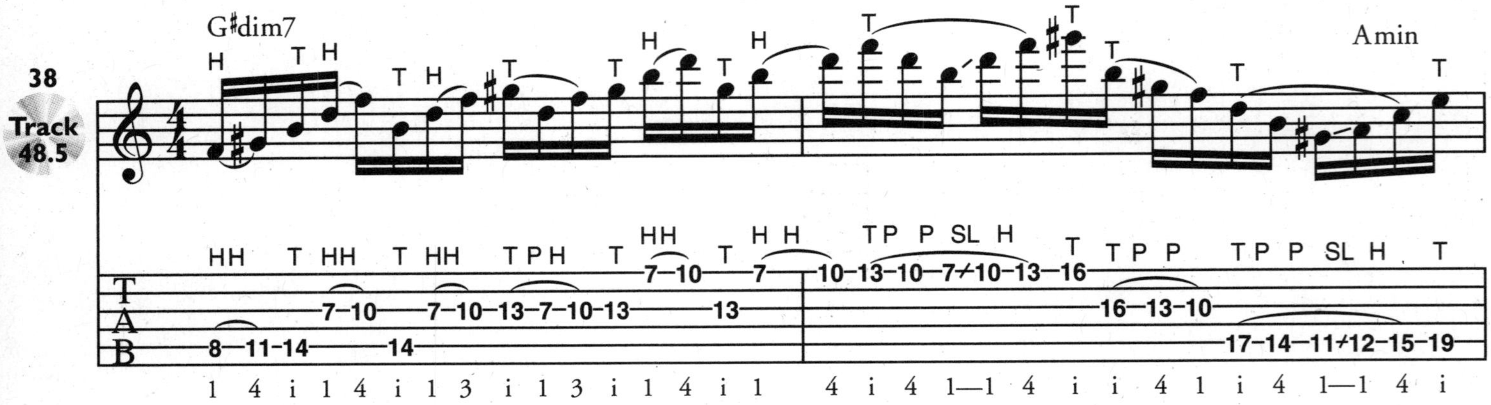

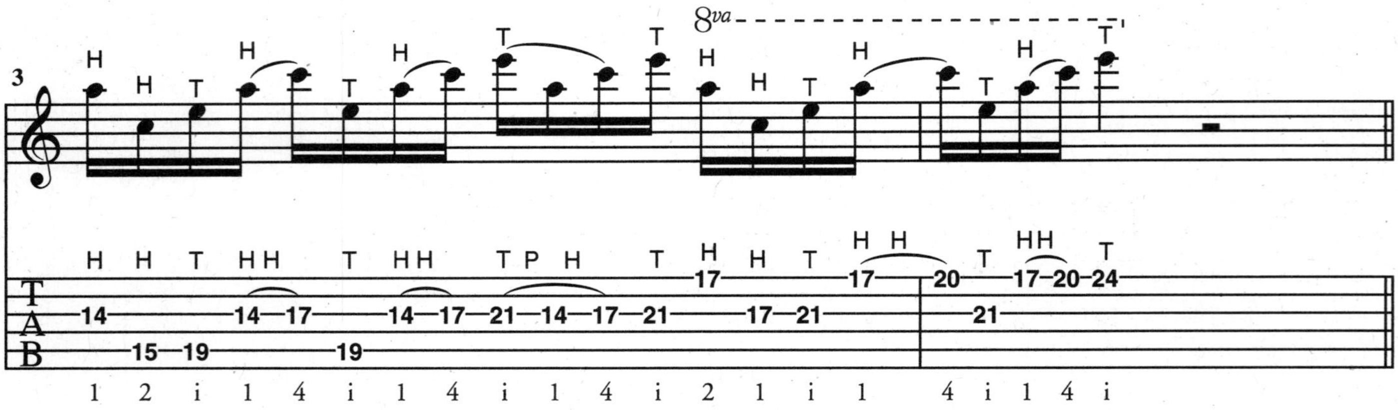

7th Chord Arpeggio Tapping

Another exciting way to play 7th chord arpeggios is to use the tapping technique. The diagrams below show the basic 7th chord arpeggio forms: major 7, dominant 7, minor 7, minor 7♭5, and dim7.

GMaj7

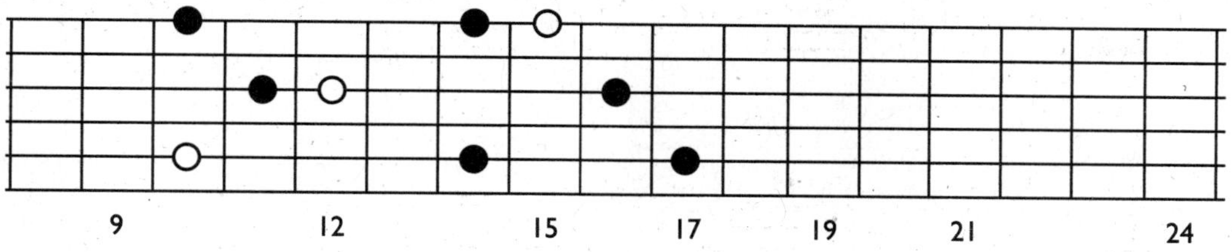

G7

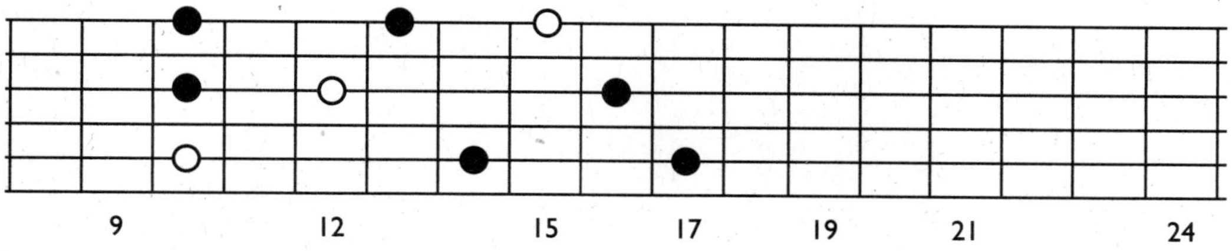

Gmin7

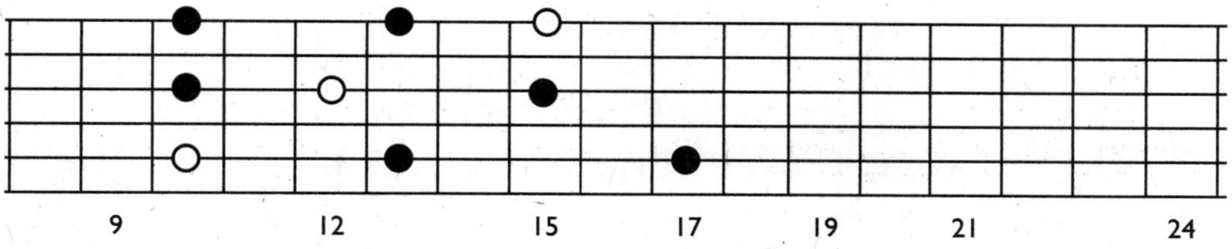

Gmin7♭5

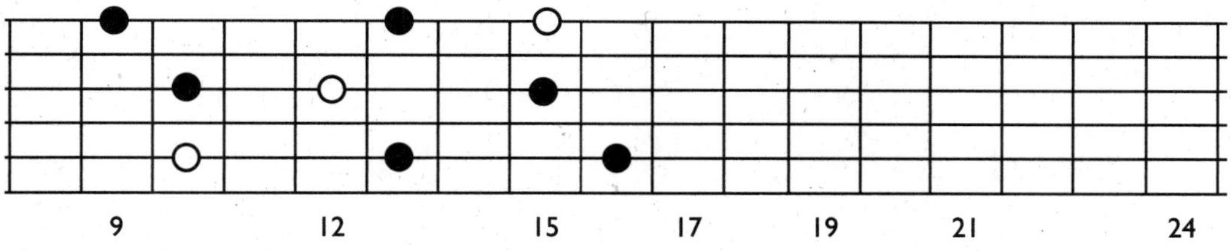

Gdim7

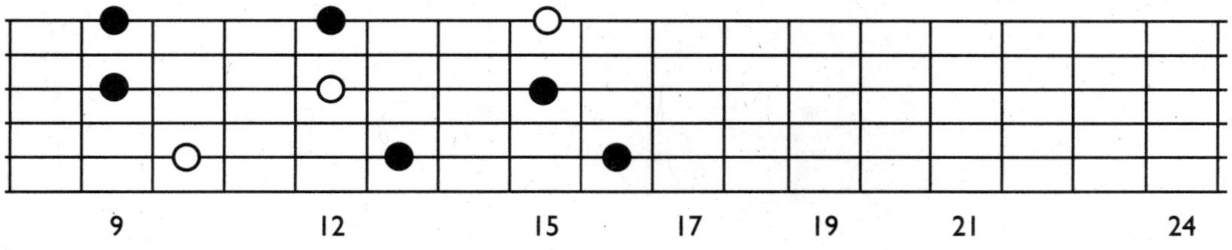

Practice these shapes all over the fretboard and use them to harmonize as many keys as the space on your fretboard allows. The shapes will also work on the other three-string set (E–D–B).

Try also the arpeggio sequences discussed in the triad section, like ascending 4ths, and so on.

The following licks feature the tapped 7th chord arpeggios. As always, practice them slowly before speeding them up.

Below is a combination of GMaj7 and Bmin7 arpeggios.

39 Track 49.1

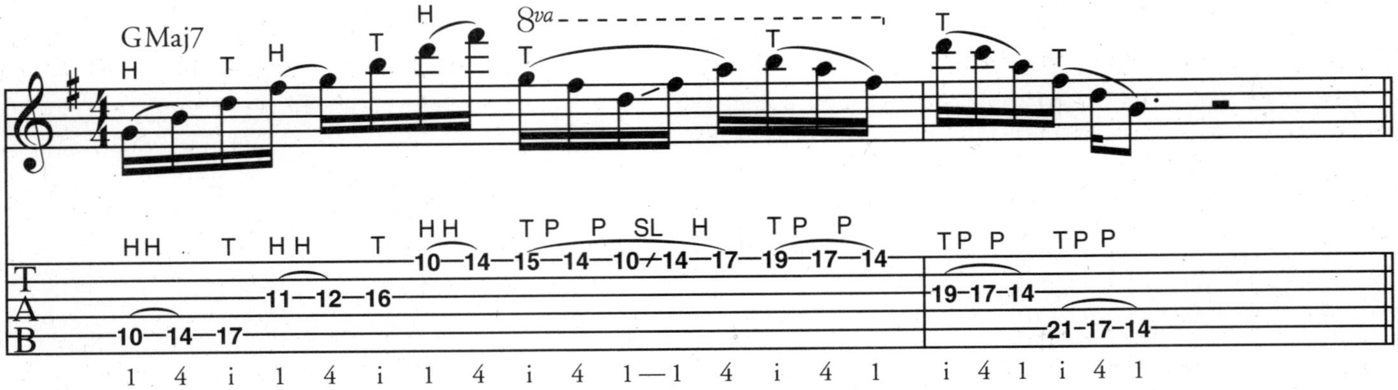

Below, we have a combination of Emin7 and Bmin7 arpeggios (transforming the tonality to Emin11) with a tap-bend.

40 Track 49.2

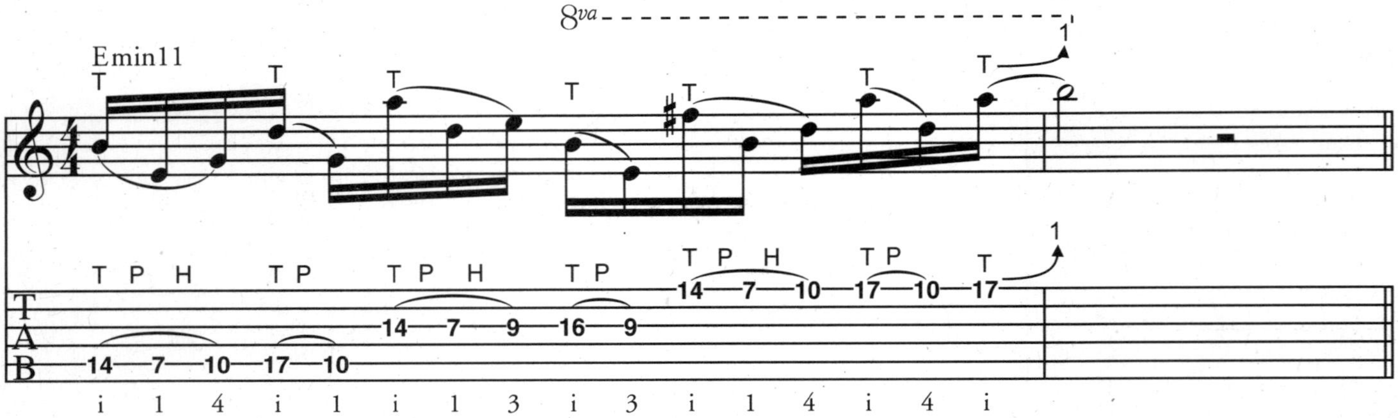

The following example combines two different arpeggios: EMaj7 and G♯min7.

41 Track 49.3

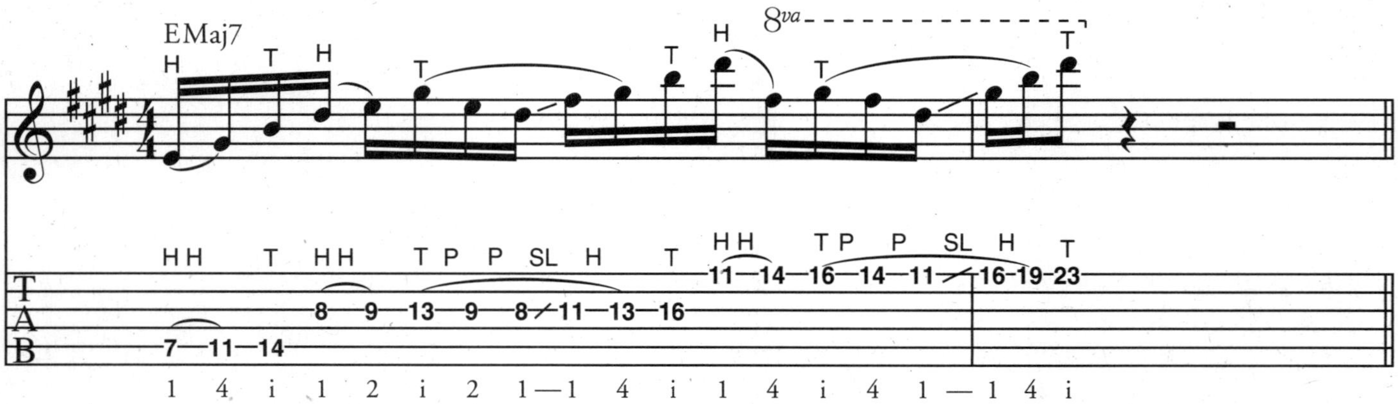

Tapping Chords

Tapping can also be utilized to play chords (in this case, referring to one-note-per-string arpeggios) and extensions, and to add ornamentations. Joe Satriani (known for his instrumental rock masterpieces), Reb Beach (of Winger, Dokken, and Whitesnake), and other guitarists use this concept to play distinct chord progressions.

The diagrams below show examples of major, minor, diminished, and augmented chords that can be played with tapping. The notes on the left side of the diagrams are to be played with hammer-ons-from-nowhere with the left hand. The notes on the right side of the diagrams, marked T1 and T2, are to be tapped with the right hand.

Major

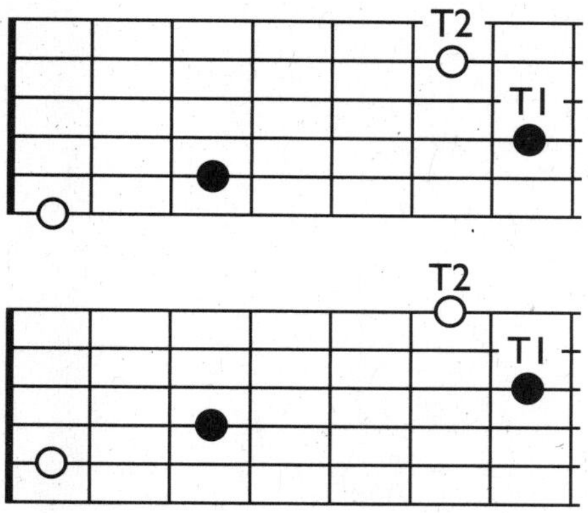

Minor

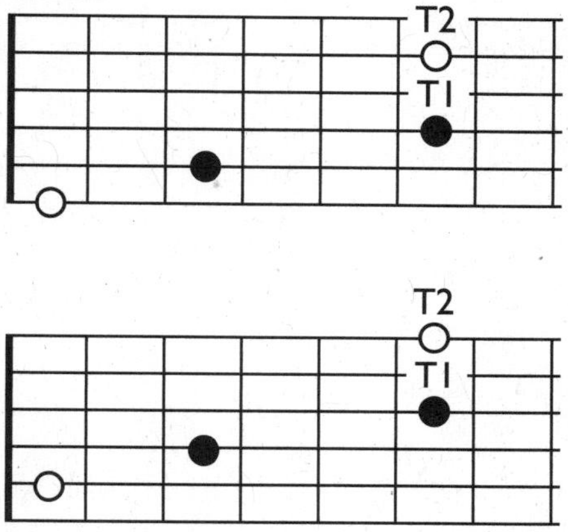

Diminished

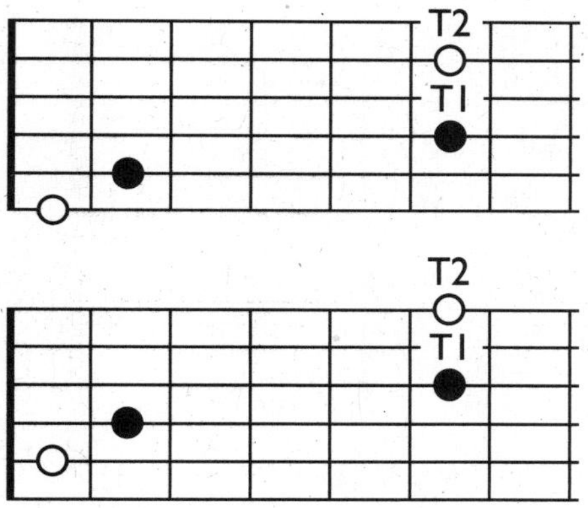

Augmented

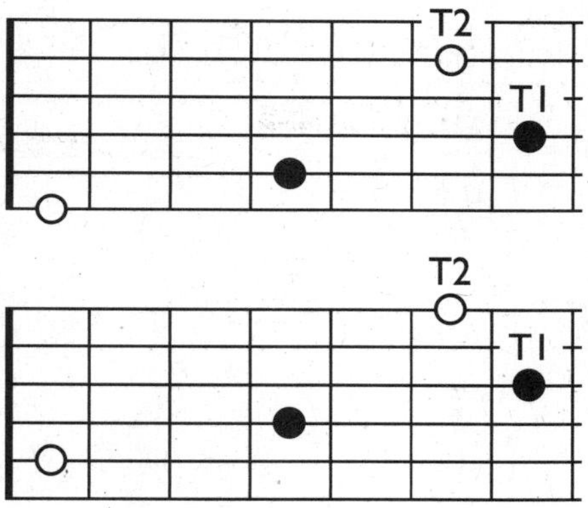

Learn all of the above shapes and use them to harmonize various keys and write different chord progressions. Of course, practice them on all possible string sets. Use these diagrams as a starting point for creating new shapes.

Below is a simple ascending tapping pattern.

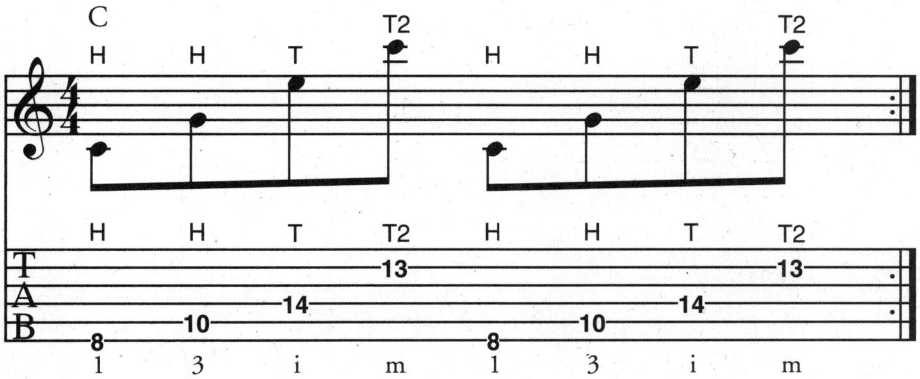

Here, we have an ascending/descending tapping pattern variation.

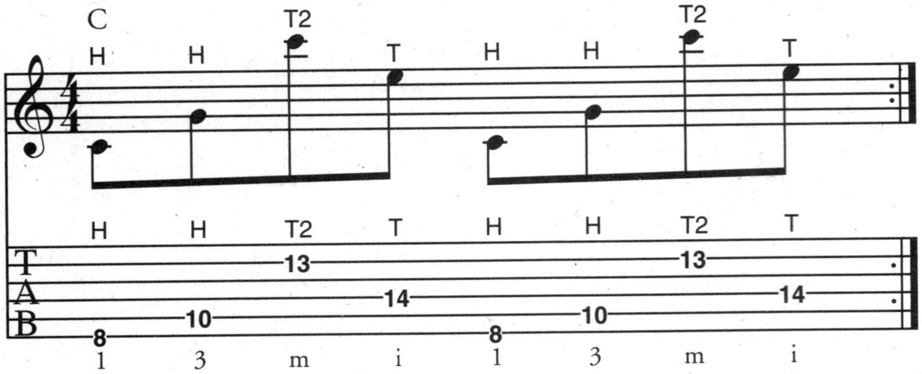

The example below is a simple C Lydian modal chord progression, which utilizes tapping to add chord tones and extensions.

42

Track 50.1

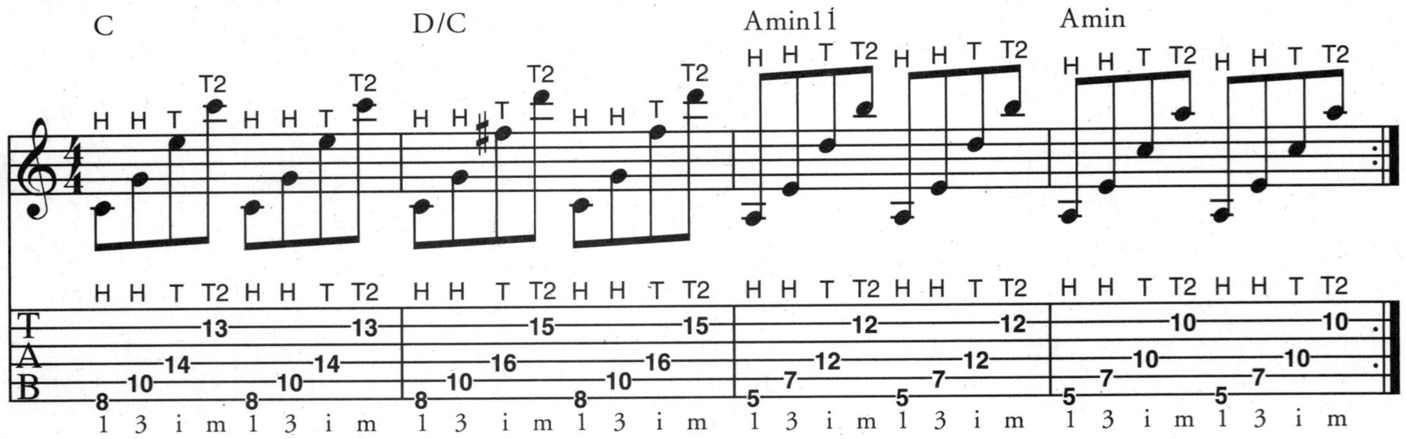

Following is a I–vi chord progression, with added 9th extensions, in D Major.

43

Track 50.2

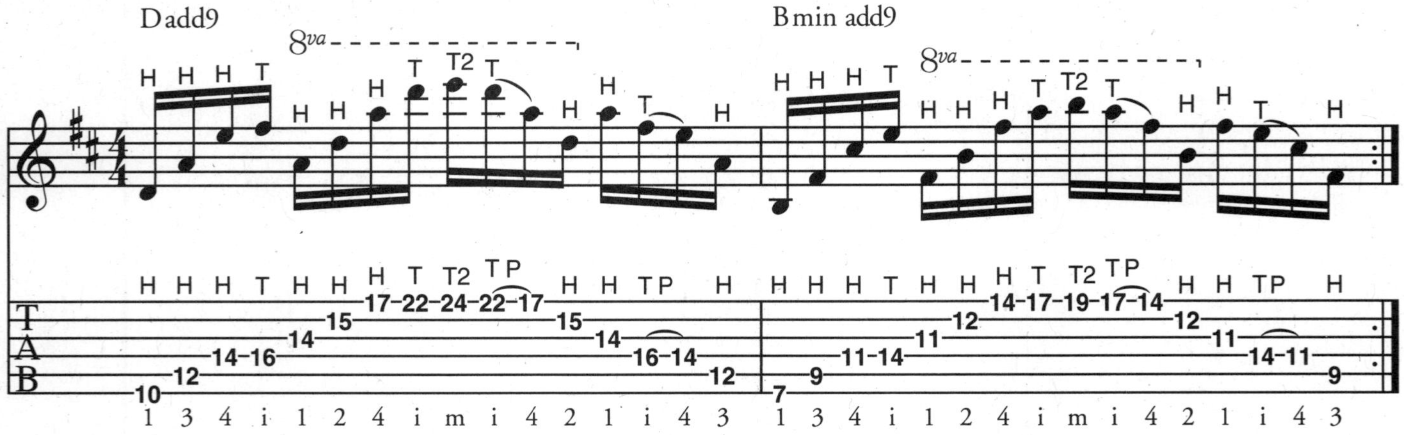

As you continue to practice, try to write similar or completely new ideas using the chord-tapping concept.

Chapter 11: The Harmonic Minor Scale

The *harmonic minor scale* is a commonly used scale in the rock and shred genre. It has been popularized by players like Ritchie Blackmore (of Deep Purple) and Yngwie Malmsteen. The genre these guitarists pioneered is often referred to as "neo-classical" rock, or shred, and it draws upon the sound of classical composers such as J. S. Bach, Ludwig van Beethoven, and Niccolò Paganini, just to name a few. But what is the harmonic minor scale, and how can you use it?

The harmonic minor scale is based on the natural minor scale. The only difference is that it has a ♮7 instead of a ♭7. So the formula for a harmonic minor scale is: 1–2–♭3–4–5–♭6–7.

Let's compare A Natural Minor to A Harmonic Minor.

A Natural Minor Scale

1 Track 51.1

A Harmonic Minor Scale

2 Track 51.2

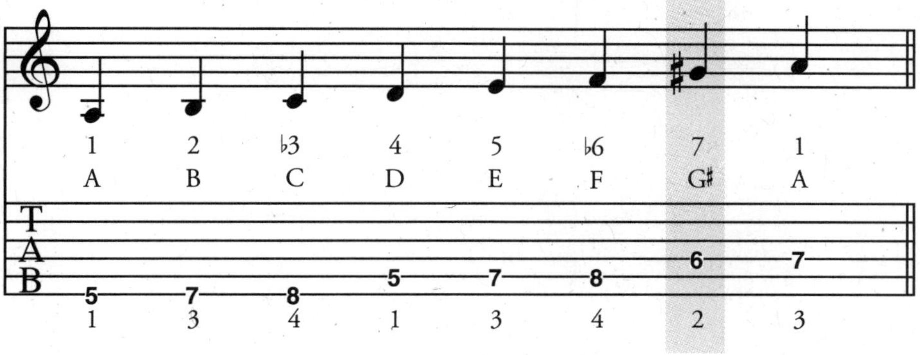

Now, what does this really mean? If you change a note within a scale, you are also altering the resulting chords.

Why was this done in the case of the harmonic minor scale? The diatonic harmony of the natural minor scale does not have a dominant chord built on the 5th scale degree, and a dominant V chord has the strongest pull towards a i chord, so it is desirable in many chord progressions. To solve this problem, we simply change the minor 3rd of the V chord (in the key of A Minor, this is Emin7) to a major 3rd. The result is an E7 chord (E–G♯–B–D). This dominant chord functions just as its counterpart in a major key, serving as a point of tension leading back to the i chord. Additionally, the G♯ acts as a *leading tone* to the tonic of the scale (A), just as the note B does in the C Major scale. (The note B is also the major 3rd of the G7 dominant chord in the key of C Major).

Following is the A Harmonic Minor scale harmonized in triads.

Diatonic Triads of A Harmonic Minor (Root Position)

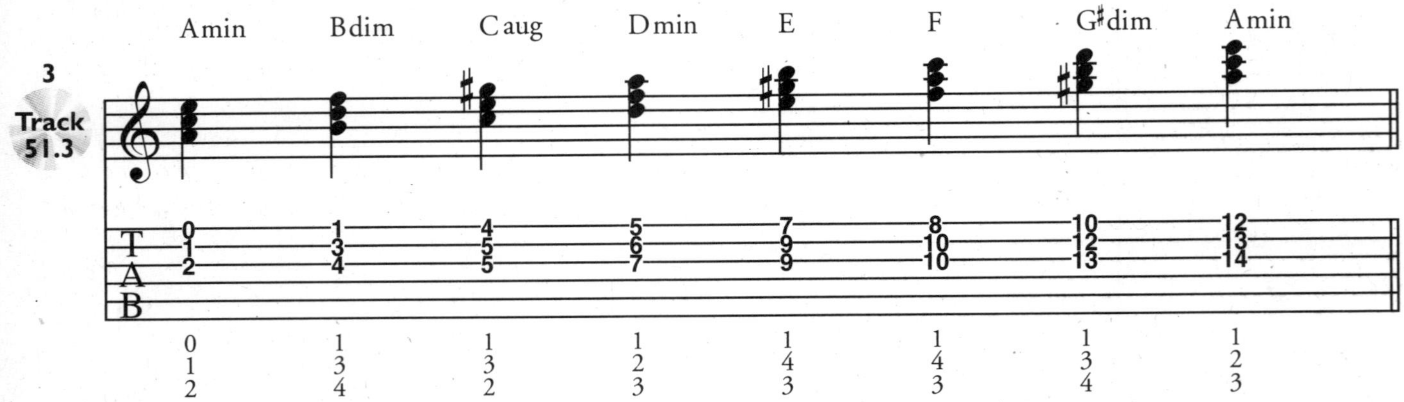

Now let's look at the inversions of this harmonized scale. As always, work out these concepts on all string-sets and keys. This will help you better understand the scale and its arpeggios.

Diatonic Triads of A Harmonic Minor (1st Inversion)

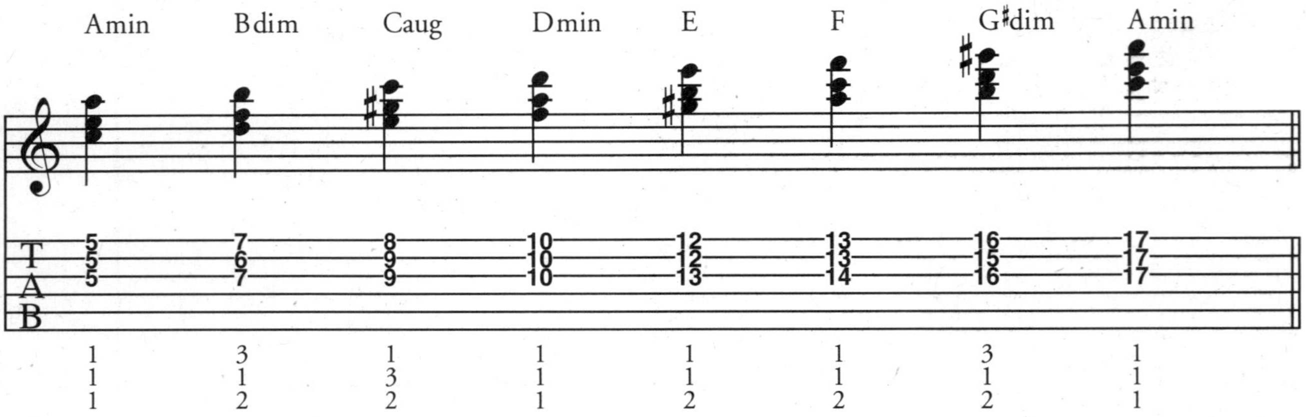

Diatonic Triads of A Harmonic Minor (2nd Inversion)

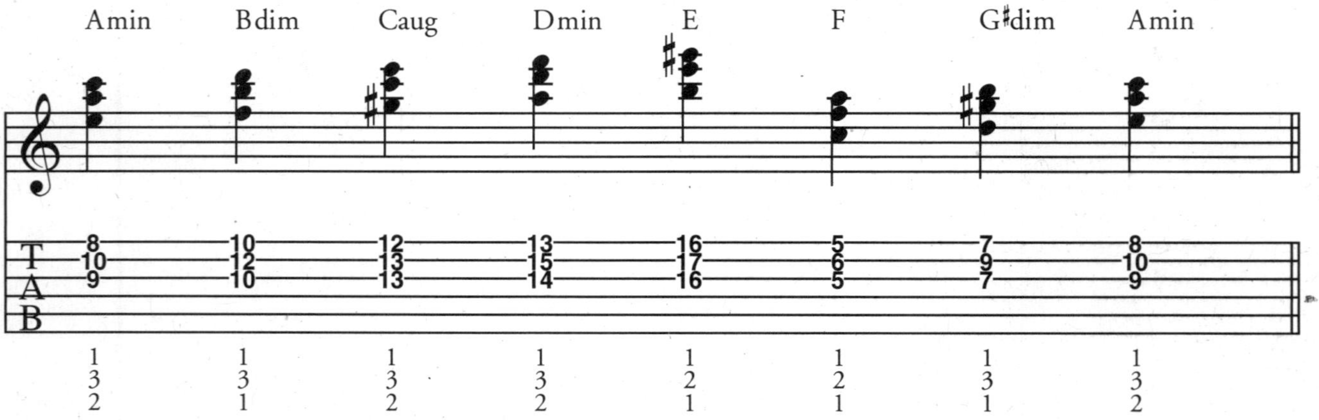

The most important chords of the harmonic minor scale are those built on the 5th and 7th scale degrees. In A Harmonic Minor, these chords are:

V = E or E7
vii° = G♯dim or G♯dim7

In order to use these chords in a minor chord progression, you "borrow" the dominant or diminished chords whenever you want to create a *cadence,* or ending, for a chord progression.

The harmonic minor scale is usually played over the V or vii° chord in a minor key. This means you have to change the natural minor scale to a harmonic minor scale when you encounter these chords in a minor key. The chord scale, or modal scale, for the V chord is also called *Phrygian dominant,* or *Spanish Phrygian dominant,* and it is the 5th mode of the harmonic minor scale.

The following example is a typical minor chord progression that will work perfectly with the harmonic minor scale.

The first three measures are in the tonality of A Natural Minor. The 4th measure is borrowed from A Harmonic Minor, with the E7 chord leading back to the A Minor chord.

Since the last chord is borrowed from the harmonic minor scale, you need to use the harmonic minor scale when playing over it.

After all this theory, let's get to the playing part. The scale diagrams below show the seven positions, or modes, of the A Harmonic Minor scale. Memorize the different scales, or since you already know the seven positions of the natural minor scale, just alter the note G to a G♯. This should be easier than learning seven "new" scales.

Once you feel comfortable with all seven positions, use the patterns and sequences from Chapters 6 and 7 to further your knowledge and chops and, of course, don't forget to practice the scale in all 12 keys!

Form 1

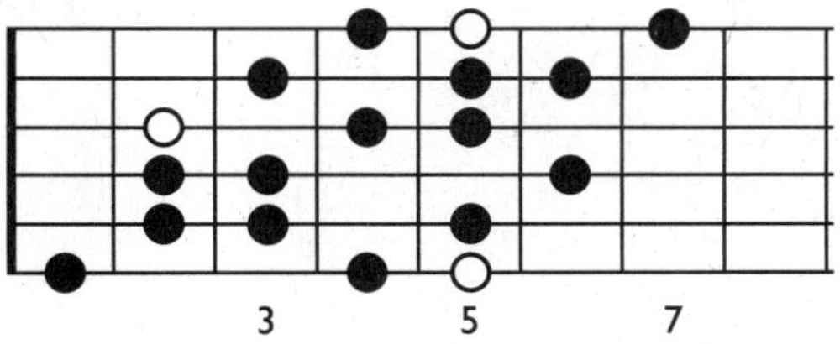

Form 2

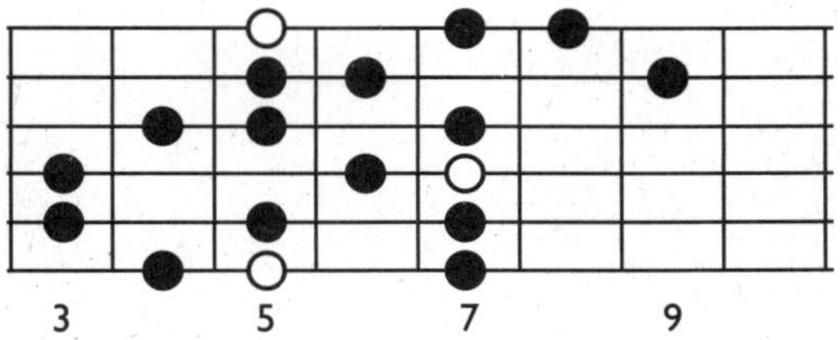

Form 3

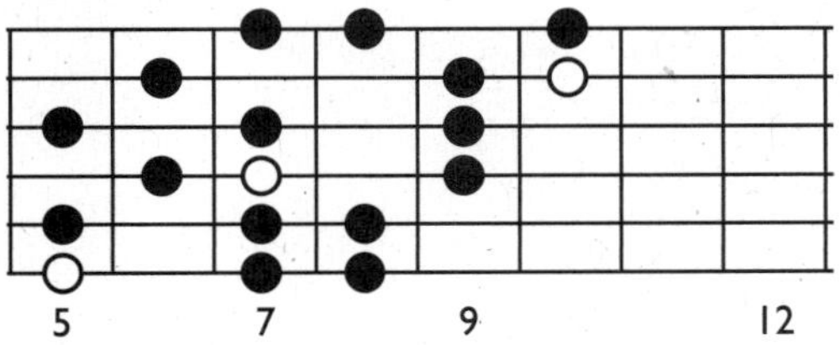

Form 4

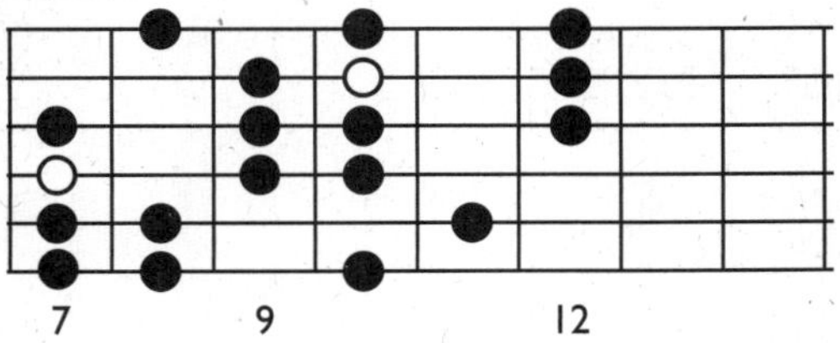

Form 5

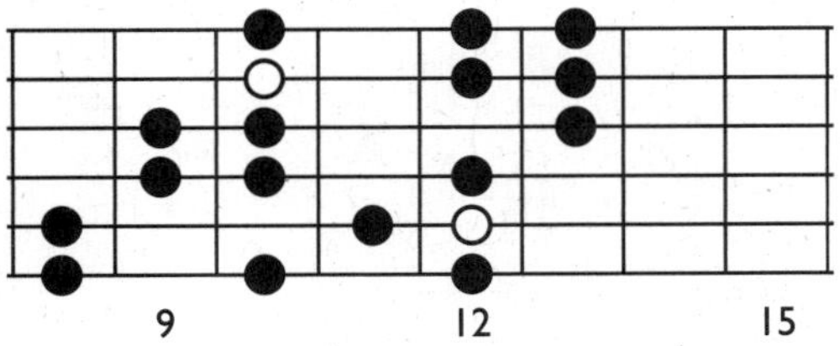

Form 6

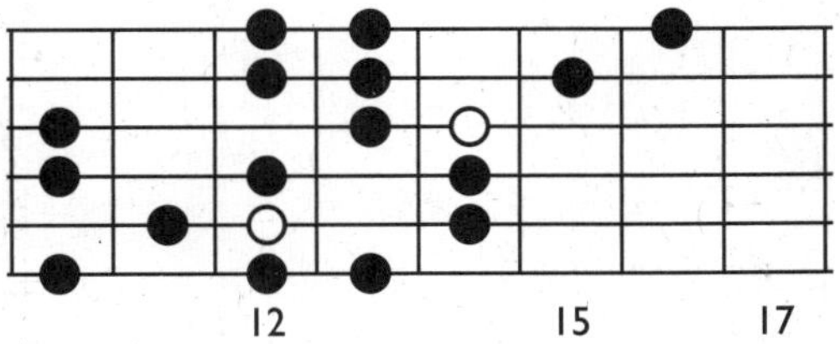

Form 7 (Phrygian Dominant)

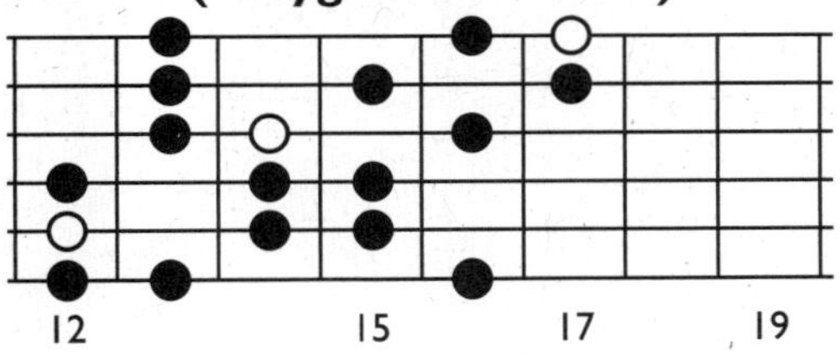

Licks and Backing Tracks

The first lick we're going to try is a pedal-tone lick in the style of J. S. Bach. Remember, a pedal tone is a repetitive note (or group of notes) played against an ascending or descending scale phrase. Yngwie Malmsteen, Vinnie Moore, and others have popularized licks like this.

4
Track 52.1

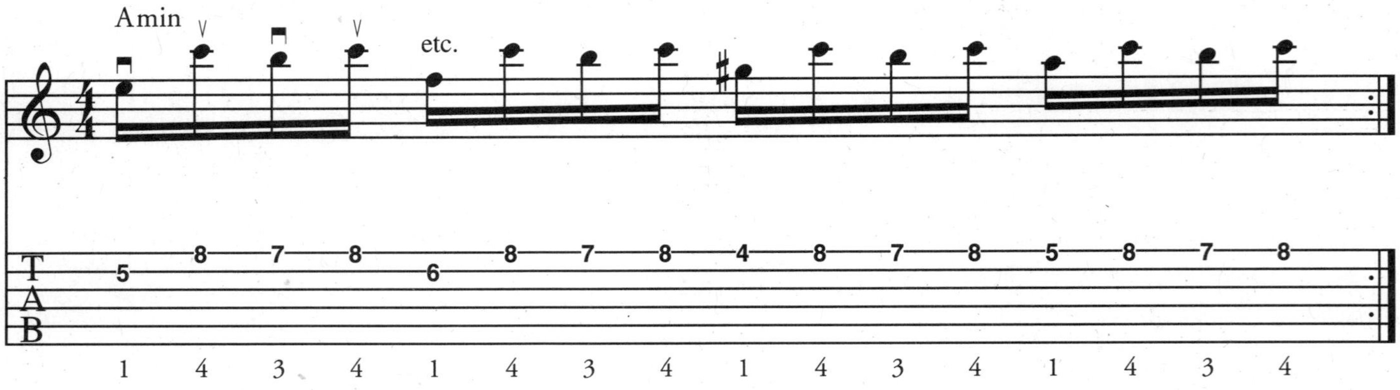

The next example is a typical pedal-tone lick in C Harmonic Minor.

5
Track 52.2

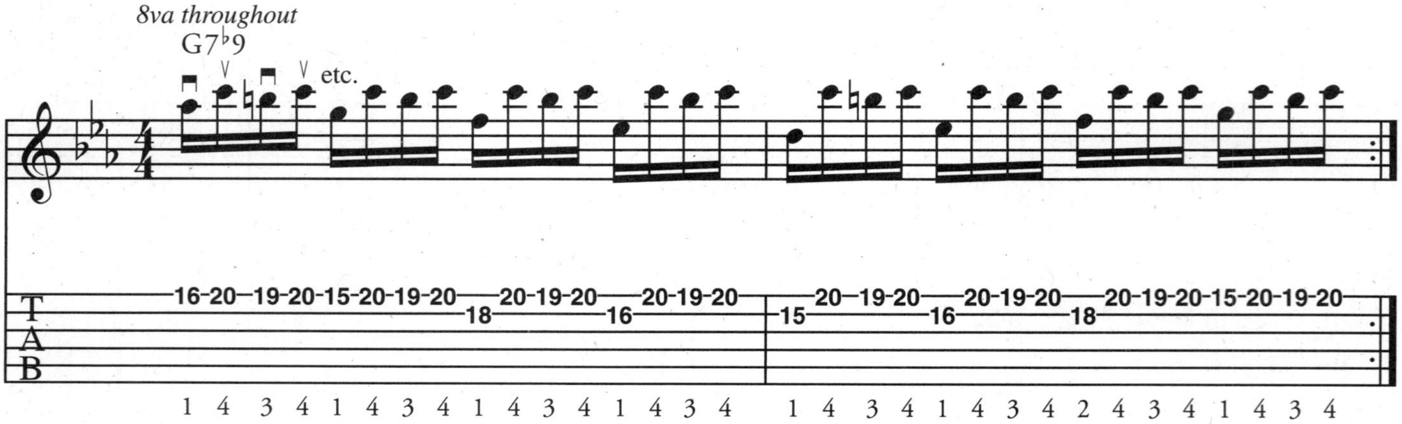

Below is another pedal-tone lick played over an A7♭9 chord. The scale we are using is D Harmonic Minor.

6
Track 52.3

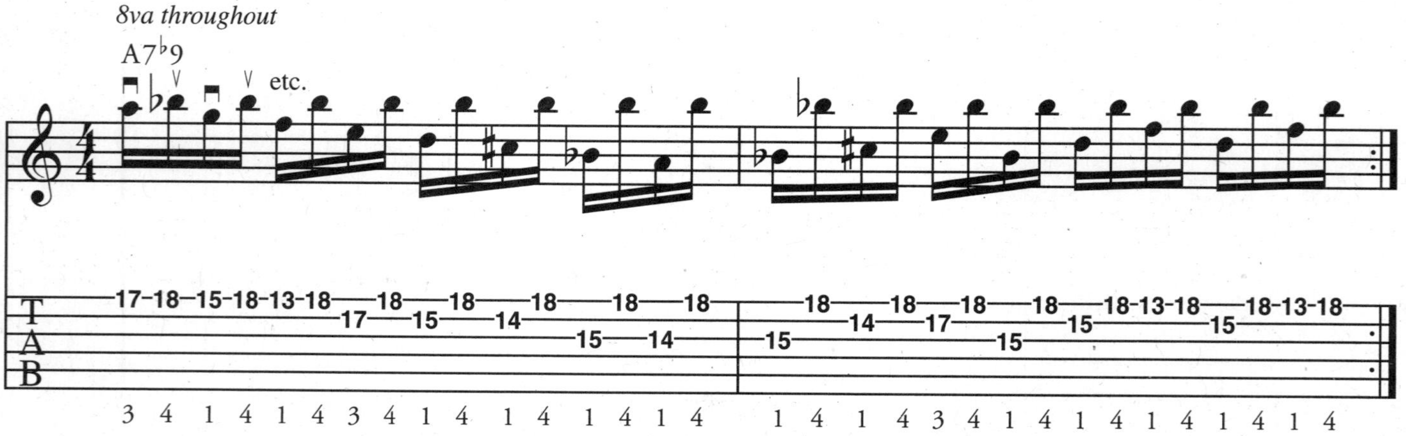

Next is an A Harmonic Minor run that ends with a simple pedal-tone lick.

7
Track 52.4

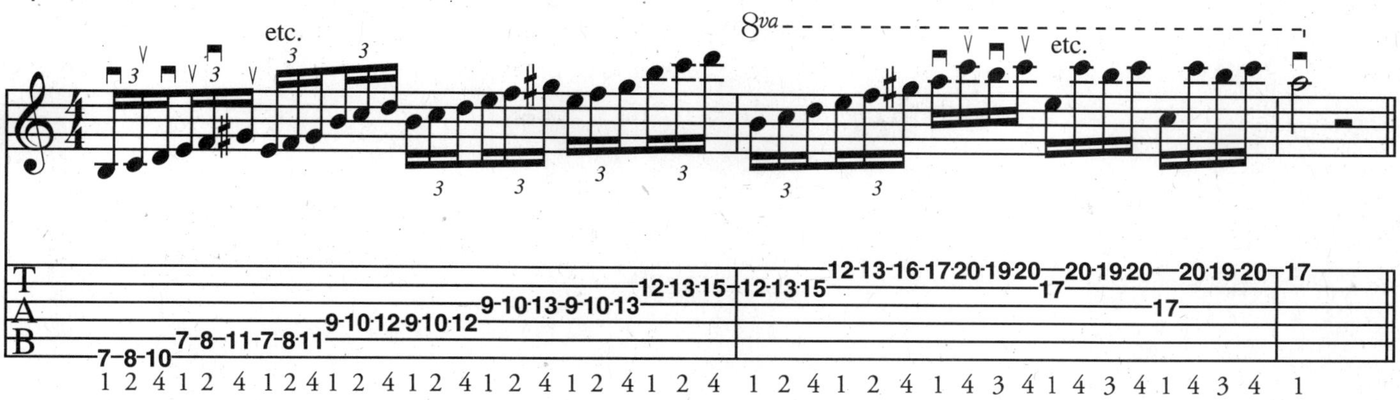

Below is a diminished arpeggio sequence ending in an A Minor arpeggio.

8
Track 52.5

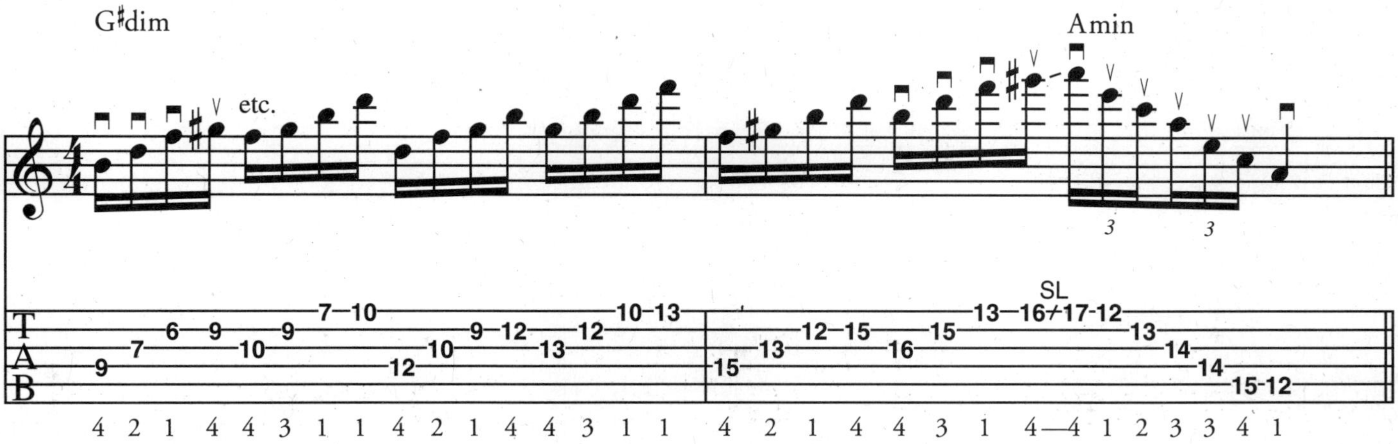

Next is a little two-string-sweep etude. The progression is Amin–F–Bdim–E–Amin. It ends with an A Minor descending arpeggio.

9
Track 52.6

The next example is an excerpt from my song called "The Final Showdown," and it includes pedal tones, octave jumps, diminished arpeggios, patterns, and scale runs. Enjoy!

The Final Showdown

(Excerpt)

On the following page is an excerpt from Paganini's *Caprice No. 2 in B Minor.* It's a great exercise for string skipping. The harmonic movement is relatively simple: it's Bmin to F♯7 and then back to Bmin. Have fun!

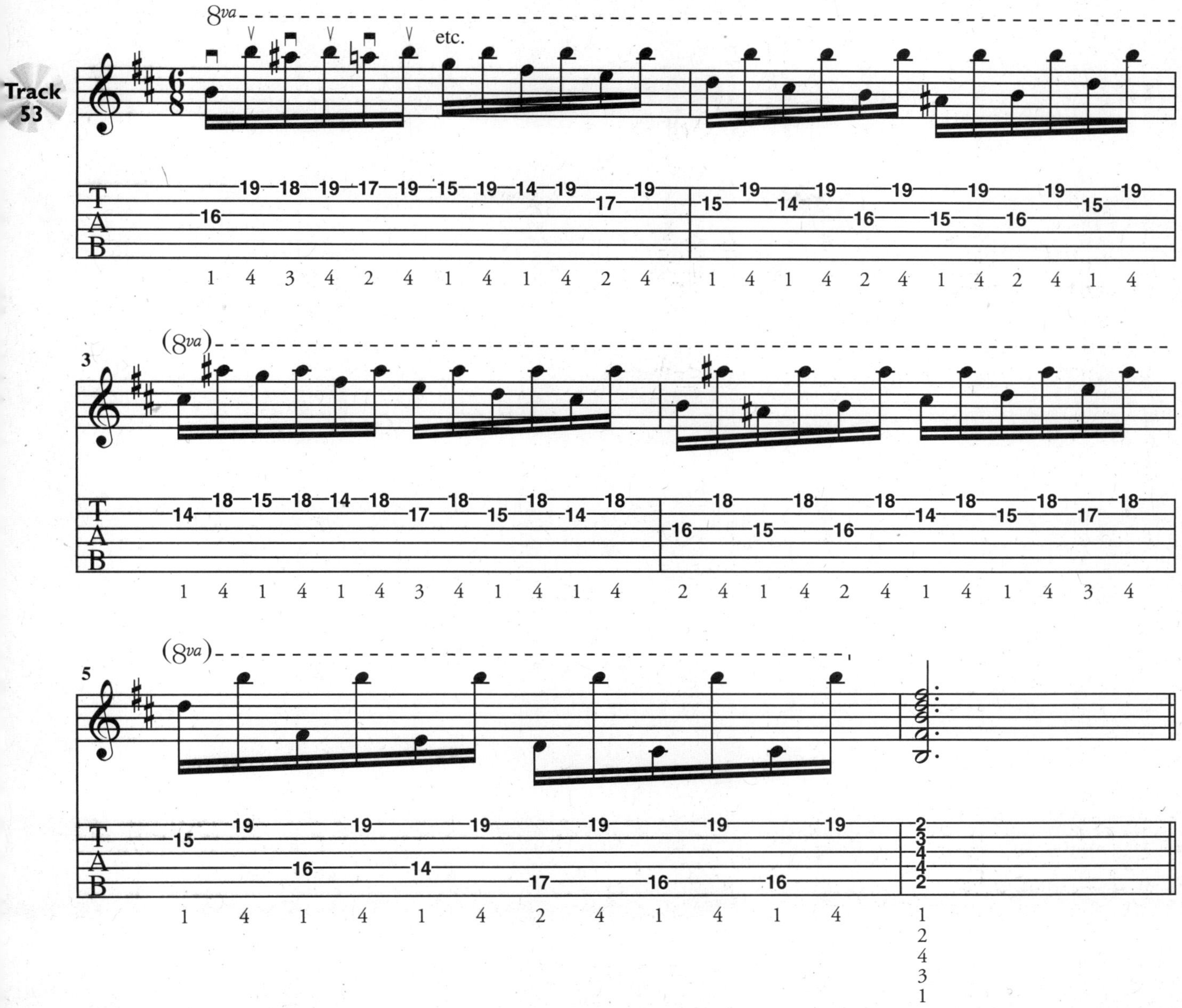

Following are two backing tracks for you to practice harmonic minor scale licks and positions. Be creative. Compose similar vamps, and work on creating licks and riffs of your own!

Backing Track 1 (Use the A Harmonic Minor scale and arpeggios)

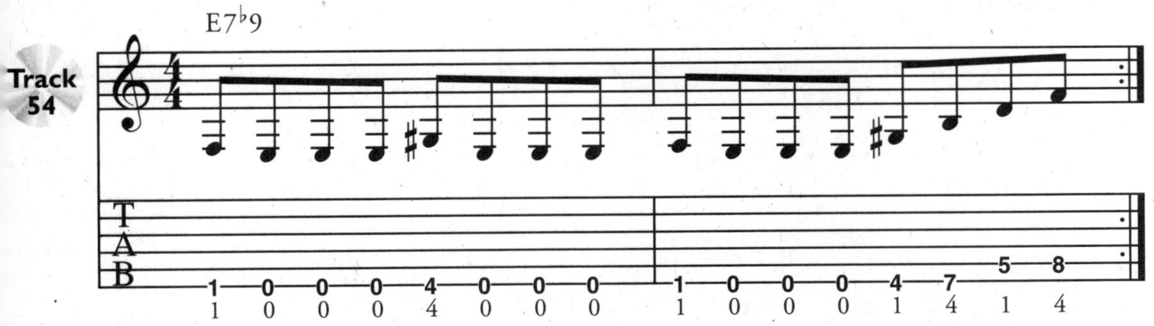

Backing Track 2 (Use the D Harmonic Minor scale and arpeggios)

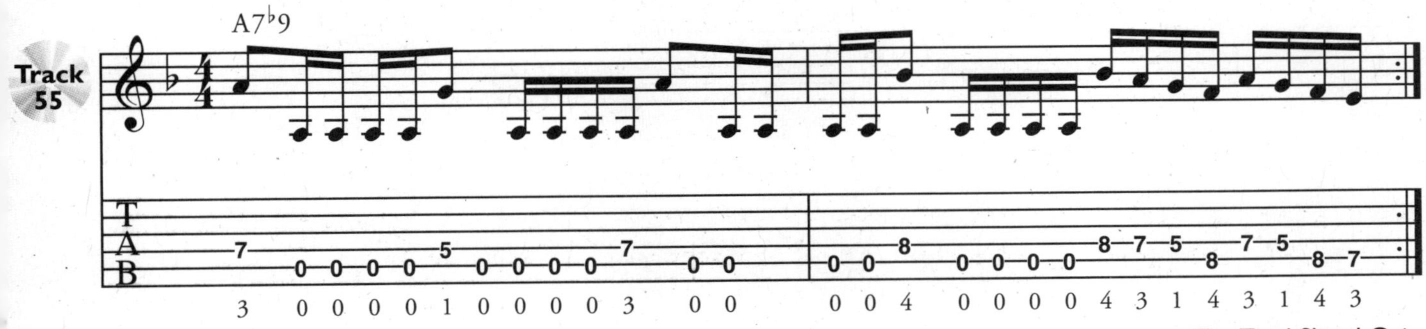

Chapter 12: The Melodic Minor Scale

The *melodic minor scale* is another important minor scale. It has an unusual, "mellow" sound, and it might not be very exciting at first, but when you examine it further, you will find that the derived modes from this scale are interesting and will definitely spice up your playing.

This scale is similar to the natural minor scale, except that it has natural 6th (♮6) and natural 7th (♮7) scale degrees.

The melodic minor scale is mostly used in an ascending context, as it utilizes the more major-scale qualities in the second half of the scale to target the root note. It is also used to avoid the augmented 2nd that occurs in the harmonic minor tonality.

The formula for the melodic minor scale is: 1–2–♭3–4–5–6–7.

A Melodic Minor Scale

1
Track 56.1

The triads that this scale creates are as follows.

Diatonic Triads of A Melodic Minor (Root Position)

2
Track 56.2

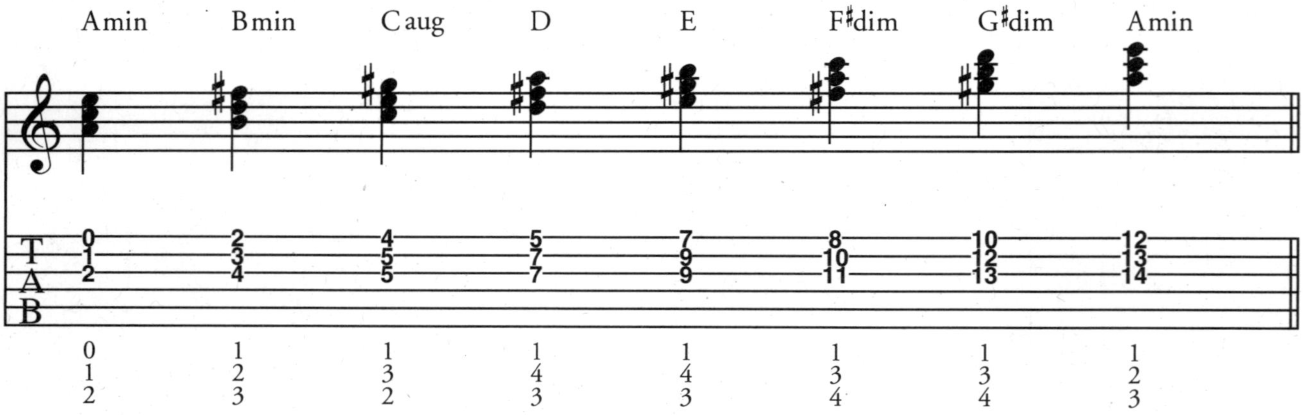

And now, the inversions.

Diatonic Triads of A Melodic Minor (1st Inversion)

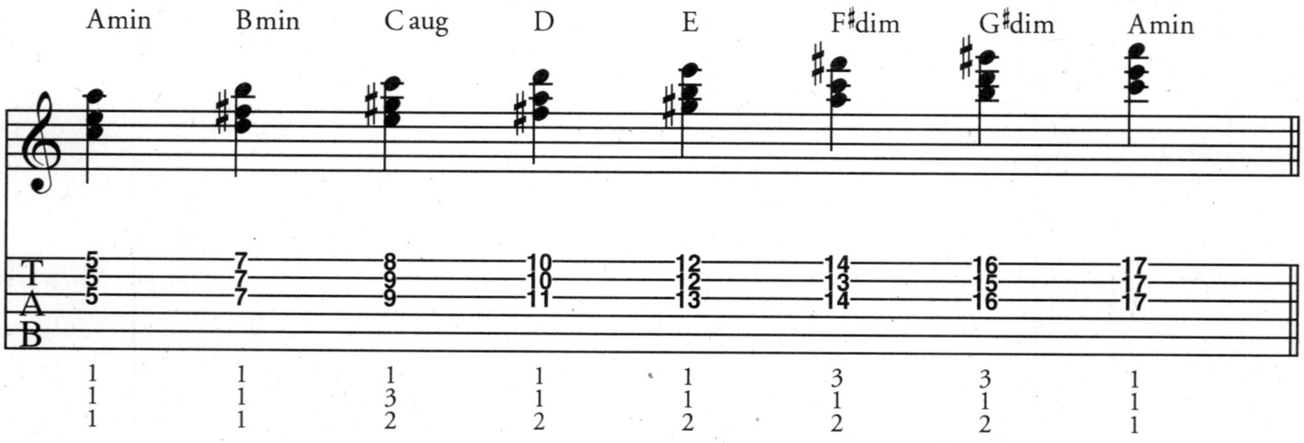

Diatonic Triads of A Melodic Minor (2nd Inversion)

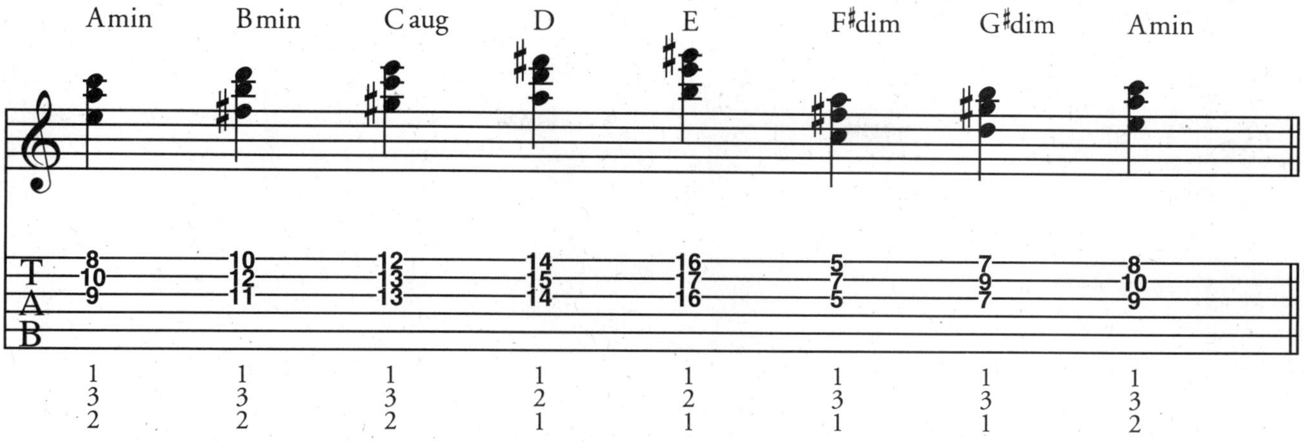

Try to learn all the inversions on all strings-sets across the fretboard. You can utilize them later in your arpeggio playing, using different kinds of techniques such as tapping or sweeping.

To be able to shred the melodic minor scale, you need to learn the seven positions of the three-note-per-string scale. Use the patterns and sequences found in Chapters 6 and 7 to build up more musical vocabulary and knowledge.

Locrian ♮2

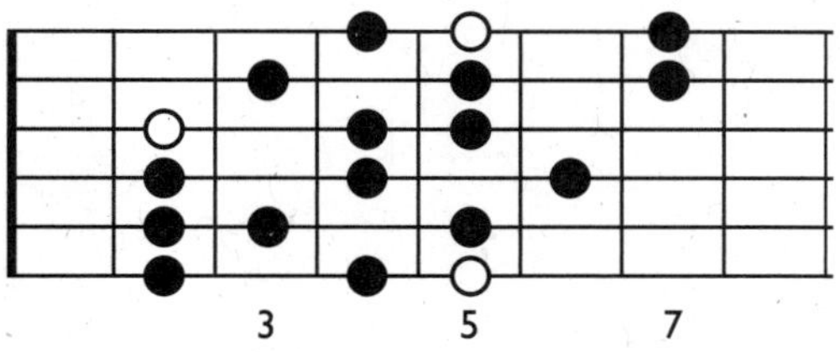

Altered Dominant

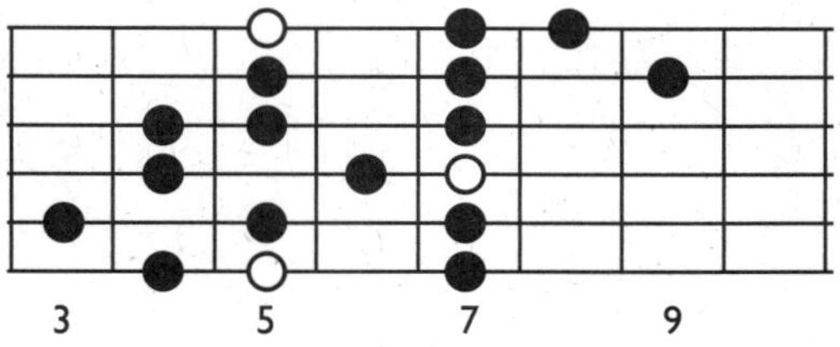

Melodic Minor

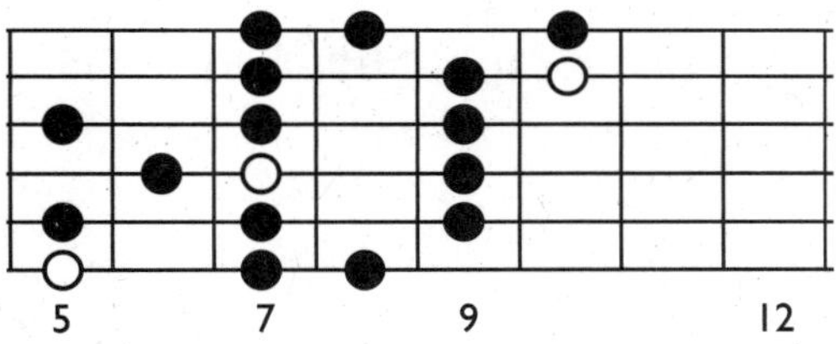

Dorian ♭2

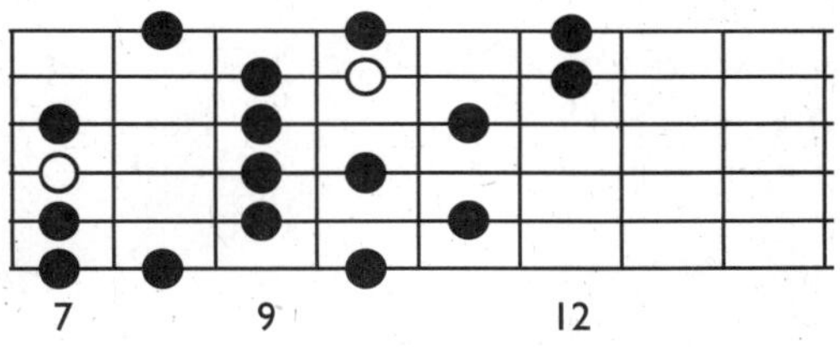

Lydian ♯5

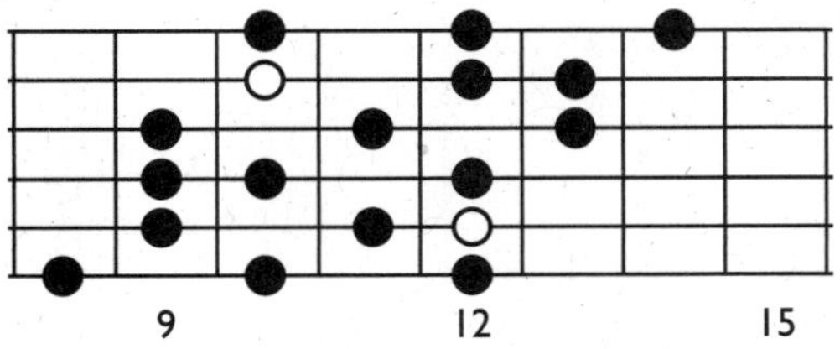

Lydian ♭7

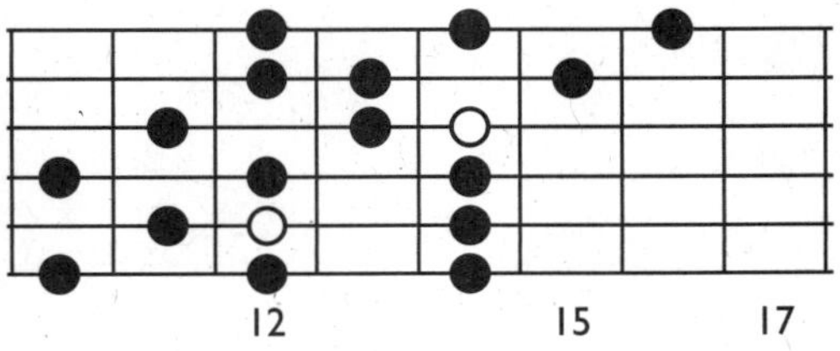

Mixolydian ♭6

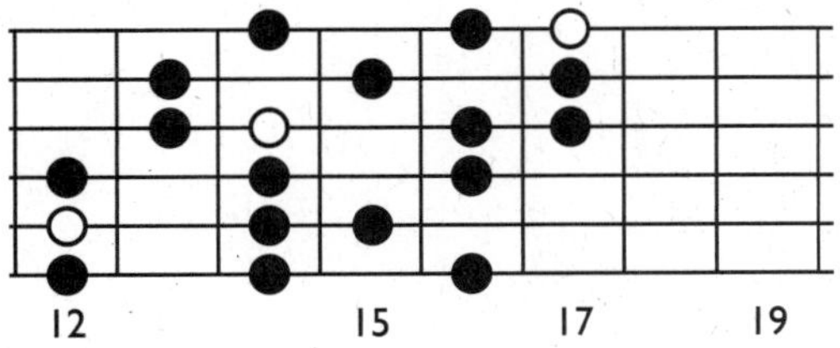

The names for the seven positions are derived from the modes of the major scale and modified to match their formulas. For example, Lydian ♭7 is the mode built on the 4th scale degree of the Melodic Minor scale. Its scale formula is: 1–2–3–♯4–5–6–♭7. As you can see, it is a major scale with a ♯4 (just like the Lydian) but then also has a ♭7.

Try using the backing track from page 115 (Track 67) to practice the positions of the melodic minor scale.

The following examples and licks utilize the melodic minor scale with different technical challenges.

The first features *hybrid picking*, tapping, and open-voiced arpeggios. Hybrid picking uses a combination of pick and right-hand fingers to sound the notes. The notes marked with *m* are to be plucked with the right-hand middle finger.

Lick 1

Track 57.1

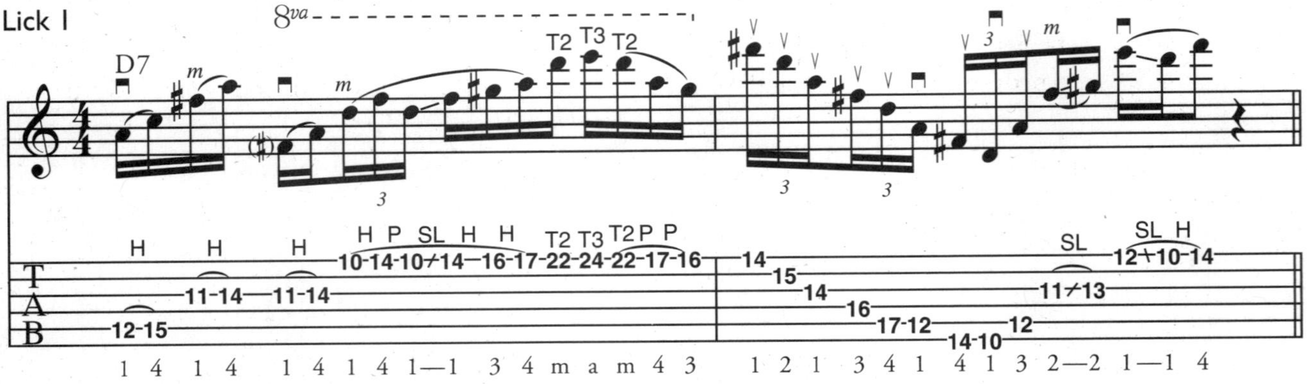

The lick below uses the triads of the melodic minor scale to sweep across the fretboard.

Lick 2

Track 57.2

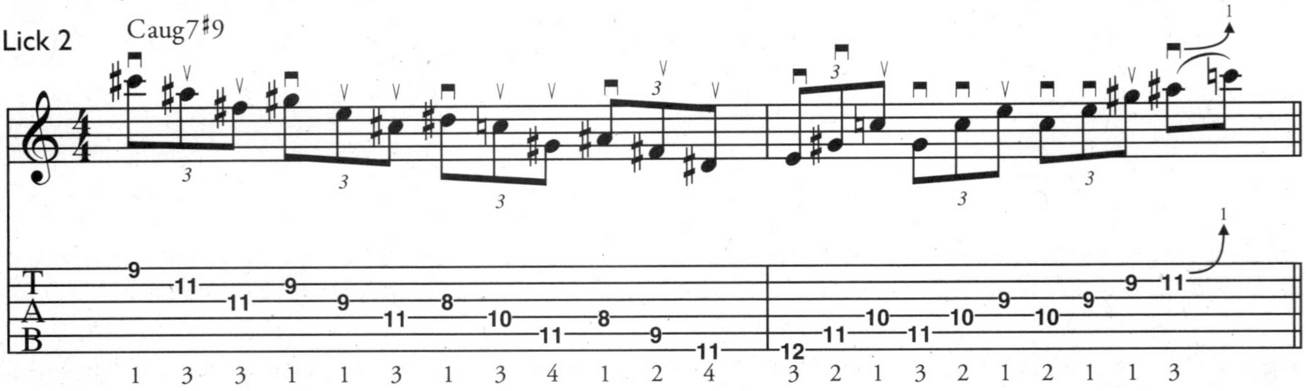

This last lick, which utilizes alternate picking and the alternate dominant scale, works great over an E7♯9 chord.

(The dominant 7♯9 chord consists of the following chord tones: 1–3–5–♭7–♯9.)

Lick 3

Track 58

The melodic minor scale and its modes are very exciting once you get used to their subtle sound and interesting applications. The modal and melodic application of this scale is endless and can keep you busy for a very long time. Try to write more riffs and licks using this scale and its modes.

Chapter 13: Exotic and Unusual Scales

In the world of shred guitar, there is an abundance of exotic and unusual scales. These scales can range from eight-note scales to simple pentatonic-based sounds. They can be applied to regular chord progressions or rock and metal-based guitar riffs.

The Algerian Scale

Let's start off with the *Algerian scale,* which is also known as *Hungarian minor,* or *double harmonic minor*. The formula for this scale is: 1–2–♭3–♯4–5–♭6–7.

Algerian Scale

1

Track 59.1

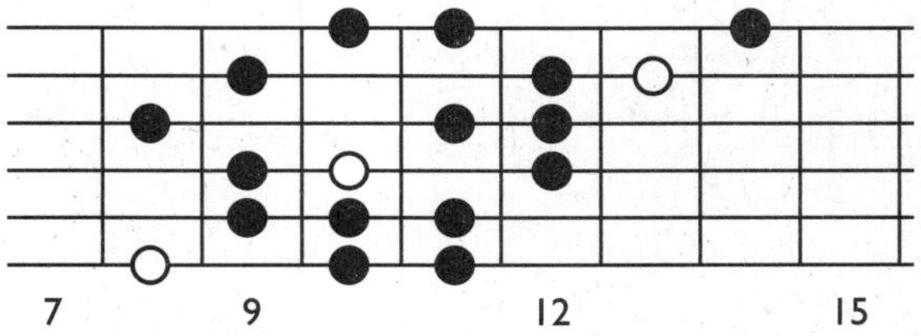

All of the following scales can be used over progressions made up of chords derived from those scales. For instance, the chords that can be derived from the notes of the C Algerian scale are: Cmin, D(♭5), E♭aug, A♭7/F♯, G, A♭, and Bmin. So, the C Algerian scale can be used over any progression consisting of those chords. On the CD, the licks are played over a straight C bass note.

The lick below is a fast Algerian scale run. Since the structure of this scale is somewhat unusual, a few very simple and repetitive patterns can be found.

2

Track 59.2

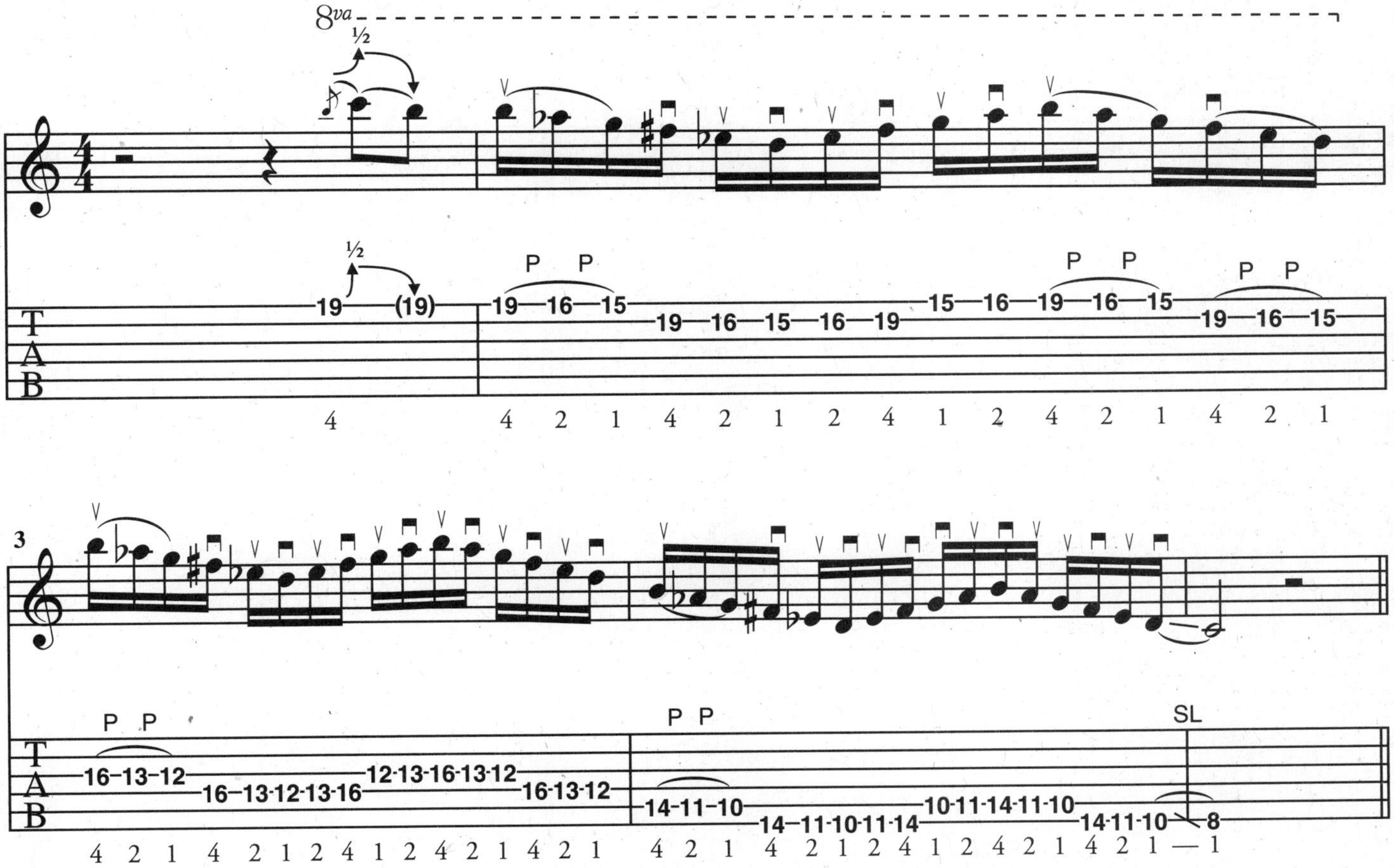

The lick below has a very different approach. It is based on the triads you can build from this scale. The triads are Bmin, E♭aug, A♭, Bmin, and E♭aug.

3
Track 59.3

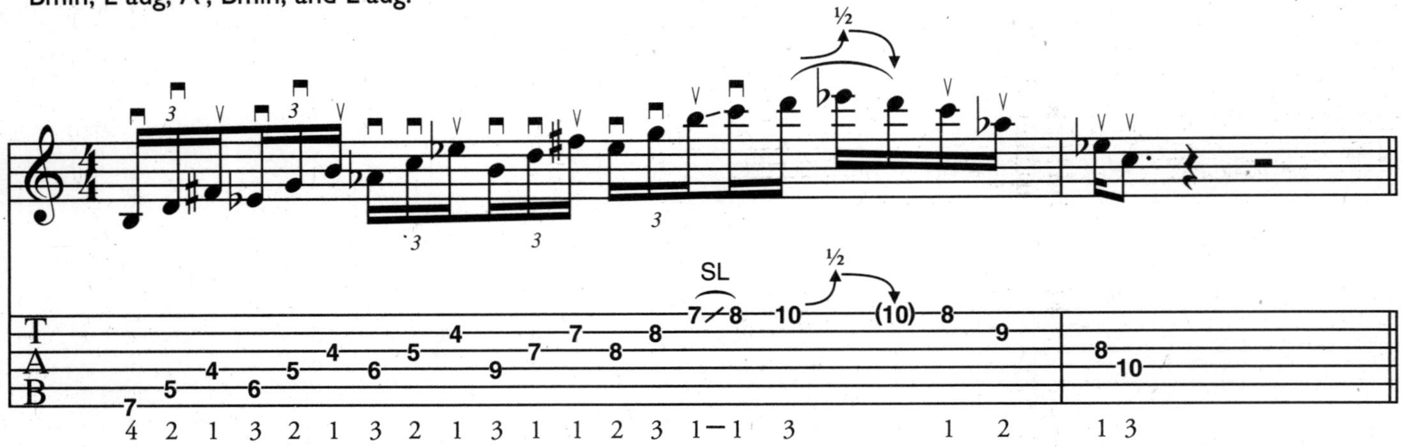

Use the backing tracks on page 113 (Tracks 64 and 65) to practice the Algerian scale and get used to the sound.

Japanese Scales

Next is one of two types of Japanese pentatonic scales. This scale is based more on a minor sound. The formula is: 1–2–♭3–5–♭6.

Japanese Minor Pentatonic Scale

4
Track 60.1

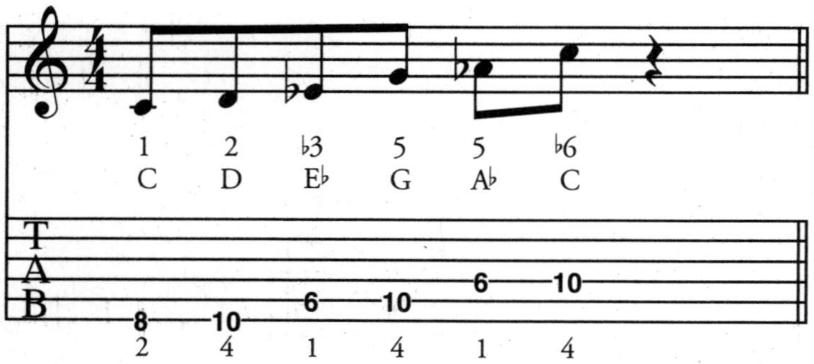

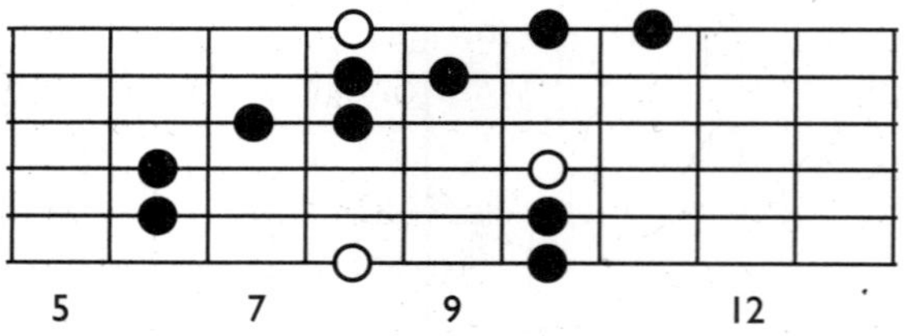

This scale can be played over progressions featuring the chords Cmin, G5, and A♭. Of course, there are more chords that can be derived from this scale, but our purpose here is just to get you started; see if you can find some more on your own.

Example 5 is a simple sextuplet scale run. Example 6 utilizes triads (C Minor and A♭ Major) derived from the Japanese scale and ends with a simple two-note-per-string ascending run. Again, use the supplied backing tracks at the end of this chapter to practice the scale and licks, as well as to come up with your own ideas.

5
Track 60.2

6
Track 60.3

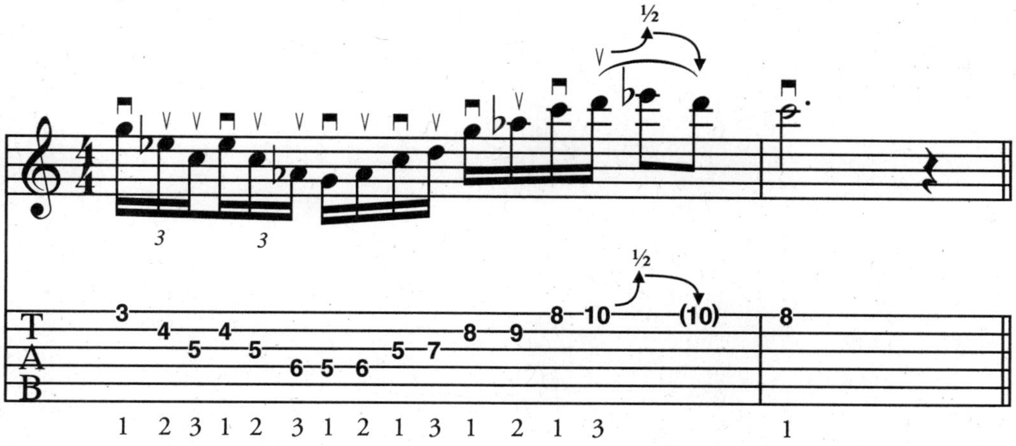

The next variation of the Japanese scale is based on a happier, major sound. The scale formula is: 1–2–4–5–♭6.

Japanese Major Pentatonic Scale

7
Track 61.1

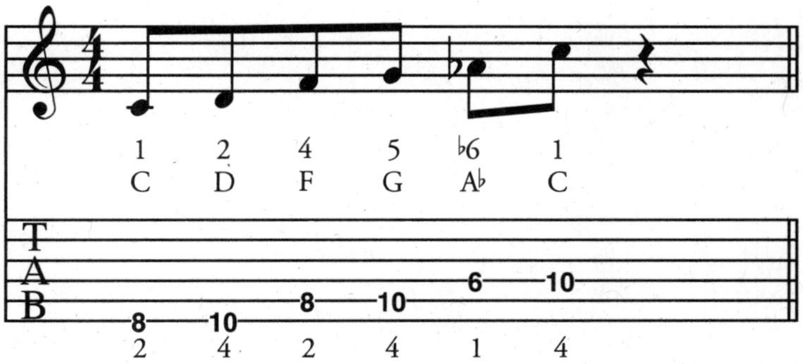

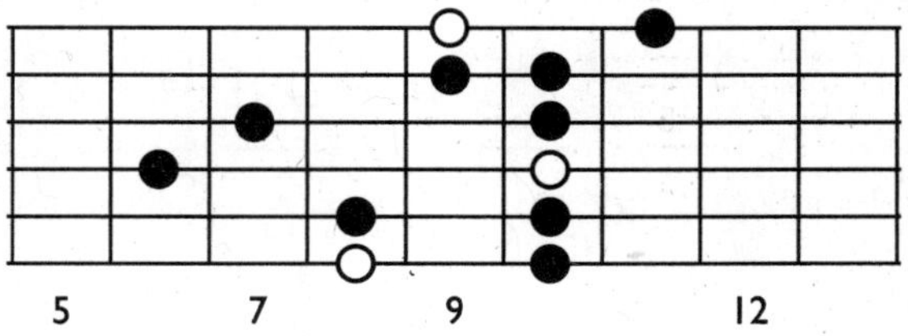

Experiment with this scale, and try to come up with different six-string fingerings.

The Japanese major pentatonic scale can be used over progressions with the following chords: Csus4, Ddim, and Fmin.

Below is a cool, really fast tapping lick that will definitely turn some heads. It is based on a two-string pattern, which is then moved in octaves.

8

Track 61.2

Every scale, whether it is a pentatonic scale or a seven-note scale, can be organized into triads or other chord-like structures that can be played as arpeggios. The lick below is based on an F Minor sweep arpeggio.

9

Track 61.3

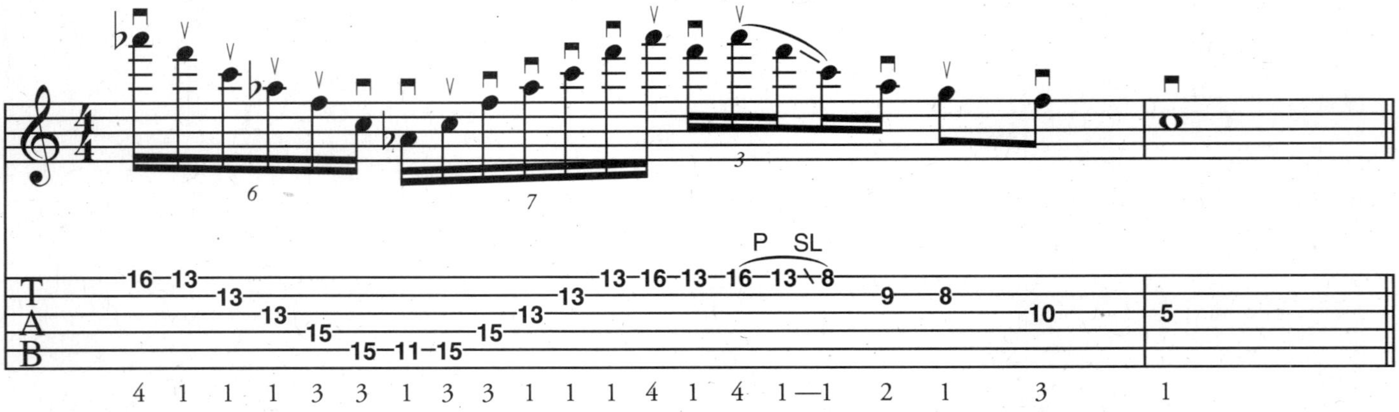

The Whole Tone Scale

The *whole tone scale* is a six-note scale consisting entirely of whole steps. This scale has an unstable, uneasy kind of sound. It is often used in the context of suspense. The formula is: 1–2–3–♯4–♯5–♭7.

This scale can be used over any augmented chord with one of its scale tones as a root (Caug, Daug, Eaug, etc.). It can also be played over a C7♯5 or C7♭13. The ♭13 is just the ♭6 in a higher octave. (The ♯5 and ♭6 are *enharmonic equivalents,* which means they are identical pitches with different note names.)

Whole Tone Scale

10
Track 62.1

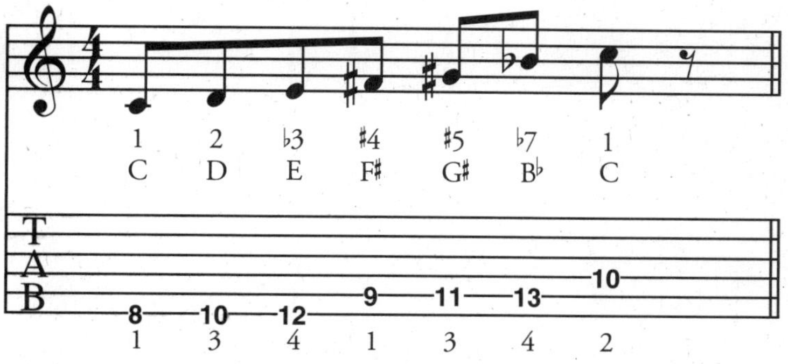

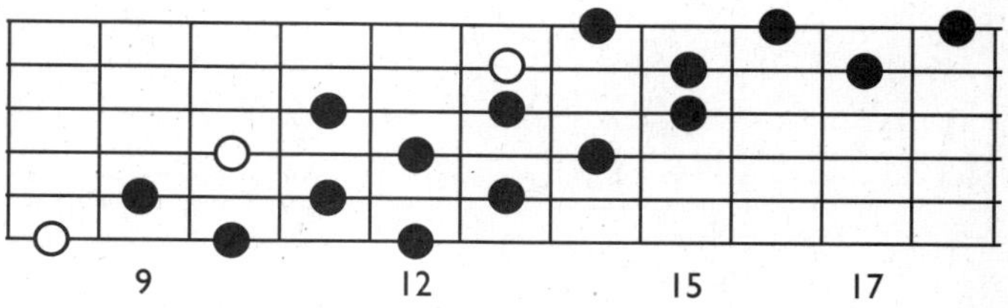

There are other possible shapes for this scale; try to work them out for yourself. Even though there are other fingerings, there are only two versions of the scale. The reason for this is that any of the six notes in the scale can be considered the root note. Consequently, the other set of six notes (remember, the chromatic scale has 12 notes) constitutes the second version of the scale.

Below is a simple tapping lick using five- and four-note groupings.

11
Track 62.2

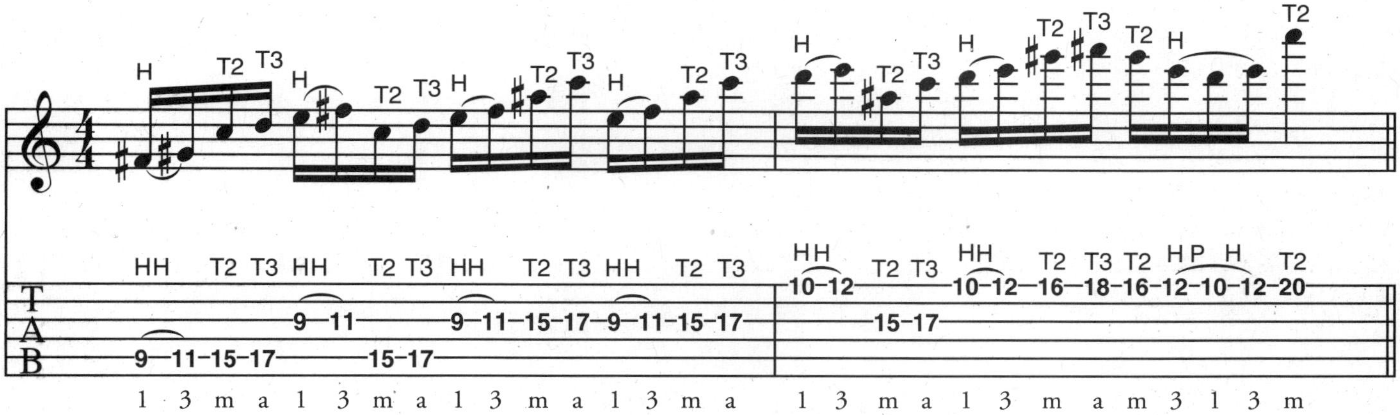

Here, we have a fast, string-skipping, alternate-picking lick in septuplets.

12
Track 62.3

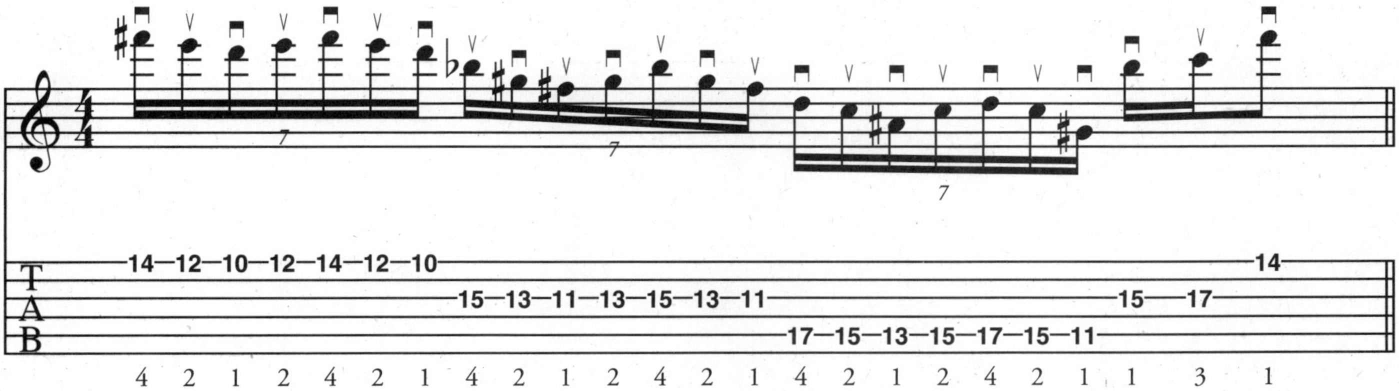

The Symmetrical Diminished Scale

The symmetrical diminished scale consists of alternating half- and whole-step intervals, and it can sound very interesting.

This is an eight-note scale, and its formula is as follows: 1–♭2–♭3–3–♯4–5–6–♭7.

Symmetrical Diminished Scale

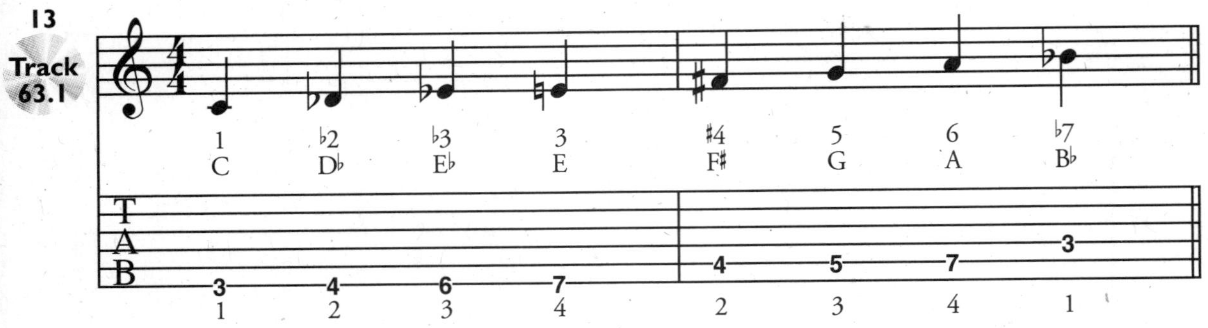

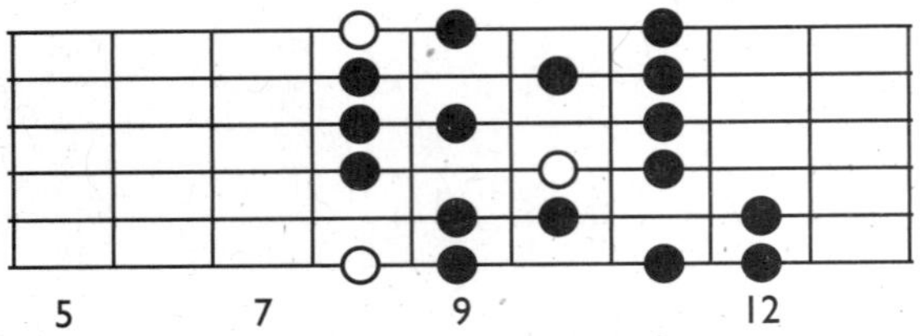

This scale also can be organized in different shapes and it is now up to you to find them. Furthermore, this scale produces a lot of different chords and sounds (in the key of C: Cdim, Cmin, Cmin7, D♭dim, E♭min, E♭, Edim, etc.). Try to find all possible triads and 7th chords. The diatonic structure and chord organization is, like the scale, very symmetrical.

Below is a strict, ascending, alternate-picking lick utilizing a repetitive pattern.

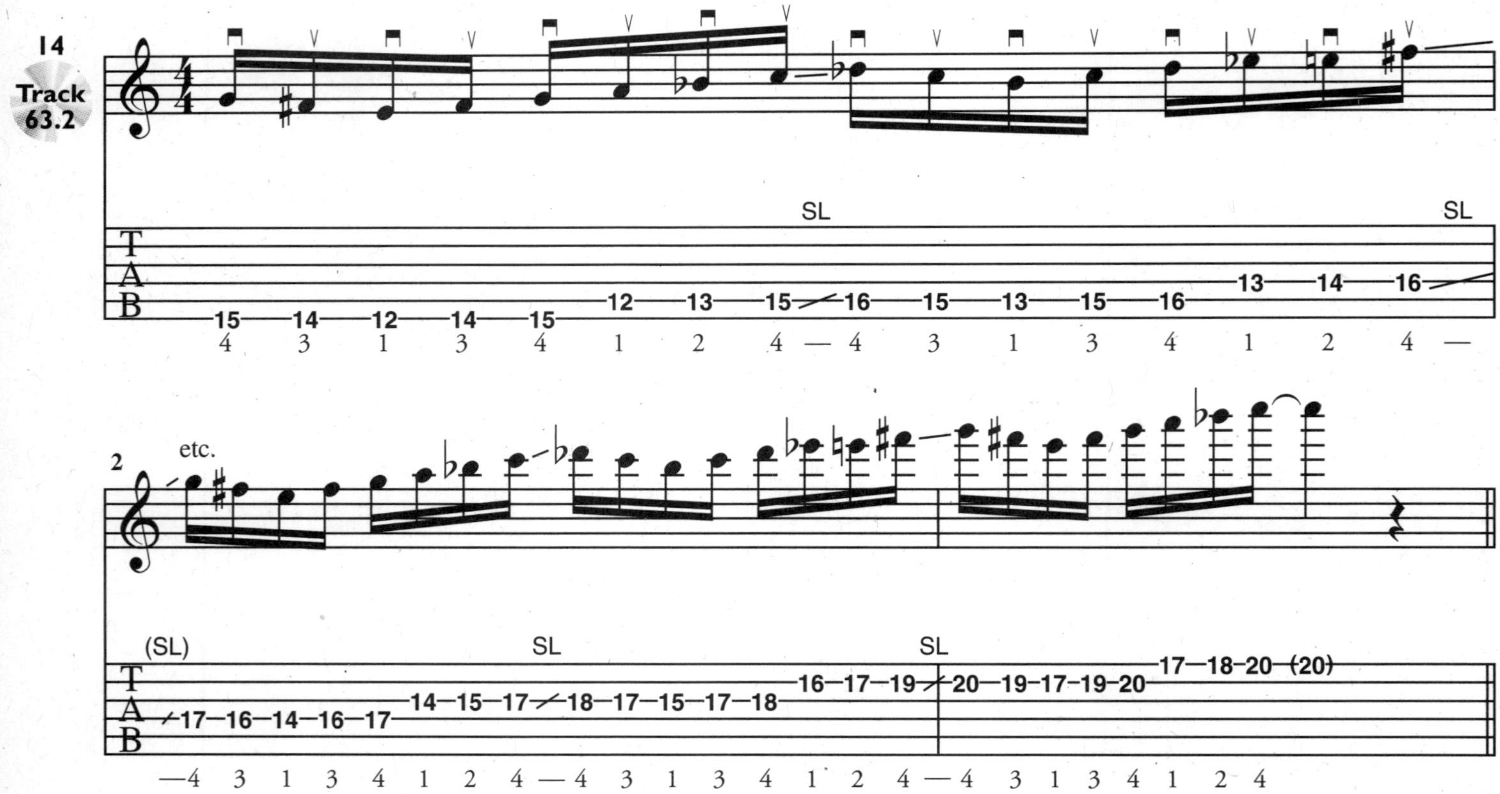

The following example is more complicated, as it employs string skipping and outside-inside picking. The phrases are grouped in fives and threes to help you clearly delineate the ascending and descending motions. The *5:4* indications under the groupings signify that there are five eighth notes in the time of four normal eighth notes (two beats). The triplet at the end of each measure lasts for the standard one beat.

15
Track 63.3

Use the following backing tracks to practice soloing with the scales covered in this chapter.

Track 64 Backing Track 1

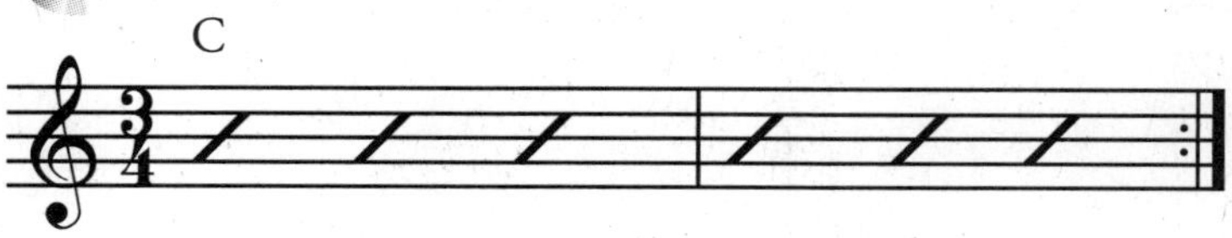

Track 65 Backing Track 2

There are so many more exciting scales that it would require a whole other book to talk about them. I would like to encourage you to do more research on this matter and develop a great vocabulary of new and interesting musical ideas.

Chapter 14: Modes

As we learned in Chapter 7 (page 43), modes are derived from the major scale and can be viewed as variations of either the major scale or the natural minor scale. To understand this better, we are going to build the modes starting from the same pitch. This way of looking at modes is called the *parallel approach*. (We have already looked at the relative approach on pages 43–44.) We'll start with the major-type modes. Our first mode is the Ionian mode, which is the major scale.

Ionian (Major)

1

Track 66.1

Compare the C Major (Ionian) scale with the Lydian mode below. All of the scale degrees are the same except for the ♯4 (F♯). This ♯4 creates a mysterious and different kind of sound. All modes have common pitches and different pitches when compared to their parallel major or minor scales. The different pitches are the *characteristic notes* responsible for each mode's unique sound.

Lydian

2

Track 66.2

When comparing the Mixolydian mode to the major scale, the characteristic note is the ♭7 (B♭). The remaining notes are the same as C Major.

Mixolydian

3

Track 66.3

Let's examine the minor modes in the same way. Compare the following modes with the Aeolian mode, also known as the natural minor scale.

Aeolian (Natural Minor)

4
Track 66.4

Dorian

5
Track 66.5

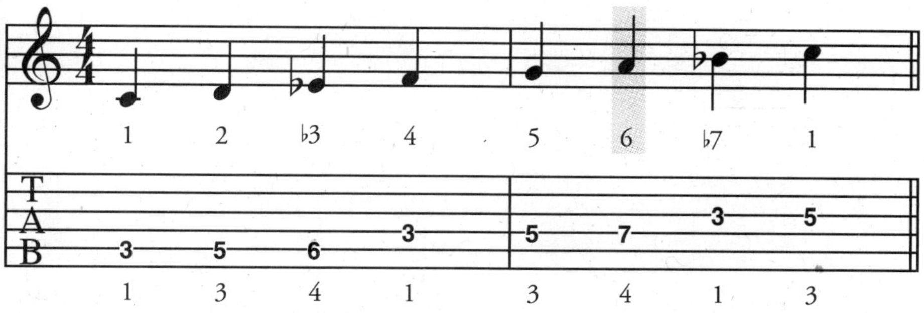

The characteristic note of Dorian is the 6 (A).

Phrygian

6
Track 66.6

The characteristic note of Phrygian is the ♭2 (D♭).

Locrian

7
Track 66.7

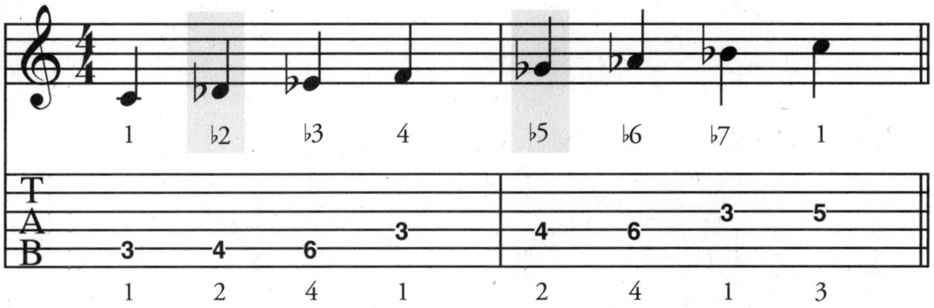

The characteristic notes of Locrian are ♭2 (D♭) and ♭5 (G♭).

Use the accompanying rhythm track to practice the modal sounds in C. This will help you develop a good ear for the different sounds of the modes.

8
Track 67

Modal Chord Progressions

Remember, according to the relative approach (discussed on pages 43–44), modes are derived from the major scale and are created from each pitch within this scale. A mode "pretends" to be an independent key but is derived from an actual major scale.

1. Ionian/Major	(C–D–E–F–G–A–B–C)
2. Dorian	(D–E–F–G–A–B–C–D)
3. Phrygian	(E–F–G–A–B–C–D–E)
4. Lydian	(F–G–A–B–C–D–E–F)
5. Mixolydian	(G–A–B–C–D–E–F–G)
6. Aeolian/Natural Minor	(A–B–C–D–E–F–G–A)
7. Locrian	(B–C–D–E–F–G–A–B)

The unique sound of each mode is created by its formula of whole steps and half steps. To create a good and independent modal chord progression, it is important to avoid diminished or dominant 7th chords, as these will lead the ear back to the original major key.

When playing a mode, you are automatically playing the notes of its relative major scale. For example, the mode C Lydian is built on the 4th scale degree of a major scale. What note is a 4th below C? The note G. So, G Major is the relative major of C Lydian. In this way, each mode can be referred back to its relative major scale, making it easier to find the right notes and chords—as they are the same.

To construct a good modal chord progression, you need to understand the importance of the characteristic note(s) of each mode and always state the modal root note. Otherwise, you will start losing the modal sound and hear only the major or minor tonality. To help you maintain the modal sound, use chords that contain the characteristic notes and avoid chords that do not.

Remember, the formula for the Lydian mode is: 1–2–3–♯4–5–6–7. If we harmonize this mode in triads, the resulting chords are: C–D–Emin–F♯dim–G–Amin–Bmin. If we harmonized the mode in 7th chords, we would get: CMaj7–D7–Emin7–F♯dim7♭5–GMaj7–Amin7–Bmin7. The characteristic note for C Lydian is the ♯4 (F♯). Let's examine all the chords that contain this note:

- D or D7 (F♯ is the 3rd)
- Bmin or Bmin7 (F♯ is the 5th)
- F♯dim or F♯m7♭5 (F♯ is the root)
- GMaj7 (F♯ is the 7th)

Remember, although diminished and dominant chords contain the characteristic note, they cannot be used, as they will lead the ear away from the mode and back to the relative major key. The other chords are called *cadence chords* and are usually played in combination with the root chord, or I chord, of the mode.

9

Track 68.1

A typical modal chord progression alternates between the I chord and the cadence chords.

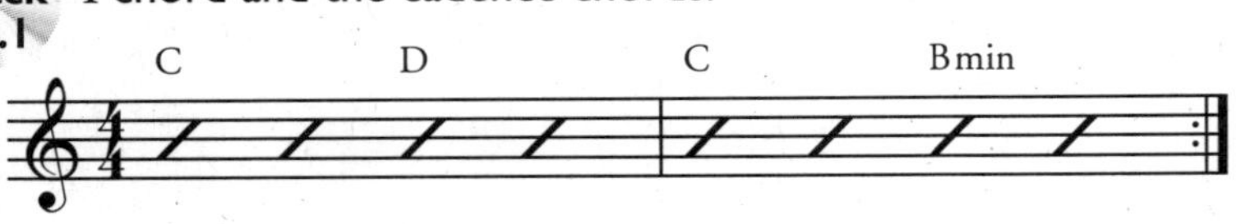

10

Track 68.2

Another approach is to play the root note of the mode below the different chords.

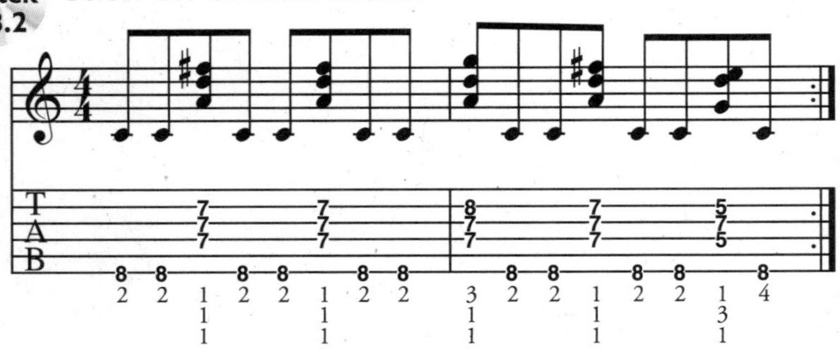

In general, triads and 7th chords can be used, but triads will sound more stable. Based on the previous example, create chord progressions for the remaining major and minor modes. The backing tracks to the right are short modal vamps, so you can practice the modes and get a better understanding of their sounds.

Backing Tracks

Track 69 Lydian Backing Track ||: E | F♯/E :||

Track 70 Mixolydian Backing Track ||: E | D/E :||

Track 71 Dorian Backing Track ||: Emin7 | F♯min7/E :||

Track 72 Phrygian Backing Track ||: Emin | F Dmin :||

Track 73 Locrian Backing Track ||: Gmin/E | B♭/E :||

Chapter 15: Speed Development

To develop fast and dependable picking speed, you must work on the synchronization between your right and left hands. This process requires a lot of patience and persistence. But with practice, everyone can pull off playing sixteenth notes at 200 beats per minute (bpm)!

The key is to work within your body's limits. For this, you need to pay close attention to your movements and how your hands work together. Use a mirror to monitor your hands while practicing. This will help you minimize unnecessary and inefficient movements.

Furthermore, always start slow and use a metronome at a comfortable speed. For example, start out at 80–90 bpm and increase the tempo by 8–12 bpm every time you have completed the lick, exercise, or riff. Once you have reached your top speed—that speed at which you start to feel a bit unstable—reduce the tempo to a more comfortable and accurate speed. The idea is that you should always push against the ceiling of your top speed and then back off to a slightly slower, but more comfortable, tempo. Over time, this process will increase your speed and stamina.

Use the following exercises to develop your speed. Make sure that you play these basic fragments across the fretboard.

Ascending

1

Track 74.1

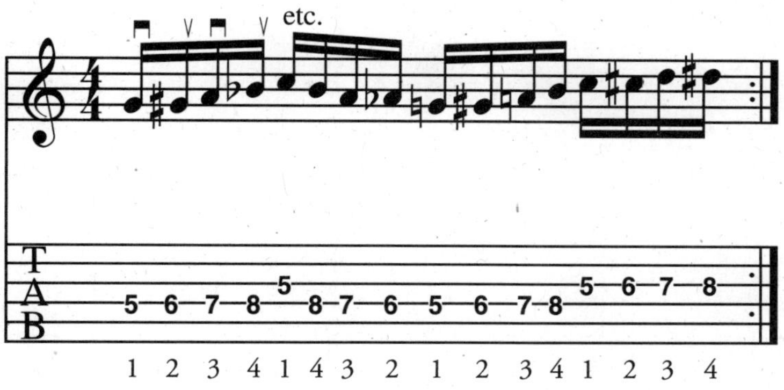

Descending

2

Track 74.2

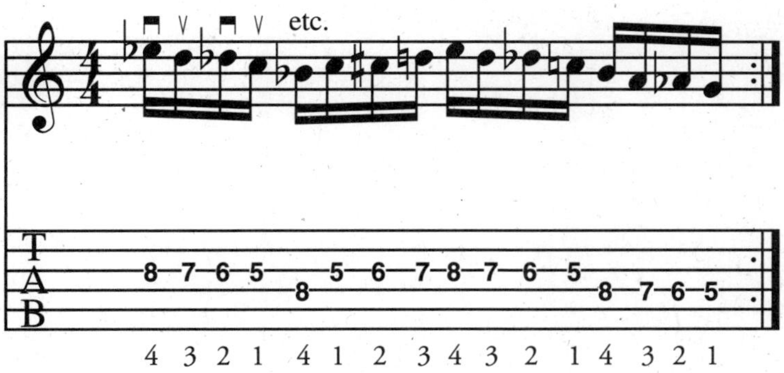

This is the entire idea from the previous page written out. Pay close attention to the alternate picking and string crossing.

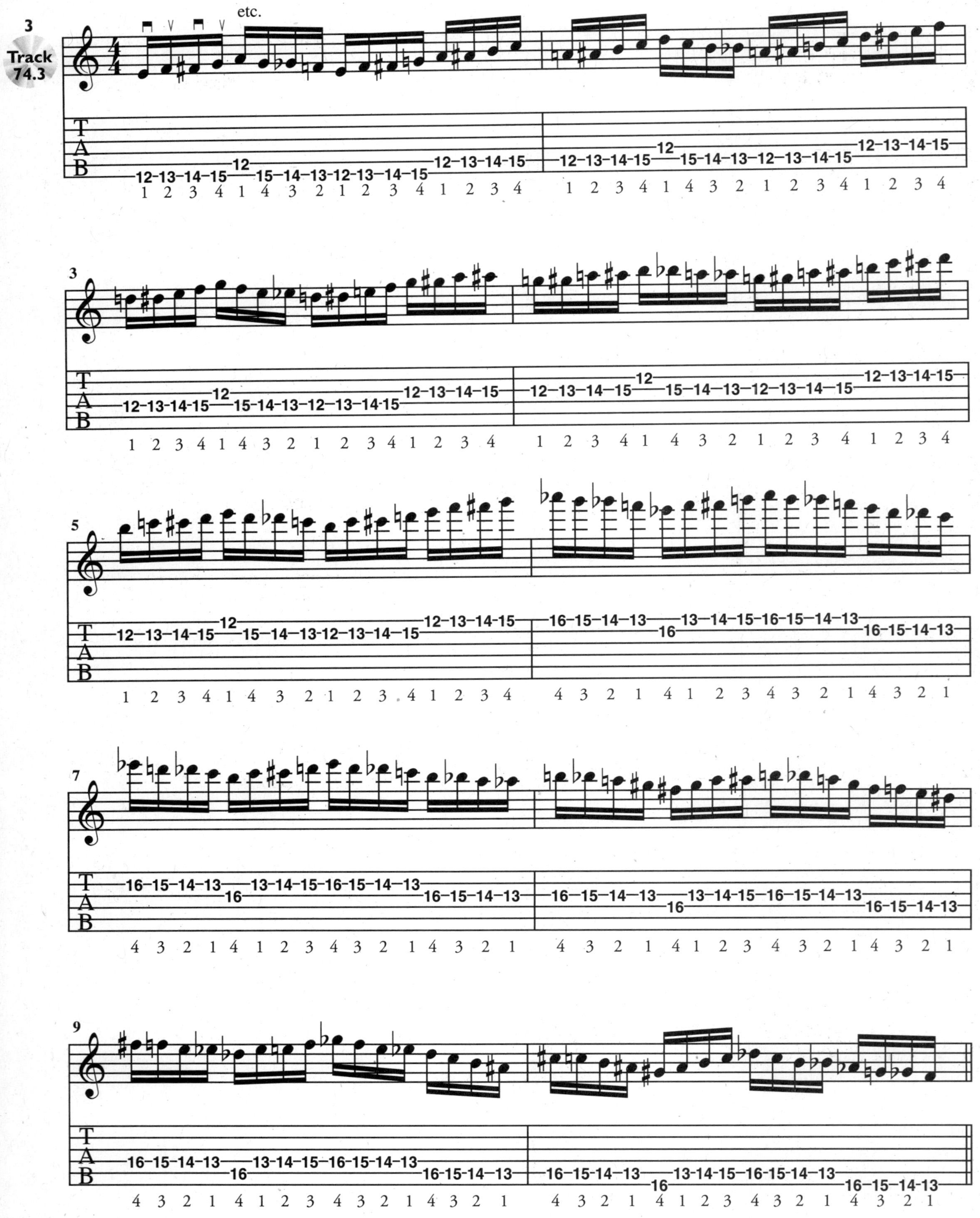

The next example is a variation of the previous idea.

4
Track 74.4 Ascending

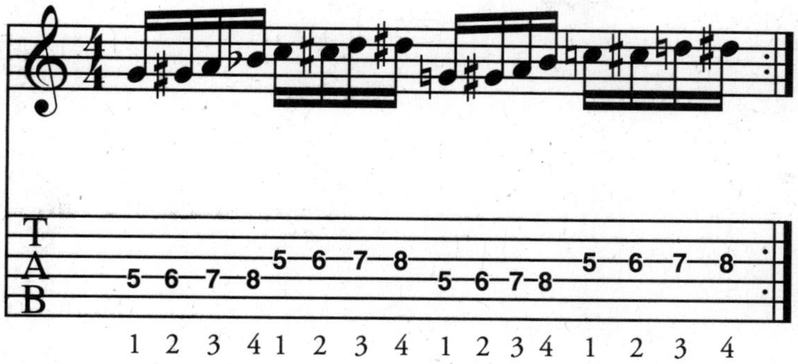

5
Track 74.5 Descending

Following is the entire chromatic phrase played across all six strings. Make sure you move it up and down the fretboard.

6
Track 74.6

Chapter 16: Miscellaneous Techniques

Outside-Inside Picking

A great alternative to sweeping, legato, or alternate picking is the so-called "outside-inside" picking technique. It combines the picking and legato styles to achieve a smoother sound. Additionally, you can skip strings much easier without worrying about missing an alternate pick strike or sounding sloppy.

The example below illustrates the basic picking and legato pattern that can easily be applied to other phrases as well. It is based on an excerpt of the D Major scale. You start the phrase with an upstroke and continue with two pull-offs. After that, you simply continue with strict alternate picking. Play it very slowly and make sure the picking and pull-offs are correct before speeding up.

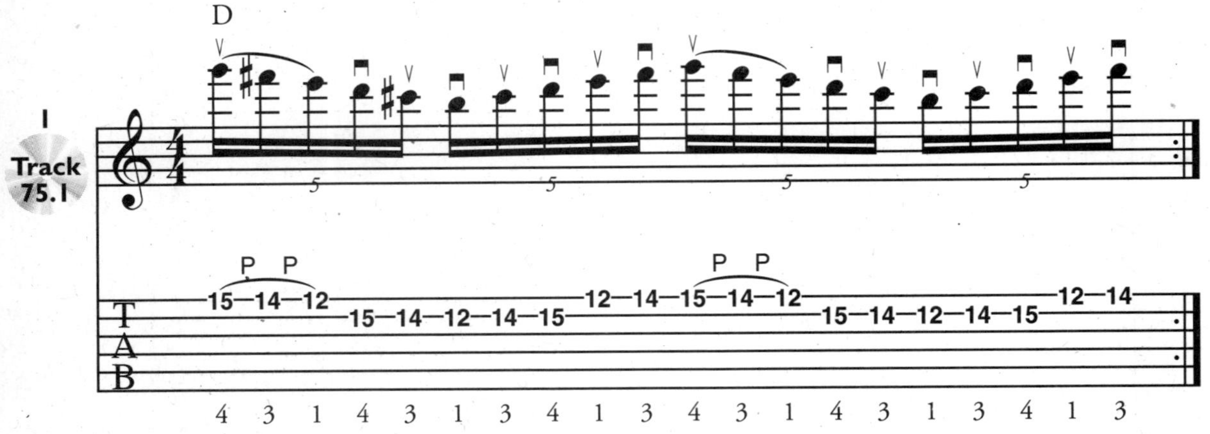

The next example shows the ascending version of the lick above. As you can see, nothing has changed except that you start on a different note within the phrase.

Now, let's focus on the great advantage that this picking technique can give you: string skipping. Outside-inside picking allows you to jump over different strings without missing a beat.

The next lick is a simple symmetrical finger exercise that can be used in the context of an E7♯9 chord. Play it very slowly and make sure the strings are not ringing too much when you skip strings. To help with this, apply some palm muting.

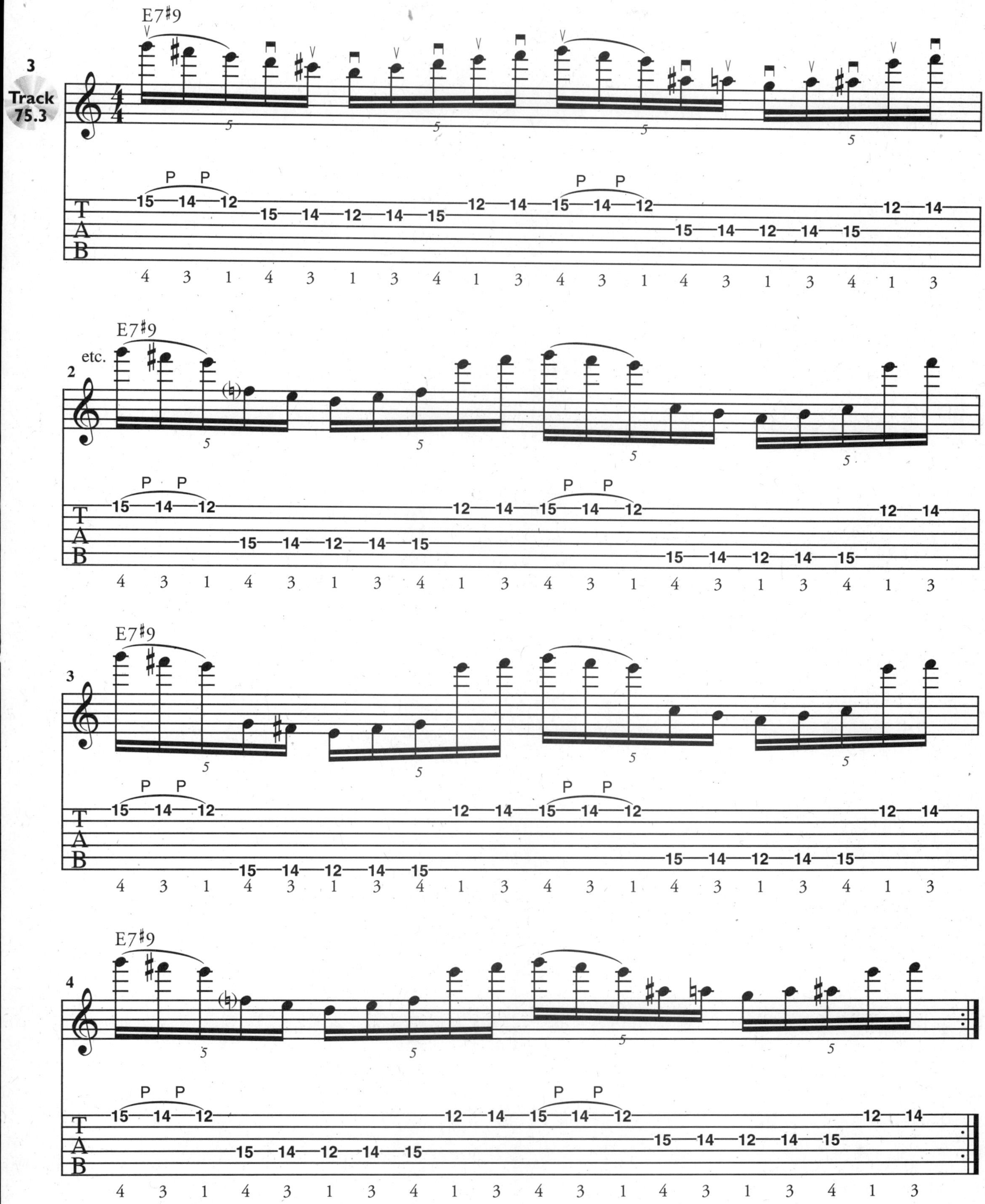

The next lick uses a short scale excerpt.

4
Track 75.4

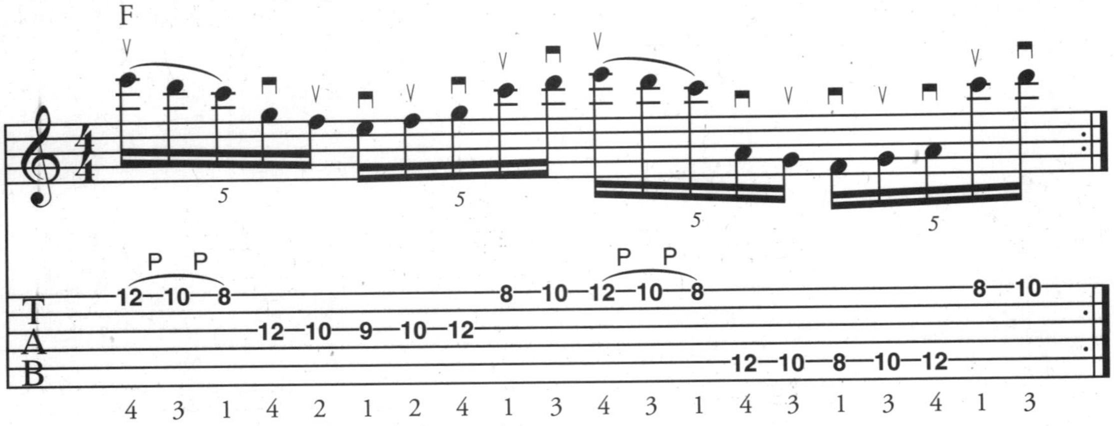

You can also add a few more notes and get a very rhythmically interesting sound. Below, we have added three notes to the sequence. The additional notes are played with an upstroke and two additional pull-offs.

5
Track 76.1

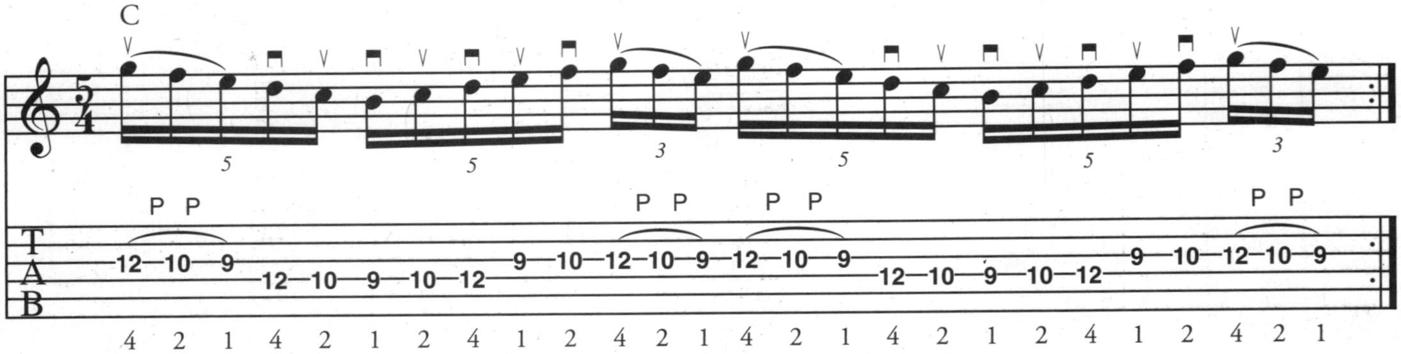

You can also play longer sequences across the strings with this picking method. After you play the following example as written, try coming up with more licks and scale runs of your own.

6
Track 76.2

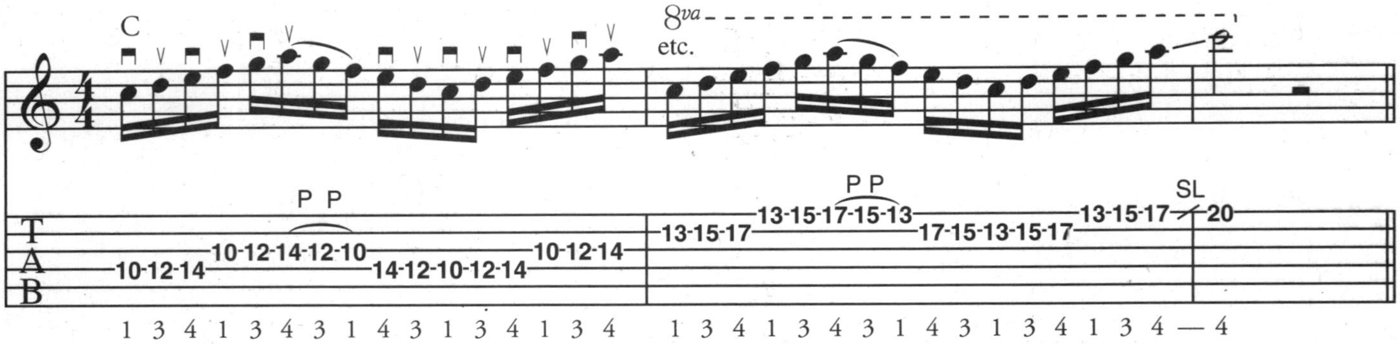

Another great way to utilize this concept is with arpeggio playing. The diagrams below show four basic string-skipping arpeggio shapes, which can also be moved to the A, D, and B strings.

Major

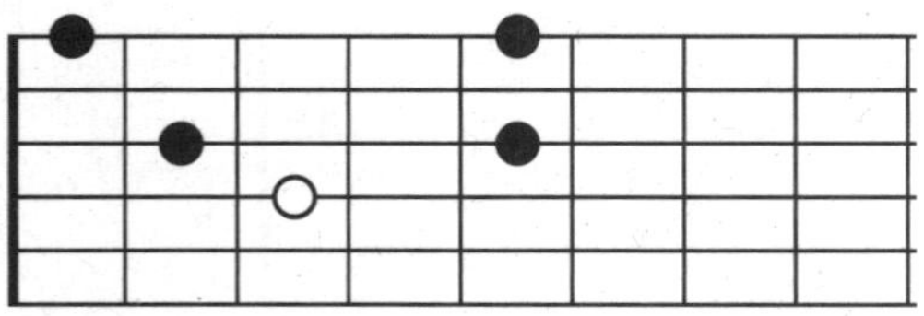

Minor

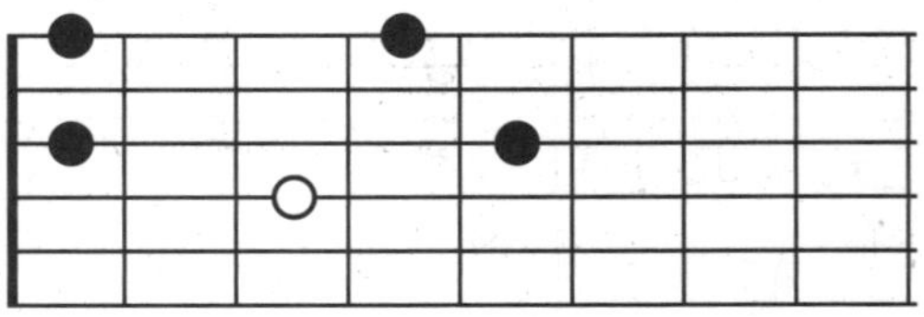

Diminished

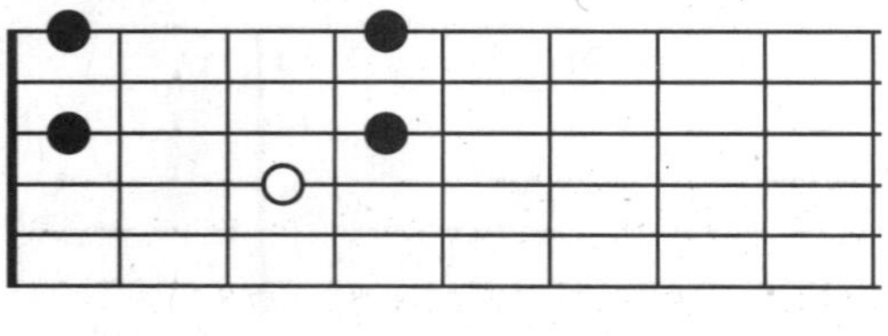

Augmented

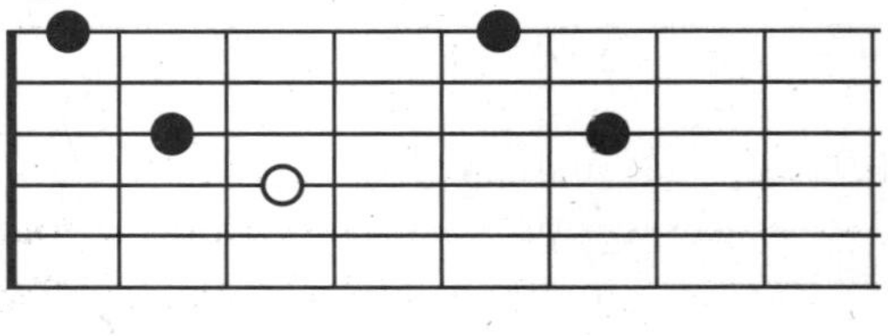

Practice the arpeggio shapes from the previous page slowly. First, use alternate picking and play the arpeggios in a simple ascending and descending fashion.

The next example is a I–vi–IV–V chord progression in the key of E Major. It incorporates an interesting triplet arpeggio pattern.

7
Track 76.3

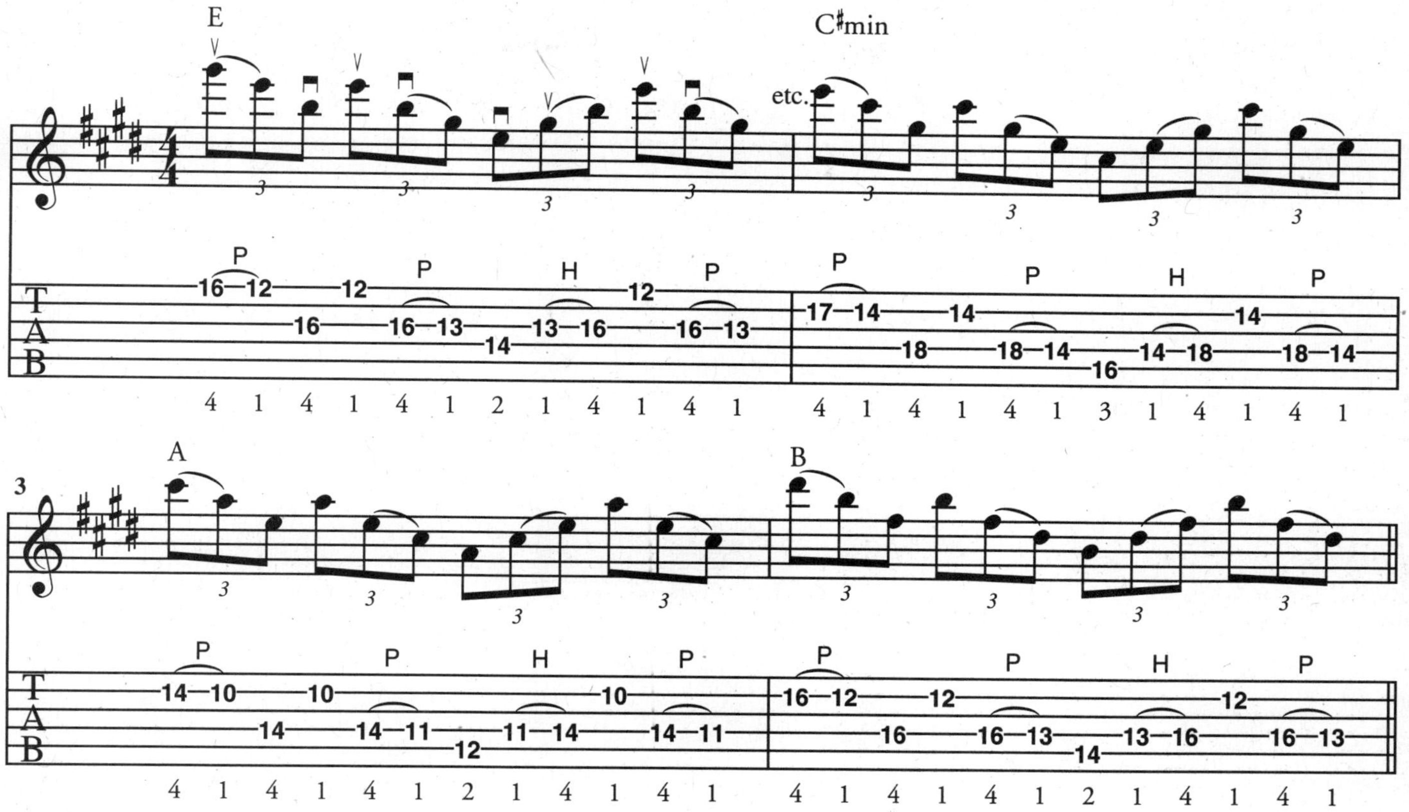

The next lick is based on the G♯ Diminished 7th arpeggio and resolves to A Minor.

8
Track 76.4

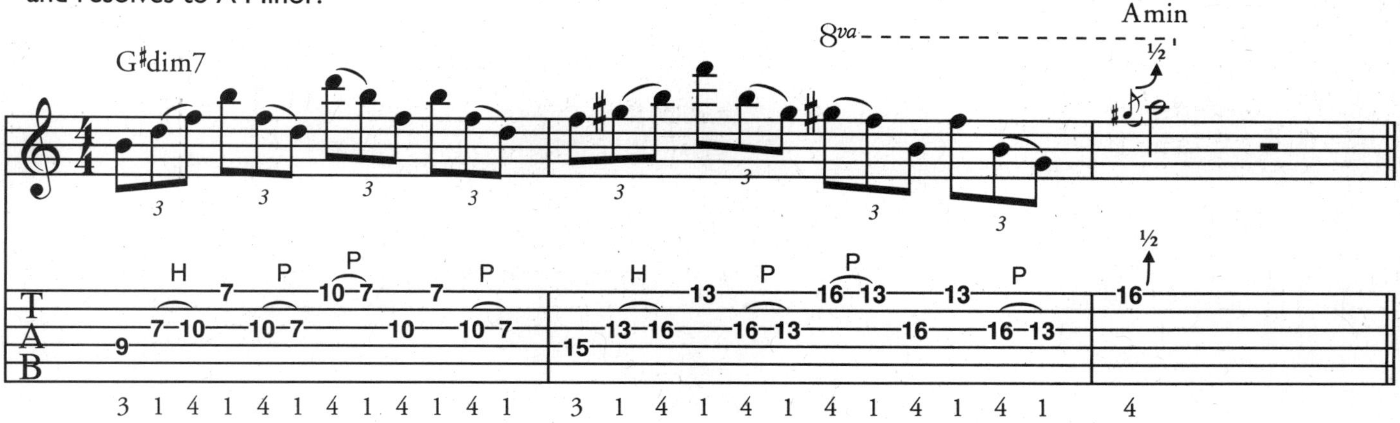

Below is a variation based on ascending eighth notes.

9
Track 76.5

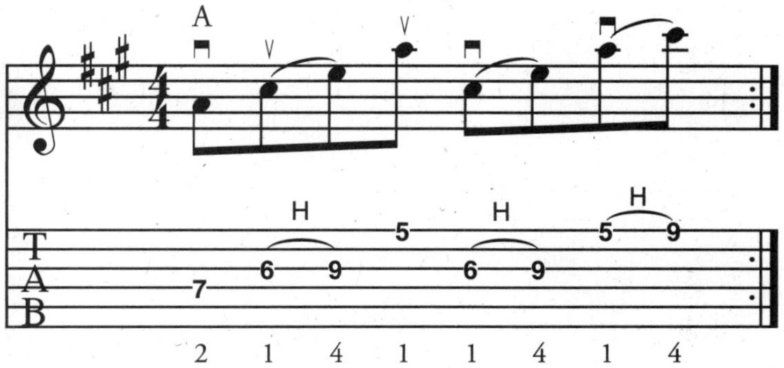

Try to incorporate all of these patterns and ideas into your playing, and use them for your own creative purposes. The outside-inside picking technique will open the door to new ideas and possibilities—explore it at your own risk!

Three-Octave Arpeggios

There are many different ways to play arpeggios: sweeping, tapping, one-position traditional arpeggios, and three-octave arpeggios.

Three-octave arpeggios are a great way to travel across the fretboard with alternate picking or legato playing. Three-octave arpeggio patterns are organized similarly to pentatonic scales: two notes per string. The basic four-note form of the 7th chord arpeggio is distributed across two strings with two notes per string.

The diagrams below illustrate the root positions of the following arpeggios: major 7, dominant 7, minor 7, minor 7♭5, and dim7. Memorize these patterns and also develop the different inversions of each chord type.

CMaj7

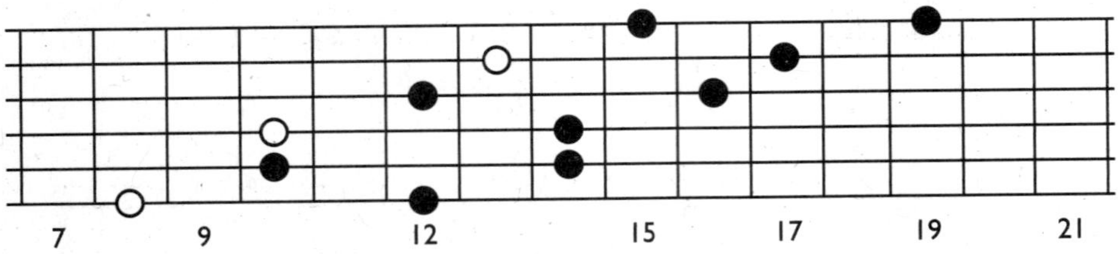

C7

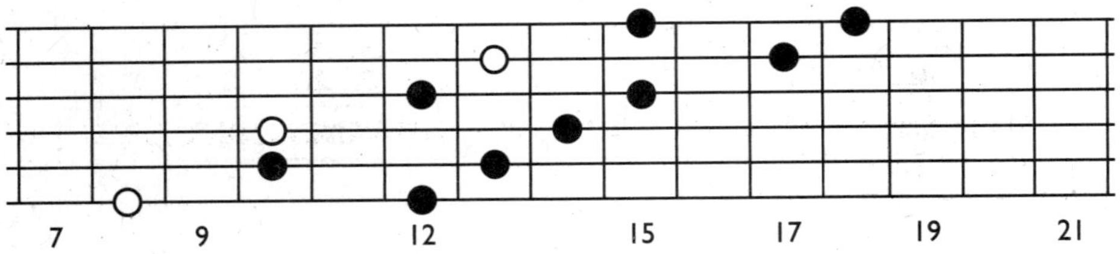

Cmin7

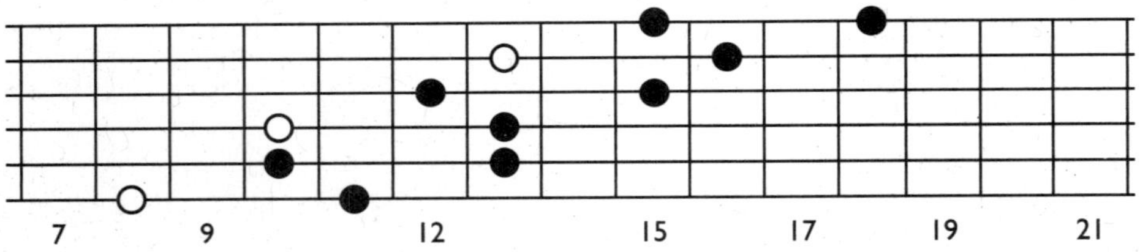

Cmin7♭5

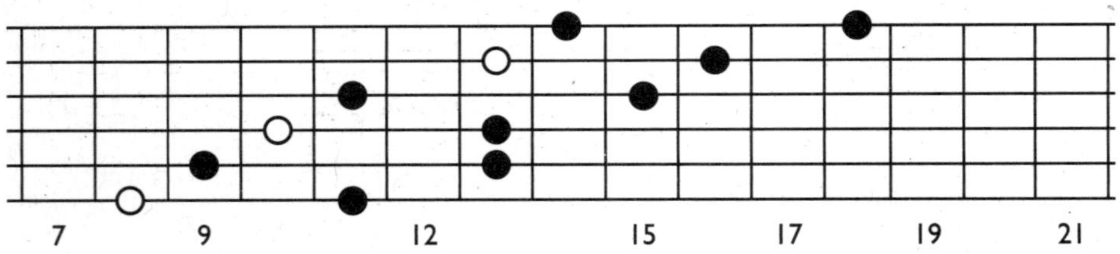

Cdim7

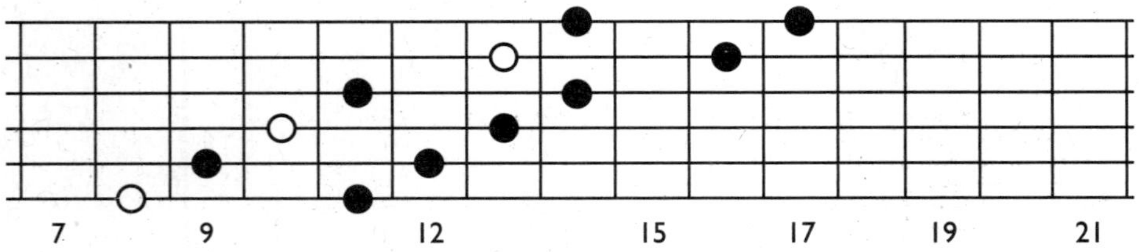

The following licks will demonstrate the use of these arpeggios with different techniques.

Below, we are playing the diatonic 7th chord arpeggios on the top two strings in E Major. This lick uses the *3rd inversions* of the arpeggios; this means the 7th is the lowest note. Try also to play this idea on the other strings (D and G, or E and A), as the shapes can be moved in octaves.

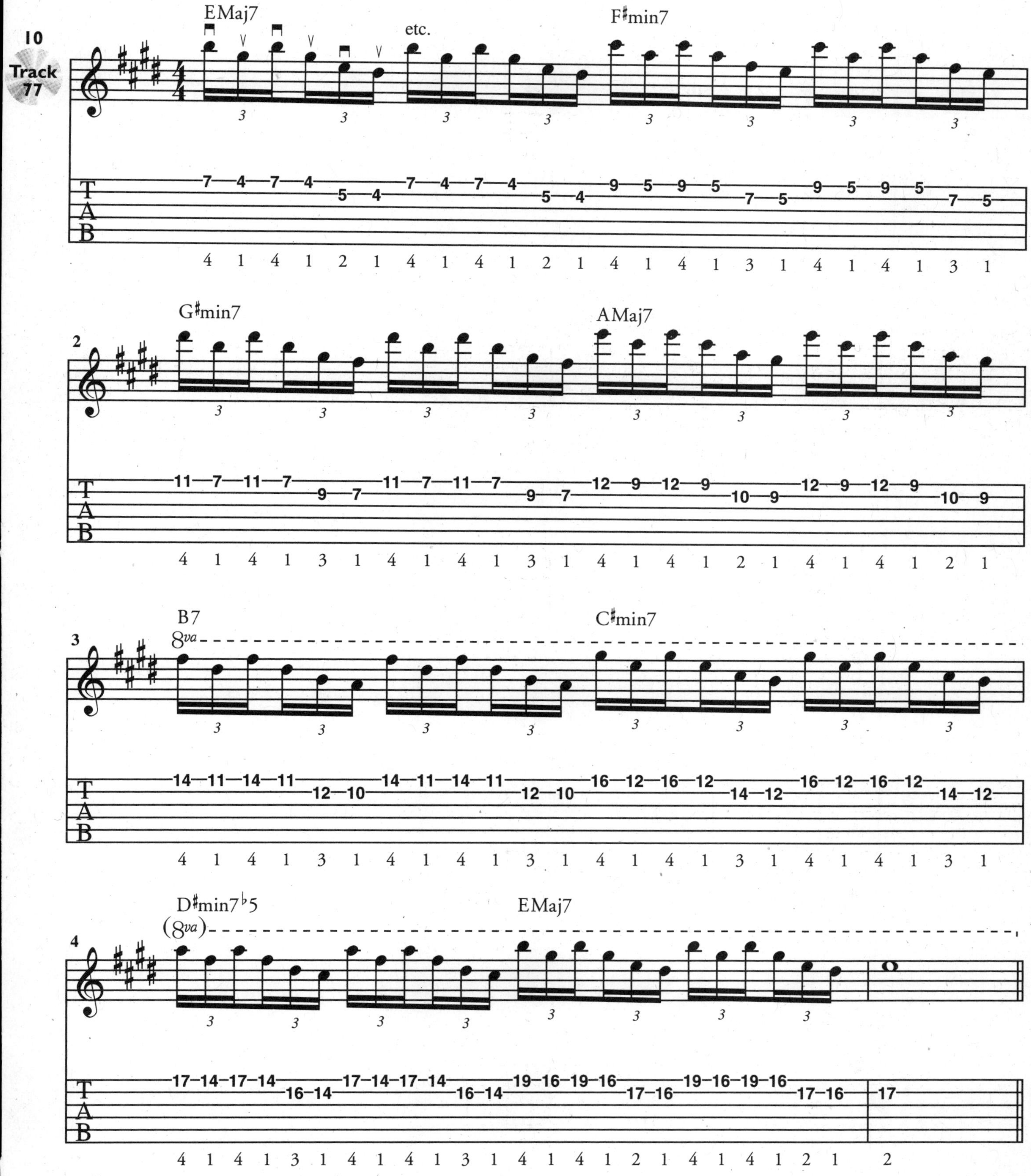

The following lick uses groupings of six to play a root-position, three-octave arpeggio in C Major. It concludes with an Amin7 arpeggio across all six strings.

11
Track 78

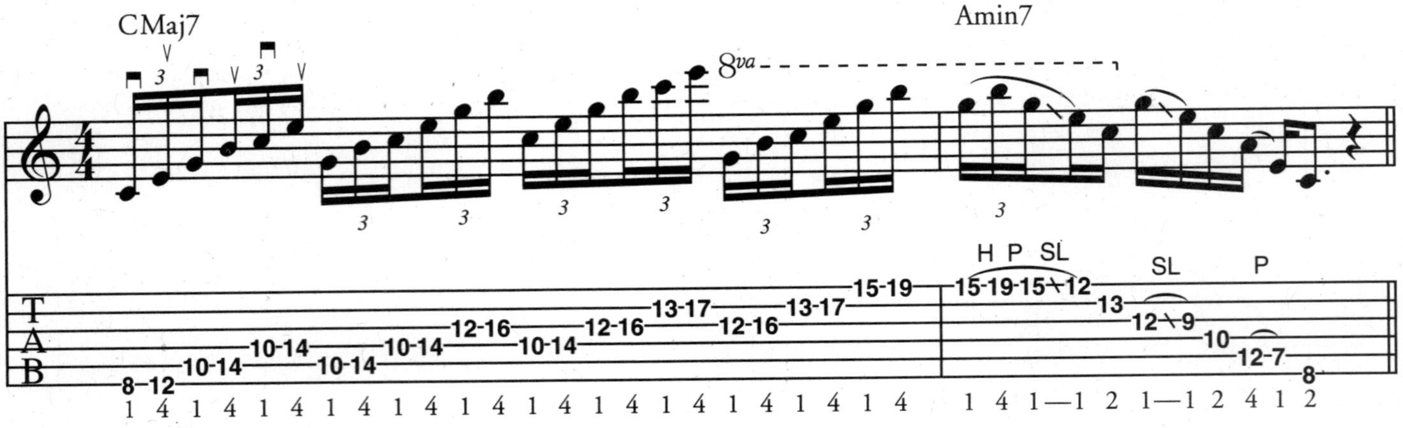

This next one uses a 1st inversion Amin7 arpeggio shape. It's played in a three-note ascending pattern with tapping.

12
Track 79

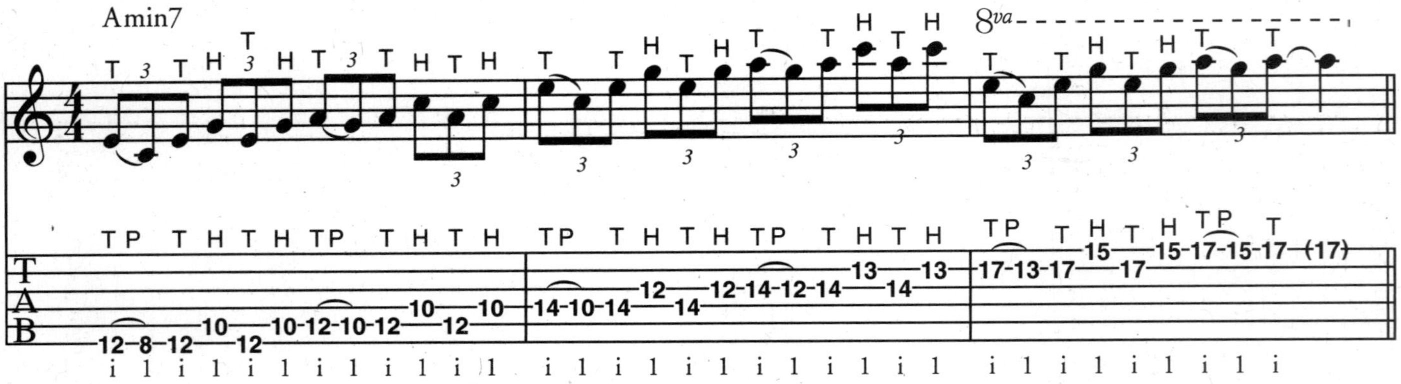

The last lick is based on a 2nd inversion G7 arpeggio shape, which has been filled in with some additional notes (6th and 2nd) to create an extended sound. The shape is played and then repeated in the next higher octave. It also uses two of the patterns from Chapter 6. Play this example slowly at first, as it will require a lot of coordination.

13

Track 80

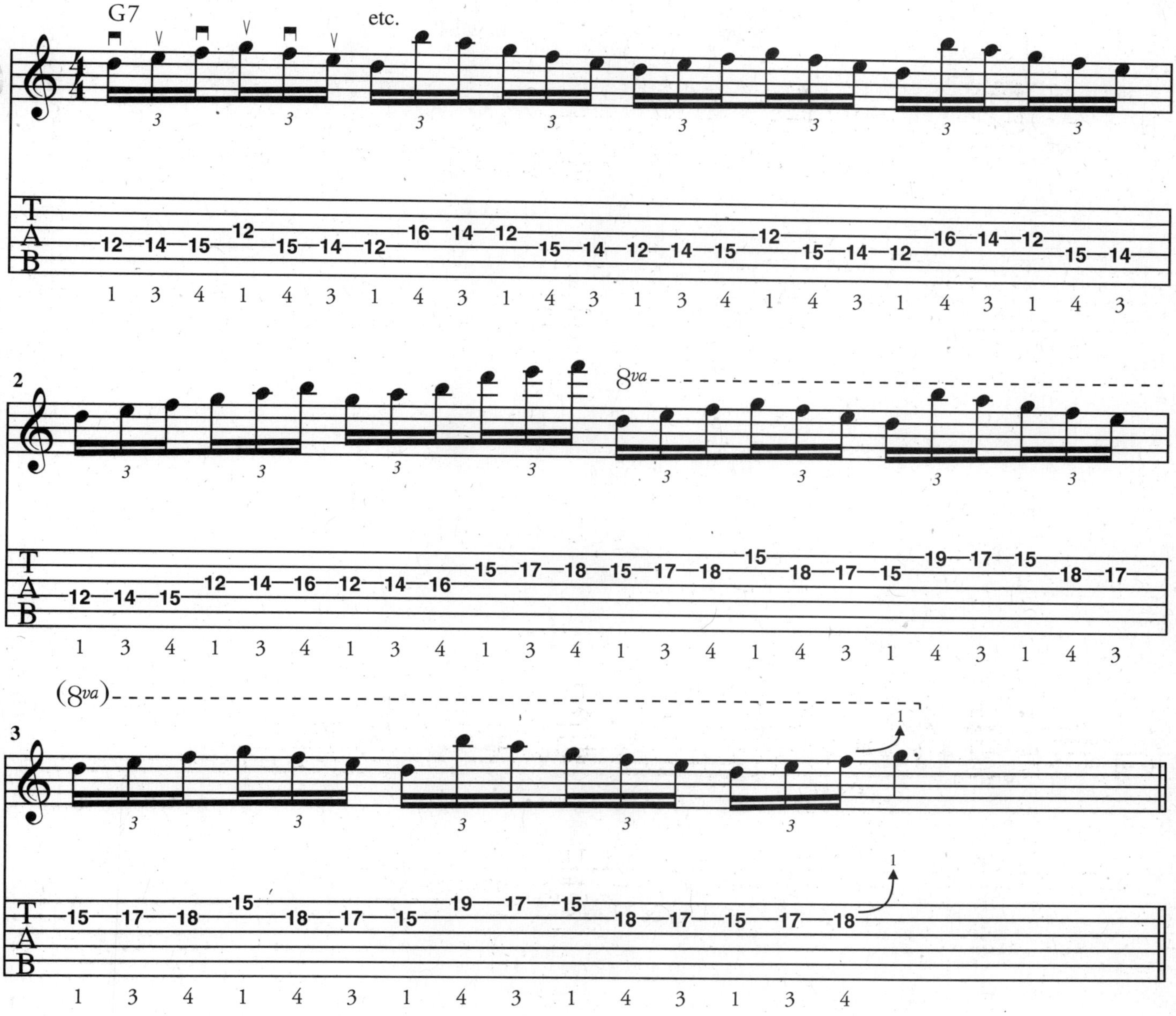

Conclusion

Developing your skills and understanding the guitar in all its aspects is an exciting and never-ending endeavor, and I can't imagine anything more rewarding. However, at times, you will feel like you are not improving—as if you are stuck. This is normal, and it happens to everyone. The important thing is to see yourself relative to where you were when you started. For this reason, I strongly encourage you to keep a music journal. This will help you understand your thoughts and goals and will give you a great reference to where you are as a student now and where you once were. Furthermore, it will help you understand your goals and help you realize that they will change along the journey of becoming a better guitarist and musician.

I have included as much content as possible in this book, but there is so much more to be said about shredding and all the amazing things still to learn. This is just the beginning!

As always, try to be creative and explore many different ideas, techniques, and concepts. Write, record, and study as much as you can, and you will see great results in your playing and in your ability to create music. It's so much fun.

Shred on!

If you love this book,
you'll love our schools!
Online...
WORKSHOPLive
The next generation of music education from the founders of the National Guitar Workshop
Take a FREE online lesson today.
workshoplive.com
...or Near You
N · G · W
National Guitar Workshop
LOCATIONS: Connecticut, Florid
Seattle, Nashville, Los Angeles,
Texas, San Francisco, Virginia
...every summer!
1-800-234-6479
guitarworkshop.com